KU-531-632

Operation Suicide

Also by Robert Lyman

Slim, Master of War: Burma and the Birth of Modern Warfare
First Victory: Britain's Forgotten Struggle in the Middle East, 1941
The Generals: From Defeat to Victory, Leadership in Asia 1941–45
The Longest Siege: Tobruk – The Battle that Saved North Africa
Japan's Last Bid for Victory: The Invasion of India, 1944

Operation Suicide

The Remarkable Story of the Cockleshell Raid

Robert Lyman

Quercus

29986001
MORAY COUNCIL
LIBRARIES &
INFORMATION SERVICES
940.542147

First published in Great Britain in 2012 by
Quercus
55 Baker Street
7th Floor, South Block
London
W1U 8EW

Copyright © 2012 Robert Lyman

The moral right of Robert Lyman to be
identified as the author of this work has been
asserted in accordance with the Copyright,
Designs and Patents Act, 1988.

All rights reserved. No part of this publication
may be reproduced or transmitted in any form
or by any means, electronic or mechanical,
including photocopy, recording, or any
information storage and retrieval system,
without permission in writing from the publisher.

Every effort has been made to contact copyright holders of material
reproduced in this book. If any have been inadvertently overlooked, the
publishers will be pleased to make restitution at the earliest opportunity.

A CIP catalogue record for this book is available
from the British Library

HB ISBN 978 0 85738 240 5
TPB ISBN 978 1 78087 251 3

10 9 8 7 6 5 4 3 2 1

Text and plates designed and typeset by Ellipsis Digital Ltd
Maps © William Donohoe

Printed and bound in Great Britain by Clays Ltd. St Ives plc

Image on preceding page: Captain 'Jock' Stewart (rear) and Major 'Blondie' Hasler (forward) in a Cockle MkII shortly after Hasler's return from Operation Frankton.

In memory of those who did not return

and

dedicated to the pupils of Wellington College,
Blondie's alma mater, who walk today in his footsteps

Contents

An extremely gallant and enterprising operation

Winston Churchill, 17 December 1942

[T]his brilliant little operation carried through with great determination and courage

Vice-Admiral Lord Louis Mountbatten, 29 April 1943

The outstanding Commando raid of the war

Korvettenkapitän Peter Popp, Kriegsmarine, 1946

Of the many and dashing raids carried out by the men of Combined Operations Command, none was more courageous or imaginative . . . an immense amount of trouble was taken over the training of the small handful of picked Royal Marines who took part under the indomitable leadership of Lieutenant Colonel (then Major) Hasler. They maintained their object in spite of the frightening losses of the first night and the subsequent ever-increasing difficulties they encountered. Although the force had been reduced to four men, the object was finally achieved. The account of this operation brings out the spirit of adventure always present in peace and war among Royal Marines. It emphasizes the tremendous importance of morale – pride in oneself and one's unit creating this morale. It also stresses the need for careful detailed planning of operations. I commend it to all as an account of a fine operation, carried out by a particularly brave party of men.

Mountbatten, 1956

I realised it would be certain death for the gallant men who took part, unless brave men and women of the resistance movement in France came to their rescue.

Mountbatten, 1964

These cruel murders of the Marine Commandos were among the vilest things the Germans ever did.

Airey Neave DSO, OBE, MC, 1969

[The raid] was carried out without any 'modern' equipment, and without any radio or electronics. A combination of very simple equipment with a high degree of human initiative, stealth, seamanship and field craft was the recipe at that time.

Lieutenant Colonel 'Blondie' Hasler DSO, OBE, 1982

Uppermost in my mind is the fact that eight out of ten men did not come back. It is easy to celebrate the glamorous side of the operation, but less easy to remember that, like most warfare, it took a tragic toll of young lives and left behind it a group of heartbroken families.

Blondie Hasler, 1982

Thanks to inspired leadership, this small group of men, taken from everyday life, and following the shortest period of training in activities entirely foreign to them, achieved the unthinkable – a raid on shipping deep into enemy territory. Operation *Frankton* demanded the highest morale, skill and 'esprit de corps', all of which their leader knew instinctively to develop and perfect. The eight families who still grieve their lost loved-ones nevertheless take pride in the overall achievement of the team, far from home, on that cold December night in 1942.

Peter Siddall (nephew of Lance Corporal George Sheard), April 2011

Preface

In December 1942 ten Royal Marines set out in collapsible plywood and canvas canoes (codenamed 'Cockles') from a Royal Navy submarine in the Bay of Biscay. They were on a five-day mission to attach limpet mines to German freighters lying in the security of Bordeaux harbour, deep within the sanctuary of the River Garonne. These ships were running the Allied blockade of the French Atlantic ports and carrying on an important trade in strategic war materials with Japan. The mission was highly risky. The man who authorised the operation, Vice-Admiral Lord Louis Mountbatten, the Chief of Combined Operations, did not expect any of the Marines to return.

What no one in Britain knew at the time was that the operation had suddenly become doubly dangerous. On 18 October that year Hitler had issued his *Kommandobefehl* (commando order), instructing that henceforth any and all captured British 'commandos' be executed without mercy. The Royal Marines on Operation Frankton had expected that, if they were captured, their uniforms, badges of rank and obvious military training and organisation would provide sufficient defence against the possibility of being mistaken and shot as spies, the traditional threat faced by soldiers fighting behind enemy lines. They did not know that a brutal new dimension had been brought to the business of warfare by a German leader enraged by the success of British commando raids across the western flanks of the Nazi empire. The chances of the ten

Royal Marines overcoming the physical and military challenges involved in penetrating the defences of Bordeaux, exploding their anti-ship mines and escaping without capture, were extremely slim. With the signing of the *Kommandobefehl* their chances of surviving, were they to be captured, had now been reduced to zero. Their escape dependent on the unlikelihood of making contact with a Resistance-run 'escape line' and making their way through hundreds of miles of enemy territory to Spain, they were on what can only be described as an impossible mission.

At the unveiling of the memorial at the St Nicholas English Church in Bordeaux in 1966, Mountbatten described Operation Frankton as 'a particularly hazardous raid' in which every 'single man showed initiative, endurance and courage of the highest order'. These men were the Cockleshell Heroes.

German Military Ranks

Oberleutnant	Lieutenant (Army)
Oberleutnant zur See	Lieutenant (Navy)
Obersturmführer	Lieutenant (SS)
Hauptmann	Captain (Army)
Kapitänleutnant	Lieutenant Commander (Navy)
Sturmbannführer	Major (SS)
Korvettenkapitän	Commander (Navy)
Fregattenkapitän	Captain (Junior) (Navy)
Oberstleutnant	Lieutenant Colonel (Army)
Obersturmbannführer	Wing Commander (Air Force)
Kapitän zur See	Captain (Navy)
Oberst	Colonel (Army)
Generalleutnant	Major General (Army)
Admiral	Vice-Admiral (Navy)

Dramatis Personae*

The 'Cockleshell Heroes'

Major Herbert (Blondie) Hasler OBE	OC, RMBPD. No. 1 *Catfish*. Survived. DSO
Marine Bill (Ned) Sparks	No. 2 *Catfish*. Survived. DSM
Sergeant Samuel (Sammy) Wallace	No. 1 *Coalfish*. Executed, Bordeaux, 12 December 1942
Marine Robert (Bob) Ewart	No. 2 *Coalfish*. Executed, Bordeaux, 12 December 1942
Lieutenant John (Jack) Mackinnon	OC, No. 1 Section, RMBPD. No. 1 *Cuttlefish*. Executed, Paris, 23 March 1943
Marine James (Jim) Conway	No. 2 *Cuttlefish*. Executed, Paris, 23 March 1943
Lance Corporal Albert (Bert) Laver	No. 1 *Crayfish*. Executed, Paris, 23 March 1943
Marine William (Bill) Mills	No. 2 *Crayfish*. Executed, Paris, 23 March 1943
Lance Corporal George (Jan) Sheard	No. 1 *Conger*. Died of hypothermia at sea, 8 December 1942†

* Ranks given as in 1942

† Assumed, as it is not recorded that his body, according to existing records, was ever found.

Marine David Moffatt	No. 2 *Conger*. Died of hypothermia at sea, 8 December 1942*
Marine Bill Ellery	No. 1 *Cachalot*. Did not disembark HMS *Tuna*
Marine Eric Fisher	No. 2 *Cachalot*. Did not disembark HMS *Tuna*
Marine Norman Colley	Reserve. Did not disembark HMS *Tuna*

Other members of the Royal Marine Boom Patrol Detachment

Captain J.S. (Jock) Stewart	Second-in-Command, RMBPD
Lieutenant William (Bill) Pritchard-Gordon	OC, No. 2 Section, RMBPD
Colour Sergeant W.J. (Bungy) Edwards	Detachment Sergeant Major, RMBPD
Sergeant King	Physical Training Instructor

Royal Navy

Captain Sidney Raw RN	Chief Staff Officer (Submarines), Admiralty
Captain Hugh Ionides RN	Commanding Officer, 3rd Submarine Flotilla
Lieutenant Dick Raikes DSO RN	Commanding Officer, HMS *Tuna*
Lieutenant Johnny Bull RN	First Lieutenant, HMS *Tuna*
Lieutenant Geoffrey Rowe RN	Pilot, HMS *Tuna*

* Assumed. His formal date of death was the date his body was found, 17 December 1942.

Combined Operations Headquarters, 1a Richmond Terrace, London

Vice-Admiral Louis Mountbatten	Chief of Combined Operations
Brigadier Godfrey Wildman-Lushington	Chief of Staff (late RM)
Commander Tom Hussey RN	Hasler's first CO at CODC
Lieutenant H.F.G. Langley RA	Hasler's second CO at CODC
Lieutenant Colonel Robert Neville RM	Royal Marines Adviser (RMA), COHQ
Lieutenant Colonel Cyril Horton RM	Planning Staff, COHQ
Lieutenant Commander G.P. L'Estrange RNVR	Planning Staff, COHQ

Commando forces

Brigadier Charles Haydon DSO	Commander, Special Service Brigade (the 'Commandos')
Major Roger Courtney KRRC	2 Special Boat Section (SBS), Special Service Brigade
Captain Gerald Montanaro RE	101 Troop, 2 Special Boat Section (SBS), Special Service Brigade
Major Gus March-Phillips	Small-Scale Raiding Force (SSRF), SOE
Captain Geoffrey Appleyard	Small-Scale Raiding Force (SSRF), SOE
Lieutenant Graham Hayes	Small-Scale Raiding Force (SSRF), SOE

Associate

Mr Fred Goatley, Saro Ltd	Designer and builder of the Cockle MkII

Britain

Dr Hugh Dalton	Minister for Economic Warfare (until February 1942)
Lord Selborne	Minister for Economic Warfare (from February 1942)
Sir Charles Hambro	Executive Head, SOE (February 1942–3)
Colonel Colin Gubbins	Head of M Section, SOE*
Lieutenant Colonel Richard (Dick) Barry	Chief of Staff, SOE
Major David Wyatt RE	SOE Liaison Officer with COHQ (until August 1942
Major Maurice Buckmaster	Head of F Section, SOE (from March 1942)
Major Robert Archibald Bourne-Paterson	Planning Officer, F Section, SOE

MI6/MI9

Lieutenant Colonel Claude Dansey	Deputy Director, MI6
Brigadier Norman Crockatt DSO MC	Director, MI9
Major James (Jimmy) Langley	MI9 (P15)
Major Airey Neave	MI9 ('Saturday')

* Gubbins, as a major general, succeeded Sir Charles Hambro in 1943.

Sir Henry Farquhar	British consul, Barcelona
Martin Creswell	MI6/MI9 ('Monday') – Madrid
Donald Darling	MI6/MI9 ('Sunday') – Lisbon/Gibraltar
Wilfred ('Biffy') Dunderdale	Head of MI6, France
Victor Farrel	British consul and MI9 agent, Geneva

French Resistance/SOE/MI9 in the field, 1942/3

Tadeusz Jekiel	Head, F2 network, Bordeaux
Robert Yves Marie Leroy ('Louis')	First SOE agent, Bordeaux, 1941
Commander Léo Paillière	Early *résistant* and SOE contact, Bordeaux
Commander Jean Duboué	Early *résistant* and SOE contact, Bordeaux
Claude de Baissac ('David')	Head, SOE 'Scientist' network, Bordeaux
Mary Herbert ('Jeweller')	Courier, 'Scientist' network, Bordeaux
Roger Landes ('Aristide')	Radio Operator, SOE Scientist network
Raymond Brard	Head of Security at Bordeaux Port; leader of Phalanx-Phidias cell (BCRA)
Comtesse de Milleville (Mary Lindell)	Head of MI9 'Marie-Claire' *réseau*
Maurice de Milleville	Courier in Marie-Claire *réseau*
Armand and Amélie Dubreuille	Member of the Marie-Claire *réseau*, 'Farm B', Marvaud Saint Coutant, *Zone Libre*
Marthe Rullier	Member of French Red Cross and of the Marie-Claire *réseau*, Ruffec

Albert-Marie Guérisse (Pat Albert O'Leary)	Head of the PAO *réseau*, Marseille
M. and Mme Martin	*Passeurs* in the Pat O'Leary *réseau*, Marseille
Maud Olga Andrée Baudot de Rouville	*Passeur* in the Pat O'Leary *réseau*, Marseille
Fabien de Cortes	Courier in the PAO *réseau*, Lyon

French civilians

Jean Raymond and his father	Fishermen, Fort-Médoc
Yves Ardouin	Oyster fisherman, St Vivien-de-Médoc
Alibert Decombe	Tenant farmer, La Présidente Farm, Portes de Calonges, near Braye
Clodomir and Irène Pasqucraud	Farm worker and his wife, Nâpres Farm, Saint Preuil
Marc, Yves and Robert Pasqueraud	Children of Clodomir and Irène
Lucien Gody	Villager, Beaunac. Did not return from deportation to Germany
Raymond Furet	Farm boy, Orignolles
Maurice Rousseau	Villager, Beaunac, aged 28. Did not return from deportation to Germany
René Rousseau	Villager, Beaunac, aged 16. Did not return from deportation to Germany
André Latouche	Villager, Beaunac. Arrested but released
Yvonne Mandinaud	Owner of La Toque Blanche, Ruffec
Alix Mandinaud	Waitress at La Toque Blanche, Ruffec
René Mandinaud	Brother of Alix and Yvonne

Edouard Pariente	Quarryman, Baigneaux
Louis and Louise Jaubert	Smallholders, Cessac
Captain Olivier	Chief of Police, La Réole, *Zone Libre*
Marcel Galibert	Lawyer, La Réole, *Zone Libre*
Marcel Drouillard	Gendarme, La Réole
Adjutant Dupeyrou	Gendarme, Montlieu-la-Garde
Fernand Dumas	Courier for the Marie-Claire *réseau*, Ruffec
René Flaud	Member of the Marie-Claire *réseau*, Ruffec
Jean Mariaud	Tax Inspector, Ruffec, and later a *passeur* with the Marie-Claire *réseau*

German armed forces

Kriegsmarine

Admiral Wilhelm Marschall	C-in-C Navy Group West, Paris
Admiral Wilhelm Meisel	Chief of Staff, Navy Group West, Paris
Fregattenkapitän Lange	Staff Officer, Navy Group West, Paris
Sturmbannführer Dr Knochen	Sicherheitsdienst (SD), Paris
Vice-Admiral Julius Bachmann	FOIC, Western France, Nantes
Korvettenkapitän Max Gebauer	Stand-in SNOIC Inshore Squadron Gascony, Royan
Korvettenkapitän Ernst Kühnemann	NOIC, Port of Bordeaux

Oberleutnant zur See Theodor Prahm	Adjutant to NOIC, Naval HQ, Bordeaux, and Execution Squad commander
Oberleutnant zur See Wild	Commander, Harbour Defence Flotilla, Le Verdon
Fregattenkapitän Dr Krantz	Commanding Officer, Dulag Nord interrogation camp, Wilhelmshaven
Hauptmann Heinz Corssen	Interrogator, Dulag Nord, Wilhelmshaven

708 Infantry Division, Royan, Charente-Maritime

Generalleutnant Hermann Wilck	GOC
Oberst von Auer	Chief of Staff
Hauptmann Rosenberger	Intelligence Officer

Abwehr, Paris

Fregattenkapitän Dr Erich Pheiffer	Abwehr (Abteilung IIIM), Paris

Security Services, Bordeaux

Oberstleutnant Lohrscheider	Abwehr (Abteilung IIIM)
Hauptmann Glatzel	Abwehr (Abteilung IIIM)
Oberleutnant Helmut Harstick	Abwehr (Abteilung IIIM)
Sturmbannführer Dr Hans Luther	Head, Sicherheitsdienst (SD)

Kapitänleutnant Franz Drey	Second-in-Command, Bordeaux SD, with special responsibility for the security of the Bordeaux docks

Prologue

It was 9.15 p.m., dark, and now that the sun had set, bitterly cold. Attempting to minimise their silhouette the four men slouched low in the gunnels of their two canoes, gazing in wonderment across the shifting black waters to the huge bulk of the two freighters on the far side of the river, illuminated in the glare of the dockside arc lamps. The fierce cold of the December night and the chilling rain that had fallen all day were forgotten in the excitement of the moment. The men and the boats in which they waited (named *Catfish* and *Crayfish*) had just emerged from a forest of eight-foot-high rushes that sprouted in profusion along the western bank of the Garonne River less than two miles from the heart of Bordeaux. They had spent the day hiding in the reeds, waiting the turn of the tide that would sweep them on to their objective.

So far as they knew they were the only four remaining at large. Ten men in five canoes had set out from the Royal Navy's T Class submarine HMS *Tuna* five nights before on a mission to attack the enemy ships lying alongside the quays in the very heart of Bordeaux, sixty-two miles from the point at which the Gironde estuary laps the waters of the Atlantic.

Leaving the iron bowels of the submarine three nautical miles off the tiny village of Montalivet-les-Bains, only three canoes were to survive the fierce challenges provided by the forces of nature that first terrible night. The remaining Royal Marines had crept up the Gironde and, when the river bifurcated, paddled south into the mighty Garonne (the left fork leads into the Dordogne), moving at night and with the tide to attempt to get to their objective, their minds fixed resolutely on the absolute need to complete their mission. The saboteurs' targets were not battleships, like the *Tirpitz* lying protected far to the north in a Norwegian fjord, but fast, ocean-going freighters preparing to run the gauntlet of the Allied naval blockade of the French Atlantic ports. Bordeaux was the European terminus of a trade in scarce commodities between Germany and Japan; and these were armed merchantmen making the long run to the other side of the world singly through the South Atlantic, around the Cape of Good Hope and thence through the Indian Ocean to the Far East, refuelling in Malaya and Singapore. It was a trade of desperation; a trade in goods which were denied to both countries because their own actions, in bringing about war on such an extensive scale, had closed to them the opportunities for uninhibited trade freely available in times of peace.

The noise of the bustle on the docks eight hundred yards away had not carried over the water during the day, leaving the four men, hidden in their canoes amidst the reeds, alone with their thoughts. What had happened to their six comrades? The fact was that two were already dead, taken by the effects of the cold water on their exhausted bodies; and two were soon to die, blindfolded and executed by a naval firing squad in a hastily dug sandpit in an anonymous wood probably no more than six miles from where the surviving canoeists lay unseen. Had they known these facts, it would have spurred these extraordinarily committed individuals even more to achieve their goal that night: the crippling of as many blockade-runners as they could find with the magnetic mines or 'limpets' now armed and piled between their legs. The silence was broken by a brief whisper from the forward canoeist. The men dipped their paddles into the water, carefully drawing away from the safety of the rushes for the dark sanctuary of mid-river, on the final stage of their mission.

What desperation led Britain's war leaders to authorise such a hazardous enterprise, deep in the heart of enemy territory more than three years into the war? What possible hope was there that a few hardy men in canoes might contribute positively to the outcome of what was now, since the German invasion of the Soviet Union in June 1941 and the Japanese declaration of war in December, a global conflagration?

One answer, of course, is that victory, when it came, would constitute the sum of a wide-ranging effort, both large- and small-scale. Some tasks, after all, could be better undertaken by small groups of men and women rather than by the big battalions. London had decided that a bombing raid against the Bordeaux docks to remove the present scourge would risk too many innocent French lives. On 8 December 1940, for instance, an RAF raid on the Italian submarines moored at Bacalan caused sixteen civilian deaths and sixty-seven wounded. Uncomfortable with the prospect of sustaining what would now be described as collateral damage, they determined that it was a job calling for skill and courage of a type different from that which entailed flying for many hours across enemy skies in thin, combustible tin coffins, and gave the task to Combined Operations. The attack would be of an alternative kind: a rapier thrust from the sea using canoe-borne raiders of the Royal Marines.

Vice-Admiral Lord Louis Mountbatten, the young and flamboyant head of Combined Operations, authorised the raid, but according to his biographer Philip Ziegler he did so with reluctance, 'since he felt it unlikely that any of the twelve participants would return'. A more appropriate name for the raid would have been Operation Suicide.

Standing at the Pointe de Grave looking across the wind-tossed sea to distant Royan is a sobering experience, for it is only when one gazes at the hostile tide sweeping the choppy grey waters of the Gironde through the narrow channel of the estuary mouth that one appreciates the immense physical and mental effort required merely to breach the natural defences *in canoes*, let alone make the journey deep inside heavily patrolled enemy territory to Bordeaux. The Gironde (combining the Dordogne and the Garonne) is one of Europe's mightiest rivers, a wide, unruly waterway riven by dangerous tidal influences and interspersed with shifting sandbanks. It seems to rejoice in catching the unwary, as many modern experienced mariners will attest. Even Ewen Southby-Tailyour, that most seasoned of sailors and Blondie Hasler's biographer, told me that navigating the Gironde in his yacht had been an unpleasant experience.

I first stood and watched these swirling waters in the warm rays of the September sun: the Royal Marines, in 1942, did so in the bitter cold of mid-December. I could but wonder at the extremes of physical fitness, of determination and sheer bloody-minded pluck that pushed their frail canvas and plywood vessels through this hostile open water, in darkness, surrounded by dangers manmade and natural, those December nights so long ago. They did it for duty, because this was what they had volunteered to do, in defence of their country, which they knew to a man to be in grave peril. They did it for Major 'Blondie' Hasler, their pernickety and fastidious but inspirational leader. But most of all they did it for themselves. They were Royal Marines. They had been trained for this moment. Although the title *Cockleshell Heroes* was made up by an Ealing hack for the 1955 film, and was one that Hasler detested, there is no doubt in my mind that the title accurately reflects what these men had managed to do, in the face of every possible obstacle and danger. Overused as the term now is, they were indeed true heroes, and the story of their raid one of the most extraordinary small-team endeavours of the Second World War.

ONE

1941 and 1942

Britain's war effort in Europe during 1941 had the effect of a mosquito biting an elephant's hide. Limited successes in North Africa and the Middle East, such as the beleaguered Tobruk garrison holding out for many months against Axis forces commanded by General Erwin Rommel, and the eradication (almost accidentally) of German influence in Iraq, Syria and Iran, were ants in the path of a bulldozer. In the big scheme of things – the massive preponderance of German military might that had subdued Western Europe in a matter of weeks and was threatening to do the same to the Soviet Union – British operations in 1941 did not seem to amount to much. But it wasn't just that the war was going badly; it was that there seemed no prospect of Britain's fortunes improving. The United States remained frustratingly far from any formal commitment as a combatant power.

In fact, the first light of a new dawn only began to appear three full years after the start of the war – in late 1942 – with the denial of Egypt and the Nile to Rommel's Afrika Korps at El Alamein in October, followed quickly by the first Allied landings in Morocco and Algeria in November (Operation Torch). For the occupants of that half of France administered by Vichy under loose German control, the Free Zone (or *Zone Libre*), this proved to be a bittersweet moment, as it prompted the Germans to sweep in and occupy the whole of France.

Germany's defeat of France and the Low Countries in June 1940 had been so comprehensive that Berlin quickly developed a sense of complacency about the security of France. Almost immediately it became a leave station. When he arrived in Caen on a sweltering day in July 1940, Private Hugo Bleicher of the Abwehr went for a stroll through the town, had a *café noir* with the pretty proprietor of the Pelican café, and promptly fell in love. The summer heat, the newness of it all and the testosterone of victory were intoxicating. Equally enamoured of her love-struck young German, Suzanne packed up her things, closed the café, and would remain by his side for the next four years.

Life with the victor was infinitely preferable to life as a victim. For the young Hamburg clerk it was a summer of love. For many young Germans, involuntary tourists in France gazing wide-eyed at all that the country even in defeat could offer, war seemed a distinctly abstract concept. The rapid end of the fighting and the balmy conditions combined to create an atmosphere for many that was reminiscent of a long, contented summer holiday. When, in June 1941, Operation Barbarossa turned Germany's triumphant war machine towards the Soviet Union – thus saving Britain from the prospect of being swallowed up – soldiers would ask to be sent on leave to France, to enjoy the pleasures of the occupation in a tranquil haven far from the violence of war in the East.

In truth, Nazi Germany expected Britain to fall and had determined that it need not waste undue effort in hastening the inevitable. Berlin was not alone in this assessment. Washington, among others, had come to the same conclusion. The French General Weygand, looking forlornly in June 1940 at the ignominious collapse of his own country, predicted the same fate for Britain. In three weeks, he declared, her neck would be wrung 'like a chicken'.

This view was entirely understandable. Britain stood on the very precipice of defeat. The bulk of her deployable pre-war professional army had been destroyed in France and its equipment left at Dunkirk: 12,200 artillery pieces, 1,350 anti-aircraft and anti-tank guns, 6,400 anti-tank rifles, 11,000 machine-guns, 75,000 vehicles and virtually all its tanks. German military strength was as unexpected (to the losers) as it was unmatched, slicing through the Low Countries in an unprecedented display of mobile combined arms superiority that brought France to her knees in six weeks and introduced a fearsome new word to the lexicon of war in the West, a word the Poles had already encountered: *Blitzkrieg*. Only the heroism of a few stood in the way of German ambitions during the Battle of Britain in 1940, but even that was insufficient, it seemed, to halt the seemingly inexorable march of the victorious German legions elsewhere in Europe, especially in North Africa.

From as early as the fall of France in June 1940, most intelligent opinion gave Britain little hope of survival. Captain Basil Liddell Hart, a noisy and initially influential English pre-war military theorist, despairing of the imminent demise of British civilisation, started circulating papers advocating surrender. Liddell Hart had a ready audience, some of whom, like Rab Butler, occupied positions in high places. Butler, Undersecretary of State at the Foreign Office, admitted to the Swedish minister in June that Britain would only fight on if it could guarantee victory. The Anglophobic American ambassador, Joseph Kennedy, reported Britain's impending ruin in regular semi-exultant tones to his masters in Washington. He fled to the countryside to escape the Blitz. Roosevelt sacked him in November following an incoherent interview published in the *Boston Globe* in which he opined that, for the United States, 'The whole reason for aiding England is to give us time . . . As long as she is in there, we have time to prepare. It isn't that [Britain is] fighting for democracy. That's the bunk. She's fighting for self-preservation, just as we will if it comes to us.'

Kennedy wasn't the only one trying to escape. Along with the gold reserves of the Bank of England, which were shipped to Canada in July 1940, went thousands of those able to afford the passage across the Atlantic, including many members of the US Embassy and the British moneyed classes. Henry ('Chips')

Channon and his soon-to-be estranged wife Honor took their five-year-old son Paul to Euston station early on 24 June, two days after France fell, en route for the sanctuary of the New World. Outside the station Channon observed a long 'queue of Rolls-Royces and liveried servants and mountains of trunks. It seemed that everyone we knew was there on the very crowded platform.' Fearful of death from the air, Liddell Hart also fled London in 1940, ending up in a country garden on the shores of Lake Windermere. The Chicago-born Channon wondered in his diary on 2 June whether this was the end of England. 'Are we witnessing . . . the decline, the decay and perhaps extinction, of this great island people?'

It certainly looked that way. Britain was now threatened by invasion from France and the Low Countries, and faced desertion by her allies. True, the Commonwealth had responded quickly to the threat faced by Britain, but France the old ally, now represented by Vichy, not only turned its back on Britain but also actively sought to support the victor. Jock Colville, Churchill's Private Secretary, observed despondently in his diary at the end of 1940 at the thought of the consequences of defeat: 'Western Europe racked by warfare and economic hardship; the legacy of centuries, in art and culture, swept away; the health of the nation dangerously impaired by malnutrition, nervous strain and epidemics; Russia and possibly the U.S. profiting from our exhaustion; and at the end of it all compromise or Pyrrhic victory.'

Despite this gloom it remained inconceivable to most Britons that the country should merely await its fate. One of the reasons for Churchill's popularity in 1940 and 1941 was that he embodied the will of the common people to fight back against the Nazi bully-boys trampling Europe under the heels of their hobnailed jackboots. They did not share the fears of those natural pessimists for whom any struggle against vast odds (especially for such nebulous concepts as 'God, King and Country') constituted pointless effort. The overwhelming feeling of the vast majority in

Britain was that they had to resist tyranny. In London the fight against pessimism was led very publicly by the Prime Minister himself. To the eager boys at his alma mater Harrow School, in 1941, Churchill thundered: 'Never give in – never, never, never, never, in nothing great or small, large or petty, never give in except to convictions of honour and good sense. Never yield to force; never yield to the apparently overwhelming might of the enemy.' Whatever his private fears, the public face of Britain in the years following 1939 was of bulldog-like resistance, a refusal to accept failure or surrender.

'Here is the answer which I will give to President Roosevelt,' he told the nation in a BBC radio broadcast on 9 February 1941: 'We shall not fail or falter; we shall not weaken or tire. Neither the sudden shock of battle nor the long-drawn trials of vigilance and exertion will wear us down. Give us the tools and we will finish the job.'

The onslaught against Britain began in earnest in the summer of 1940, following the humiliation – dressed up as victory – of Dunkirk. What had become known as the 'Blitz' was in full swing in the months that followed France's surrender through to May 1941, German bombers from France nightly crossing the English Channel and the Irish Sea to unburden their payloads of high explosives on defenceless civilian populations below. It was the horrifying smell of excrement and disinfectant that greeted the novelist Brian Moore, then working as an air-raid warden in Belfast, in the aftermath of a Luftwaffe raid on the city on 15 April 1941. Heaped bodies, contorted in the inelegant postures of death, confronted him in a mortuary, 'body on body, flung arm, twisted feet, open mouth, staring eyes, old men on top of young women, a child lying on a policeman's back, a soldier's hand resting on a woman's thigh, a carter still wearing his coal sacks on top of a pile of arms and legs'. It was later estimated that Belfast had suffered over fifteen hundred dead and seriously injured in a single night.

If it was the Battle for France and the Battle of Britain that dominated 1940, it was the onset of the Battle of the Atlantic in 1941 that very nearly brought Britain to her knees. In the North Sea German surface raiders such as the battleships *Bismarck* and *Tirpitz* threatened to join the massive U-boat campaign in the Atlantic against shipping en route to the British Isles, a shockingly effective offensive that could have strangled the country's lifeline to the free world and starved her into submission. Churchill later described the Battle of the Atlantic as the only thing in the war that ever really frightened him. He had every reason to be worried. The U-boat campaign very nearly won the war for Germany in 1941. In that year alone 875 Allied ships were sunk traversing the Atlantic – a total loss of 3,295,000 tons – 432 of them by submarine. These were catastrophic losses that could not be sustained indefinitely.

It was the inability of the government, despite the rhetoric of defiance from Downing Street, that most plagued the conscience of those trying to hold back the unseen menace from the deep and the threat from the vapour-trails in the sky. As horrible as indiscriminate obliteration from the air was the prospect of death by way of the storm-tossed sea. When seventy-six children died in the cold, grey, swirling seas of the Atlantic when the SS *City of Benares* was torpedoed by a U-boat in September 1940, it was not only their parents who grieved. The nation, which could not even protect the most vulnerable, was humiliated. Churchill demanded that the evacuation of children to the New World cease, and within weeks it did. But the threat from the sea grew. The worst month of the Battle of the Atlantic was November 1942, when more than 700,000 tons of shipping was lost. With the loss of life came the sinking of war equipment from the United States purchased on credit (the final instalment in Britain's war debt to the USA and Canada was paid only in 2006), urgently required to replenish Britain's empty armoury.

In 1941 food was severely rationed as a consequence of the

success of the 'wolf packs' in sinking vast quantities of precious shipping. The Japanese invasion of South-East Asia in December 1941 also had mercantile implications for Britain, as at a stroke supplies of rubber, tin and rice from Malaya stopped. In the following year taxes rose, the basic rate of income tax reaching an unprecedented 50 per cent. At the same time the National Service Act was extended to introduce conscription for unmarried women between the ages of twenty and thirty, to add to that for men which had been brought in at the outbreak of war.

In these dark days in which she stood alone against Germany, aided only by her empire and Commonwealth, Britain had to find practical ways to resist the might of the all-conquering German war machine. She had few resources. After Dunkirk the country had only fifteen divisions available for home defence – fourteen infantry (one of which was Canadian) and one armoured. The Wehrmacht alone had deployed ninety-three divisions in its attack on the West. In Britain the RAF was outnumbered three to one, with the bulk of the Luftwaffe flying day and night sorties over British cities. With no means of retaliation Channon's 'great island people' began to stare at the demoralising inevitability of defeat. Unless it could feel that it was striking back and that there remained the possibility, however fleeting, of eventual Axis defeat, the motivation to continue the struggle became much harder to sustain.

One of the few means available of 'doing something' at the time was aerial bombing. The other was commando-type raiding on the enemy coast. The former was limited by the number and type of aircraft to do the job, as well as the number and quality of the munitions available to drop on strategic targets in Germany and occupied countries. Both were embarrassingly limited, a product of Britain's abject failure to take the defence of the country seriously during the interwar years. In the case of raiding, very little expertise existed outside of the advocacy, enthusiasm and personal drive of a small number of extraordinary men. Little existed in terms of doctrine or practical ideas for raiding in either the Army or the Royal Navy, and had to be assembled almost entirely from scratch. A large part of the British Army had been destroyed in France, and despite the 'miracle of Dunkirk' it required considerable time, effort and expense to reconstitute. Clearly, help in the short term at least could not come from this source. Likewise, the Royal Navy was impossibly stretched from the Atlantic to the Mediterranean, not to mention her global commitments.

The strategic imperative, however, was clear. The physical reality of Britain's military impoverishment banished any thoughts other than of fighting the enemy where they threatened most directly. This meant no choice but the allocation of all available resources – fighting men, tanks, guns, armoured cars and aircraft – to North Africa and the Middle East, for it was here that Britain was confronted directly by Axis action.

But while these struggles were under way across a vast sweep of territory stretching from Libya to Iran, Churchill fretted about the seeming impotence of Britain's forces in the home territories, the country watching timorously behind the grey Channel moat as the helmeted legions over the water exerted their tyranny unimpeded. It was in this context, of fighting back regardless of the odds, that raiding operations were to develop and thrive. The fact that they represented a tiny, perhaps even foolhardy, response to the might of the Teutonic behemoth bestriding the remnants of European civilisation acted as an even greater stimulus. Britons understood, perhaps even relished, the concept of the underdog – as the enduring success of the television programme *Dad's Army* so strikingly attests.

Churchill had demanded continuous violent action to be undertaken against the enemy coast until such a time as a full-scale reconquest of the Continent could be launched, an eventuality he knew could be many years away. On 4 June 1940 – the final day of the Dunkirk evacuation – he had a memo sent to his Chief of Staff, General Hastings ('Pug') Ismay:

> The completely defensive habit of mind, which has ruined the French, must not be allowed to ruin all our initiative. It is of the highest consequence to keep the largest numbers of German forces all along the coasts of the countries they have conquered, and we should immediately set to work to organise raiding forces on these coasts where the populations are friendly. Such forces might be composed of self-contained, thoroughly-equipped units of say 1,000 up to not more than 10,000 when combined. Surprise would be ensured by the fact that their destination would be concealed until the last moment. What we have seen at Dunkirk shows how quickly troops can be moved off (and I suppose on) to selected points if need be. How wonderful it would be if the Germans could be made to wonder where they were going to be struck next, instead of forcing us to try to wall in the Island and roof it over! An effort must be made to shake off the mental and moral prostration to the will and initiative of the enemy from which we suffer.

Two days later he reprised this theme, telling Ismay – in case the message had not been clear enough the first time – that he wanted the joint chiefs of staff to propose 'measures for a vigorous, enterprising and ceaseless offensive against the whole German-occupied coastline'. The chiefs of staff agreed to the establishment of a force of five thousand men from across the British Army, to be formed into 'striking companies'.

On the same day – 6 June 1940 – Colonel Dudley Clarke, a South African-born officer in the Royal Artillery, was instructed to set up a group of uniformed guerrillas who were to be responsible for carrying out, in part at least, the Prime Minister's new instructions. Clarke found himself in Section 9 of the Military Operations Directorate of the War Office, or MO9 for short. The name he gave to these new troops – 'commandos' – was picked straight out of the title of Deneys Reitz's exciting account of the activities of mobile columns of Boer fighters: men who, despite their inferiority in numbers and supplies, had struck back vigorously and successfully against the British in South Africa forty years before.

The tale of forced marches, ambuscades, night attacks and narrow escapes was, to Clarke, the perfect description of Churchill's requirement. Despite some resistance, the name stuck. A new organisation – Raiding Forces – was created, and Lieutenant General Sir Alan Bourne of the Royal Marines was appointed Commander of Raiding Operations. He did not hold the post for long. A deeply cerebral man, he made the mistake one evening over dinner at 10 Downing Street of giving the Prime Minister, according to one observer, an ill-judged 'dissertation on strategy'. His appointment nevertheless began a close relationship between the Royal Marines and Combined Operations. For much of its life the senior planning and operational posts in Combined Operations were held by officers of the Royal Marines.

Raids began immediately, but, without the benefit of much prior planning or preparation, achieved little of substance. Nevertheless it was a start, and valuable lessons were quickly learned, especially about the need for proper training and equipment, most notably purpose-designed landing craft. Colonel John Durnford-Slater, whose baptism of fire with the newly raised No. 3 Commando this was, concluded that one of the raids, on Guernsey, was 'a ridiculous, almost comic, failure'. Churchill, whose inclination was to support raids of any kind so long as they dealt the enemy a bloody nose, was horrified at the early efforts of the hastily assembled raiders, describing them, a little unfairly, as 'silly fiascos'. He thought the problem was their scale, demanding that 'pinprick raids' be avoided in favour of raids of such seriousness that the Germans would be forced to worry where the next blow might fall.

Churchill had in mind a series of substantial raids against the entire extent of the Nazi seaboard, which would harass the occupiers and compel them to tie down troops. He wanted operations in which armoured vehicles would debouch on to an enemy shore, 'do a deep raid inland, cutting vital communication, and then back, leaving a trail of German corpses behind them'. Guerrilla-style 'pinprick raids' against the coast by small groups of commandos followed by 'fulsome communiqués is one strictly to be avoided', he directed. His vision instead was to work up to a point where 'large armoured eruptions' reaching as far, perhaps, as Paris, would provide the overall tenor of offensive operations in the years before the reconquest of Europe would be possible.

The sort of raid the Prime Minister envisaged was confirmed by his appointment of the legendary figure Admiral Sir Roger Keyes, on 17 July 1940, to the post of Director Combined Operations (to replace the hapless Bourne). Keyes, as the commander of Dover Port in 1918, had led the famous raid of German-held Zeebrugge, a largely ineffectual though successfully propagandised enterprise that gained ennoblement for Keyes together with a cheque from a grateful nation for £10,000. He had a huge and genuine personality, and was desperate to re-enter the fray. He had been at Gallipoli and knew what landing operations required in order to be successful. With a sensible plan, the right equipment and rehearsals, together with effective training for all those involved in or in support of a raid, even the smallest and seemingly insignificant operation could bring results that far exceeded the resources committed to it.

The immediate purpose of these raids was to force the Germans to disperse their forces across the length and breadth of the coast, to maintain morale in Britain and to keep the fighting spirit alive in the armed forces. Amphibious strikes against the enemy coast would tell British (and later, American) military planners much about what would be required to prepare for the reconquest of Europe. But the capacity to launch even small-scale raids was extremely limited, there being only nine heavy landing craft in Royal Navy service at the time, and only six of these in British waters. Likewise, difficulties in raising the units, training the men, finding the ships, designing seagoing craft able to deposit assault troops directly on to an enemy-held shore – and all in the teeth of every other priority of the moment – proved too much for even the legendary Keyes to solve. Keyes thought he knew where the problem lay, writing to Ismay that even the Prime Minister could not solve the problems he faced 'unless he starts afresh and gets two or three ardent offensive spirits – free from everlasting Committees – to help him do so'.

This was only partly fair. Keyes expected far too much, too quickly, of Britain's shattered army. In the days and months following Dunkirk, the country was starved of trained fighting units which could be moved into the new raiding organisation. There were a few defence battalions guarding key points across the British isles, four battalions of the Royal Marine Light Infantry, and an organisation in the Royal Marines charged with defending harbour installations: the Mobile Naval Base Defence Organisation (MNBDO). But precious little else.

What there was in abundance – despite Keyes' advancing years (he was sixty-nine) – was fighting spirit, enthusiasm and talent. The commando units and independent companies set up in the days immediately following Churchill's injunction served to attract, on the one hand, an eclectic assortment of talented adventurers and, on the other, a number of shirkers, according to the actor David Niven. Niven had returned from Hollywood to rejoin the colours (he had been commissioned into the Highland Light Infantry from Sandhurst in 1930) and found himself appointed to MO9 with Clarke in the early days of raiding.

In 1940 Roger ('Jumbo') Courtney, the well known African big-game hunter and canoe enthusiast – he had once canoed down the Nile from Lake Victoria, a distance of 2,300 miles, carrying a sack of potatoes and an elephant spear, his only possessions other than the clothes on his back and the boots on his feet – managed to persuade Admiral Keyes of the potential offered by canoes to target enemy shipping in harbour with magnetic mines that could be attached by hand to their hulls. He presented a paper proposing an attack from the sea using folding canoes – called Folbots, named after the first commercially viable folding kayak made by the German Johannes Klepper, the *Faltboot*, in 1906. This was initially dismissed out of hand on the grounds that ships were too large and complex to be boarded, let alone damaged, by one man. But the forty-year-old Lieutenant Courtney persisted, demonstrating spectacularly to a sceptical naval staff the validity of his idea, namely that in certain circumstances ships at anchor were uniquely vulnerable to sabotage.

He proceeded to swim out undetected to the commando ship HMS *Glengyle* anchored in the River Clyde and removed the cover from one of its anti-aircraft guns to prove where he had been, before swimming back to shore. He then interrupted, still in his dripping swimming trunks, a meeting of naval officers, throwing the pom-pom cover melodramatically on to the table. On another occasion he planted huge white chalk marks down the side of a vessel to demonstrate the ability of swimmers or canoeists to get close to ships without being seen, and to lay mines against their hulls.

The idea of using canoes – canoeing was a fast-growing pre-war water sport popular on both fresh and sea water – to launch pinprick raids against the enemy was one that came to a number of inventive minds at the beginning of the war. On 15 July 1940 Engineer Lieutenant G.M.D. Wright RN of HMS *Triumph*, for example, wrote to the commander of the 2nd Submarine Flotilla on HMS *Forth* (a submarine support ship) suggesting the use of the well known civilian single and two-man Folbot collapsible canoes against the enemy. In addition to carrying a load of up to four hundred pounds, Wright argued, a canoe could, in suitable conditions, be 'sent from a submarine into a harbour where enemy ships were suspected of lying [to bring about] considerable damage'. Wright listed the virtues of canoes:

1 complete silence
2 no silhouette
3 easy manoeuvrability
4 a man in training could maintain 4 knots for over an hour
5 seaworthy qualities in a small breaking or large unbreaking sea
6 when collapsed would take up no room in a submarine.

Courtney's point, and Wright's arguments, were made. Vice-Admiral Max Horton, then the Vice-Admiral (Submarines) at the Admiralty, asked on 2 August 1940 for permission to supply a one-man Folbot for trials. These were satisfactorily carried out at the Special Service ('Commando') training centre at Lochailort; and Keyes authorised Second Lieutenant Courtney to raise, confusingly, a 'Folboat' troop of eleven men as part of No. 8 Commando. Thirty Folbots were ordered from their manufacturer in London's East End.

During 1941, from Malta and Alexandria, Courtney did much to develop the art of raiding from the sea with a group of men in the Special Boat Section of the Army Commandos. Launched from submarines in the Mediterranean, small detachments of men would paddle into the shore, attacking airfields, bridges, roads and trains and carrying out reconnaissances of the enemy coast. The idea was mooted as to the efficacy of doing something similar against targets in Europe, and on 8 September the Deputy Combined Operations (Bourne) sent a letter to Brigadier Charles Haydon, Commander of the Special Service Brigade (the Commandos), asking that early examination be undertaken of the capabilities of two-man Folbots and RAF rescue dinghies.

Courtney's deputy, Captain Gerald Montanaro of the Royal Engineers, was the commander of 101 Troop of the Special Boat Section (also part of the Special Service Brigade) based in Dover harbour, and was tasked with identifying answers to the following questions:

1 In a slight or moderate sea what quantity of explosive (max. weight and size) can safely be carried in addition to a crew of two with personal equipment, weighing together 350lbs?
2 What speed can be maintained, fully loaded, and for what continuous period?
3 Are they capable of towing a Folbot or raft carrying additional stores, and at what speed can this be done under the above sea conditions?

The only way to answer these questions was by close engagement with the enemy. On the night of 12 November 1941 a canoe reconnaissance was undertaken on Les Hemmes beach between Gravelines and Calais. A motor torpedo boat dropped the canoes some two thousand yards from shore. One of the two Folbots employed capsized in the surf and Lieutenant Keith Smith was lost, and later captured. Then, on the night of 11 April 1942 Montanaro, together with Private Preece of the King's Shropshire Light Infantry, launched their Folbot from a motor torpedo boat in the dark three miles from Boulogne harbour in a live operation against the enemy.

Their target was a heavily laden German freighter, perhaps of 4,000 tons, carrying a cargo, as it turned out, of copper ore. The canoe carried eight of the newly designed limpet mines, activated by acetone fuses. The two crewmen wore kapok-lined survival 'Octopus' suits of the type that had just begun to be issued to fighter pilots, which were designed to keep a man afloat and warm enough to survive for twenty-four hours at sea. Under cover of darkness and with blackened faces they made their way through the heavily defended harbour, brightly lit by searchlights, to place eight limpet mines (all on four-hour fuses) on the hull of the vessel. Some drunken Germans at one point threw a beer bottle into the water, wetting the men with the splash.

Their collapsible canoe was scarcely up to the task, however, and was damaged during the approach to the target when it struck a submerged concrete ledge. 'I ordered Preece to ram his cap-comforter into the hole,' recalled Montanaro, 'and to start all chemical fuzes, thus committing us to the attack.' They found that they had to scrape the barnacles off the hull before the magnets on the limpets would stick, at least one refusing to hold and dropping into the sea. They then slipped away into the night, the Folbot wallowing dangerously with four inches of water inside it, making the task of paddling exhausting and the vessel ungainly and difficult to control. The two men only just managed to find their way back to the waiting motor launch and drag themselves back on to it before the Folbot sank beneath them. The launch then powered its way home to Dover. Aerial photographs the following day showed that their target had sunk, but later intelligence suggested the Germans had executed a number of innocent Frenchmen, believing that the sinking was the result of sabotage by the Resistance.

TWO

The Hand of Steel from the Sea

Keyes struggled to achieve the success for Combined Operations that he repeatedly promised. But even this valiant old warhorse – for all his faults, and immodesty was his chief failing (Ismay described him as 'the bravest of the brave') – could do little to bring about the offensive capability for which he had been tasked. No major raids followed his appointment for eight months and those then undertaken comprised attacks on largely peripheral outstations of the newly expanded Reich. This was not, however, for want of planning. In their new headquarters in Richmond Terrace (opposite Downing Street) where Keyes had deliberately taken the new Combined Operations organisation so that it could be independent of Admiralty influence, a string of ambitious operations was conceived throughout 1940 and 1941, most of which foundered on the rocks of insufficient resources or opposition from the service chiefs.

Combined Operations was regarded by some in the more traditional services to be immature and premature, and viewed jealously. The personal prejudices, agendas and vendettas of individuals had a significant role to play in the decisions that were made in the early years of its existence. Plans were drawn up to install the Free French in Dakar, to capture the Azores from Portugal and the Canary Islands from Spain, as well as to seize the Italian island of Pantelleria between Sicily and Tunis, and thus a potential aid in the defence of Malta. Major General John Kennedy (Director of

Military Operations at the War Office) also affirmed that by the end of 1940 planning was under way for the eventual descent on the Normandy coast, even though most recognised that this event would be many years ahead of them. '[The] correct raiding policy at this period of the war,' Kennedy argued, 'was to harry the enemy with small detachments on a wide front, and thus force him to maintain troops all along the coast-line for the purposes of defence.'

In Europe, three major raids were carried out by Combined Operations in 1941.* In the first of these, in March, two requisitioned Dutch passenger liners, carrying five hundred commandos and protected by a screen of five destroyers, landed on the Norwegian Lofoten Islands, surprising the German occupiers and destroying 800,000 gallons of fish oil from factories that supplied glycerine to the German war economy. There was little opposition. Local Norwegians initially assumed that it was a German exercise, but before long were plying the commandos with ersatz coffee. One young British subaltern commandeered the German telegraph office at Stamsund and sent a message addressed to Mr A. Hitler, Berlin: 'You said in your last speech that German troops would meet the British wherever they landed. Where are your troops?'

War was still something of a game to this young adventurer. The truth was that the Germans had more serious fish to fry. On 27 March a coup in Yugoslavia overthrew the pro-Axis government. A week later both Yugoslavia and Greece were invaded in a lightning attack that forced Yugoslavia to surrender on the 17th, and Greece to capitulate ten days later. The Lofoten Islands raid was an insignificant sideshow that the Germans recognised for what it was: the last and futile flailing of a dying state. A second raid on the Lofoten Islands took place in late December 1941.

This relative lack of vigour was not entirely the fault of the fledgling Combined Operations organisation (or of Keyes himself) as it struggled to find resources, penetrate the prejudice of the

* In addition to three conducted in the Mediterranean.

existing services, overcome the jealousy of other officers unable to challenge Keyes' relationship with the Prime Minister or compete with the defensive demands of a country expecting a German invasion at any moment. Nor could it provide the wherewithal to engage the enemy in Europe when almost the entirety of Britain's offensive capability on land in 1941 was concentrated on the Mediterranean, North Africa and the Middle East.

Nevertheless, Keyes' constant battles with the chiefs of staff led to his undoing. A reluctant Prime Minister was forced to retire his old friend and replace him with someone less strident and more amenable to the chiefs. He was not going to ask them to nominate an appointment, however. As Minister of Defence (as well as Prime Minister), Churchill reserved this prerogative for himself. It was important that the new incumbent owed his loyalty to him personally, and not to any of the three service heads. So it was that the young, flamboyant and even aggressively impetuous Captain Lord Louis Mountbatten was intercepted in Los Angeles, one day in October 1941, by the British consul waving an urgent telegram. Mountbatten was ordered to return to London without delay. He had recently been appointed captain of the aircraft carrier HMS *Illustrious*, then being refitted in Norfolk, Virginia, following a hard season in the Mediterranean. He had taken the opportunity to visit Hawaii and to examine the vast US Pacific Fleet anchored safely at Pearl Harbor.

Irritated by the loss of his command Mountbatten returned home as ordered, making the long and difficult journey by plane. None too pleased to be losing the chance to command a capital ship, he demonstrated something of this displeasure when, called to meet the Prime Minister at Chequers on his return, he was told that he was to replace Keyes. On responding that what he really wanted was command of a ship, an exasperated Churchill blurted out that he was a fool: he warned him that, as with his recent experience when he had been sunk off the coast of Crete in HMS *Kelly*, persisting in pursuing a ship command would inevitably lead to him being sunk again – the only difference now being that it would be in a more expensive ship.

Being sunk once (and surviving) could be considered glorious, but twice would be sheer recklessness. Did Mountbatten not recognise the promotion that the appointment of 'adviser' to Combined Operations entailed?

Despite his reservations, Mountbatten accepted the appointment. Churchill recognised in him a man who, while lacking military seniority and the experience of higher command, was nevertheless instinctively suspicious of the committees that had bedevilled Keyes, unworried by the requirements of due process, hateful even of bureaucracy and, if his time in command at sea was anything to go by, complacent about the sort of risks that might vex someone more conservative. He was also young and subservient, a man who would seek to please rather than, like Keyes, antagonise the chiefs. In short, Mountbatten was rash enough, and not too calculating of risks, to make the business of raiding a success.

'You will continue Commando raids,' instructed the Prime Minister, 'for they are important for the morale of this country and of our allies. But the primary task will be to prepare for the great invasion, for unless we return to the Continent and beat the Germans on land we shall never win the war.' Seeking to inject pace into his newly inherited empire, Mountbatten called for two raids a week. Anything would be considered.

Churchill chose well. The King's cousin was single-minded, a natural enthusiast and vain enough to want to be successful in his new post, which – despite his earlier reservations – he now set about with gusto. Keyes had lost his battle with the three chiefs of staff to be the independent director of a fourth, combined service. His refusal to accept demotion to that of mere 'adviser' to the War Cabinet, instead of being an integral part of it, had led inevitably to his demise. The fighting calibre of the man was amply demonstrated when he accused the assembled chiefs to their face of being 'yellow'; but in his efforts to create a fourth service he was trying to push water uphill.

Churchill explained in unequivocal terms what he expected Mountbatten to achieve. At a time when the prospect of the invasion of German-occupied Europe was still a distant dream, his task was to re-energise the plan to launch commando raids against the occupied coast from the North Cape to the Bay of Biscay, while at the same time preparing the plans and forces necessary for the re-invasion of France. Promoted from captain to commodore (but still far junior in rank to his predecessor), Keyes, who was to complain in a letter to Ismay a mere two months later that the chiefs of staff had conceded to Mountbatten all that they had refused him. This was because, as the historian of Combined Operations Hilary St George Saunders was to suggest, Mountbatten did not, like Keyes, 'make the mistake of Icarus, and soar too close to the sun'. On handing over his responsibilities to Mountbatten, Keyes observed bitterly: 'Dicky, the trouble is that the British have lost the will to fight. There's no spirit of attack any more. The Chiefs of Staff are the greatest cowards I've ever met.'*

Throughout 1941 responsibility for raiding the enemy coast lay in the hands of the Army commands on the southern and south-eastern coasts. The idea was that the Army would ask Combined Operations for the requisite resources and then undertake the operations themselves. The process did not work well, lacking coordination and strategic coherence. As a consequence, few serious raids took place on the French coast that year and Combined Operations found that its operations tended to be in Norwegian waters, far from the purview of the regional Army commanders-in-chief.

At the end of the year a second attack on German-occupied Norway was mounted against the islands of Vaagso and Maaloy, between Bergen and Trondheim, by 570 men of Colonel

* Mountbatten was elevated from 'adviser' to 'Chief of Combined Operations' on 18 March 1942, and promoted from Commodore to Acting Vice-Admiral.

Durnford-Slater's No. 3 Commando, together with elements from three other Commandos. The Cruiser HMS *Kenya*, four destroyers and two landing craft together with the 'T' Class submarine HMS *Tuna* arrived off the target on the morning of 27 December, and began a preparatory bombardment. RAF Hampdens, Beaufighters and Blenheims, flying at the edge of their range from bases in Scotland, bombed targets and defended the airspace above for seven hours as the commandos landed and destroyed with explosive charges the power station and coastal defences, the radio transmitter, factories and lighthouse. The raid was marked by fierce infantry combat, in which for the loss of 112 British casualties and eleven aircraft the enemy suffered 252 casualties, lost nine merchant ships and four Heinkel bombers.

The raid did much to develop Britain's understanding and experience of raiding as well as demonstrating the worth of the raiding principle: the Germans believed that the two raids on Norway that year constituted an attempt to find an access point with a view to invading Europe, and redeployed a further thirty thousand troops to Norway to meet this threat. It also added to Hitler's increasing hostility towards the commando menace.

Under Mountbatten the Combined Operations organisation grew rapidly in size, competence and capability, the HQ at Richmond Terrace alone increasing from twenty-three to over four hundred, responsibility for the planning and coordination of raids (but not always control) coming under their remit. COHQ thus became a critical focal point for planning raids that would then be carried out by whatever fighting organisation proposed them. Pug Ismay noted gratefully in March 1942 that Mountbatten's new broom was working well, Combined Operations 'functioning in complete accord with the Service departments and Home Forces'. Although many were less generous, particularly those with tribal drums to beat, what is undoubtedly true is that Mountbatten's arrival as Commodore, Combined Operations (CCO) served to energise COHQ. His eagerness to engage staff from outside the traditional ranks of service officers introduced much needed genetic variety into the Combined Operations corporate body. A remarkably eclectic mix of adventurers, scientists, university dons and writers offered ideas and suggestions far from the beaten track of military orthodoxy: the many technical successes of Operation Overlord in June 1944 were due in large measure to Mountbatten's iconoclasm in 1942. When first introduced to Richmond Terrace early that year, Major 'Blondie' Hasler, newly appointed to the Combined Operations Development Centre, was struck by COHQ's efficiency and hyperactivity.

At about that time Mountbatten appointed Brigadier Godfrey Wildman-Lushington to be his Chief of Staff. Wildman-Lushington, an experienced Royal Marine who had also earned his wings as a pilot in the fledgling Royal Naval Air Service, became to all intents and purposes the head of planning and chair of the principal decision-making Examination Committee, which determined what raids and operations would go to Mountbatten (and thence to the chiefs of staff) for approval and final planning. The Search Committee within COHQ would first identify targets, or develop those presented to it from outside agencies. Within the planning section were Colonel Robert Neville (Chief Planning Co-ordinator) and Lieutenant-Colonel Cyril Horton. At this stage of the war the Royal Marines were not 'Commandos', which were instead on the Army's establishment.* They were nonetheless an integral part, with the Commandos and independent companies (formed for the Norwegian Campaign in 1940), of the combat element of Combined Operations. The significant role played by the Royal Marines in the planning and control of Combined Operations HQ ensured they would receive their fair share of operational tasks.

At the same time as the uniformed services were building their

* It took some time for the new organisation to settle down. By March 1941 the 'Special Service Brigade' comprised eleven Commandos, each of which was about half the size of an infantry battalion, with 390 men.

raiding capability, an organisation was created that was dedicated to taking subversive activity into the heart of enemy territory. The Special Operations Executive (SOE) found its initial shape in July 1940, and was given the task of planning and undertaking subversion and sabotage in countries occupied by the enemy. Dr Hugh Dalton, the Minister for Economic Warfare, had persuaded Churchill to support the principle of sabotage in occupied territories. 'We have got to organize movements in enemy-occupied territory comparable to the Sinn Fein movement in Ireland, to the Chinese Guerrillas now operating against Japan, to the Spanish Irregulars who played a notable part in Wellington's campaign,' Dalton argued. '[It] must use many different methods, including industrial and military sabotage, labour agitation and strikes, continuous propaganda, terrorist acts against traitors and German leaders, boycotts and riots.' Churchill agreed, and appointed him head of SOE forthwith. The new organisation, however, remained separate from the Ministry of Economic Warfare. Dalton inherited a small part of the War Office's Military Intelligence organisation that had been set up in 1939 to research guerrilla warfare methodologies as well as the relatively new Section D of MI6,* established originally to investigate sabotage and propaganda.

Ultimate success for Britain in the war nevertheless remained uncertain, the prospect of victory a desperate hope rather even than a possibility, in 1941. Two factors changed everything, however, that year. The first was Hitler's megalomaniacal surge into the limitless geography of the Soviet Union in June. The second was the arrival in the war of the United States, propelled by Japan's offensive in the Pacific and the Far East. Within days of the attack on Pearl Harbor on 7 December 1941 Churchill was on RMS *Queen Mary*, in great secrecy, to embrace his new co-belligerent. It was a moment for which he had long hoped, recognising that without the might of the United States on Britain's side, it was only a matter

* Sometimes also referred to as Section IX of MI9.

of time before she too succumbed and slid beneath the waves of the Nazi tsunami that had already drowned the old countries of Europe in blood and violence.

It was a good visit, but tensions were apparent from the outset. Roosevelt and his advisers readily accepted the principle that defeat of Germany came first, but from the outset talked big. The immediate aim, they argued, should be to flood Britain with newly recruited US troops during 1942 (Operation Bolero) in preparation for an assault on Fortress Europe in 1943 (Operation Sledgehammer). Churchill disagreed. Britain was at that time fighting the enemy in North Africa and could not afford to divide its meagre forces across two battlefronts. The Axis forces would need first to be defeated in the desert, before attention could turn to fighting them on the Continent.

But in Europe proper, Britain could still play the role of the mosquito. While America built up its forces Combined Operations would increase the intensity of raids on the enemy coast under their dynamic new chief, and Mountbatten was well known to the Americans. The Prime Minister's emphasis on raiding did not please Roosevelt, who worried that it would serve to divide forces and reduce the impact of the planned-for Second Front, but in the end the British view prevailed. Britain's 'Continental Policy' for 1942 was 'confined to a series of small raids', agreed the Chiefs of Staff Committee on 1 June 1942, 'together with one larger scale raid'. Substantial raids would maintain offensive spirit, encourage morale, take the war to the enemy and serve to prepare for the eventual invasion of Europe. At a time when the bulk of forces in the British Isles were defensive, Combined Operations was to be aggressively and distinctively offensive.

As the New Year of 1942 arrived, planning for these mini-offensives, under Mountbatten's keen eye, accelerated. In fact, for Britain in Europe, insofar as land operations were concerned, 1942 was the year of the hit-and-run raid designed to bloody the enemy's nose and keep him on his toes. Mountbatten's Examination

Committee soon found itself evaluating a wide range of ambitious prospects, to build on those successfully launched in 1941. They did not all fit the same pattern. Some were tiny – a few brave men carried in flimsy craft launched from a submarine – while some were considerably larger, designed to test the techniques necessary to launch, in due course, the invasion of the Continent. A few entailed approach by parachute, but the vast majority were amphibious. These included the idea of sailing an explosive-filled destroyer into the heavily guarded port of St Nazaire, and detonating it in the lock gates of the dry dock, the only one on Brittany's Atlantic coast that could provide sanctuary for the German battleship *Tirpitz*. Also included was the idea of a parachute raid to destroy a new German radar installation at Bruneval at Cap d'Antifer, as well as a large-scale raid on a Channel town, perhaps Bayeux or Dieppe, later in the year.

The ideas that crossed the Examination Committee's desk included many that depended on the skill and courage of small groups of men, the success of whom was ultimately determined by their audacity, but which did not pass Churchill's 1940 test for size. The previous year had, however, presented a number of examples of small-team operations, which varied in effect, but all of which provided a pattern for successful raiding and a precedent for well thought out pinprick raids of the kind Churchill had originally detested.

Following the eight raids mounted in 1941 a further fifteen were launched in 1942, conducted or coordinated by Combined Operations.* The raids were carried out by a variety of fighting organisations. On 27 February 120 newly trained men from C Company, 2nd Battalion, Parachute Regiment led by Major John Frost, who two years later was to achieve fame commanding his battalion at Arnhem's 'bridge too far', parachuted into the Pas de Calais to seize the German radar station at Bruneval, twelve miles

* See Appendix 3.

north of Le Havre. The raid was spectacularly successful. Parts of the Würzburg radar array were dismantled and recovered back to Britain, with the troops evacuated by motor torpedo boat (MTB). The following month an even more spectacular feat of bravery saw the old destroyer HMS *Campbeltown*, packed with high explosive, ramming the dock gates at St Nazaire and explode a day later, putting the dry dock out of action until 1947. This hazardous and audacious raid, accompanied by commandos who carried out demolitions in the port, was, as the historian Brigadier C.E. Lucas Philips described it, without doubt 'the greatest raid of all'. Both raids were heavily publicised to boost morale in Britain.

On 19 August a force of six thousand troops and tanks landed at the Normandy port of Dieppe (Operation Jubilee) in a raid designed to test the principles of amphibious assault. Planned by Mountbatten's Combined Operations, it proved an expensive lesson. Nearly 60 per cent of the participating troops were killed, wounded or taken prisoner, but it is clear that this raid taught significant lessons that would be used to plan the Normandy landing two years later. Vilified by the Canadian official historian for the plan, Mountbatten asserted in response: 'I have no doubt that the Battle of Normandy was won on the beaches of Dieppe. For every man who died in Dieppe at least ten more must have been spared in Normandy in 1944.' The lessons of Dieppe included the folly of assaulting a heavily defended enemy port head on, and the need for heavy aerial and naval bombardment to suppress shore defences during the assault.

Elsewhere, across the Mediterranean, during 1941/42 commandos of various kinds were to demonstrate unequivocally the effectiveness of the submarine-launched canoe raid. Likewise, on the occupied French coast the pinprick raid was allowed to thrive during 1942. Operating from a requisitioned Elizabethan manor near Poole Harbour, the fifty-five men of the secret Small-Scale Raiding Force (SSRF), which came under the control of Combined

Operations for tasking and under SOE for administration, and operated under the cover title 'No. 62 Commando', carried out raids in which the initial journey to the French coast was made by MTB and the final few miles to the shore via canoe. Led by commando officers Major Gus March-Phillips, Captain Geoffrey Appleyard and Lieutenant Graham Hayes, who had worked together in a successful commando-type operation in West Africa earlier in the year,* the SSRF achieved a considerable measure of success in mounting armed reconnaissance of the northern French coast. The MTB they used was a one-off built by Thorneycroft, which had such an extraordinary top speed (40 knots) that her crew nicknamed her the *Little Pisser*.

Their raids were audacious but they also stirred up a hornet's nest, not least in Berlin where the SSRF's success goaded March-Phillips was brave, but his courage sometimes verged on the foolhardy. The first raid on 14 August 1942 killed three Germans and wounded six others; the second raid, on the Casquets lighthouse on the island of Alderney on the night of 2 September, spirited back to Britain the entire German garrison, caught in their pyjamas. A week later a further raid on a small island off Alderney was equally successful. Churchill, in a lecture he gave in Edinburgh on 9 October, described the raids as a 'hand of steel out of the sea'.

But on the night of 12 September No. 62 Commando's luck ran out. The eleven men of Operation Aquatint planned to make their way to Sainte-Honorine-des-Pertes on the Normandy coast, then climb hundred-foot cliffs to attack an ammunition depot and bring back some German prisoners. The first part of the raid went well, despite the men landing two and a half miles from their intended point. The twelve-man collapsible assault boats were designed and built by Mr Fred Goatley (who had shipbuilding works at Cowes on the Isle of Wight) and had been introduced to them on 3 August

* Operation Postmaster.

that year by Major Blondie Hasler of the Southsea-based Royal Marines Boom Patrol Detachment (of which more later).

With the boats safely hidden on shore and guarded by one of their number, the party departed on its reconnaissance. On their return, however, disaster struck. Confronted by a German patrol as they were preparing to embark from the beach they were involved in a fierce firefight, during which German reinforcements (men who had been accommodated locally) quickly arrived. Canoes were sunk by machine-gun fire and the MTB under the command of Appleyard, who had not gone ashore because of an earlier knee injury, sustained hits to the engine. March-Phillips and two others were killed instantly, while others were wounded and taken prisoner. Of those who went ashore Graham Hayes alone managed to escape the fate that awaited the rest, swimming nearly two miles to the west, coming ashore near the village of Asnières-en-Bessin. He was then smuggled through France to Spain by members of the French Resistance, but was betrayed by some of his rescuers and shot in Fresnes Prison, Paris, on 13 July 1943. Appleyard's *Little Pisser* managed to creep home, badly damaged, with a German bullet in its engine.

In the same month a daring raid was made on the power station at Glom in northern Norway that provided the electricity for a nearby aluminium plant. Operation Musketoon comprised ten commandos from No. 2 Commando and two Norwegian corporals working for the SOE. Transported by the Free French submarine *Junon*, the men then completed a difficult overland route to approach from the rear, and successfully destroyed their target. Four of them made good their escape to Britain but eight were captured, one of the Norwegians – Corporal Erling Djupdraet – dying of his wounds three days later. The captives were first taken to Colditz Castle before, ominously, being escorted in civilian clothes to Sachsenhausen Concentration Camp outside Berlin.

Meanwhile, under Appleyard's command the SSRF launched a raid on the island of Sark on the night of 3 October 1942, during which a number of German prisoners were captured and tied up to facilitate their removal to Britain. In the ensuing exchange of gunfire, however, all but one of the prisoners were killed. When the news reached Berlin that British commandos had deliberately slaughtered captured prisoners, Hitler reacted furiously. On 7 October he personally drafted a note, which was published in the Wehrmacht's daily communiqué: 'In future, all terror and sabotage troops of the British and their accomplices, who do not act like soldiers but rather like bandits, will be treated as such by the German troops and will be ruthlessly eliminated in battle, wherever they appear.' Then, on 18 October, these instructions were formalised in a secret order Hitler had drafted relating to future treatment of captured enemy commandos.

The infamous *Kommandobefehl*,* which had an initial distribution limited to only twelve copies, ordered the execution of all Allied commandos encountered by German forces in Europe and Africa, even if in uniform or if they attempted to surrender. Any individual or group of commandos captured by German forces was to be handed over immediately to the Sicherheitsdienst (Himmler's Security Service, the SD)† for 'annihilation'. The order made it clear that failure to carry out these orders by any commander or officer would be considered an act of negligence punishable under German military law.‡ On 19 October the Wehrmacht's Chief of Staff (Colonel General Alfred Jodl) distributed further copies, with an appendix stating that the order was 'intended for commanders only and must not under any circumstances fall into enemy hands'.

Four days later, at Sachsenhausen, the seven survivors of

* See Appendix 1.

† The SD was the intelligence service of the SS and the Nazi Party, not to be confused with the Abwehr (the intelligence arm of the armed forces), nor with the Gestapo, the Geheime Staatspolizei (GIS, Secret State Police), the official secret police of Nazi Germany and the SD's sister organisation. Totalitarianism grows such organisations like viruses. All three operated across France.

‡ The *Kommandobefehl* was signed by Field Marshal Keitel on Hitler's behalf, an act that earned him a death sentence at Nuremberg.

Operation Musketoon were duly executed in accordance with these orders. Just before dawn on 23 October they were each killed by a single shot to the back of the neck and their bodies immediately cremated. Subsequent members of raiding forces captured by the Germans were afforded no mercy and refused the basic protections allowed for them under the 1909 Hague Conventions (and the Third Geneva Convention of 1929), to which Germany was a signatory.

At the time they were deployed the Royal Marines of Operation Frankton had no inkling of the danger they would be in, were they to fall into enemy hands. If captured they would be treated as scum to be eliminated, with no more rights than the hated *francs-tireurs* of the Franco-Prussian War, or the partisans even then being encountered by the Germans in large numbers in the East. Had they known this, it is certain that more attention would have been paid to the importance of keeping the evading saboteurs out of the hands of the enemy.

Despite all this raiding activity, minuscule in comparison with the huge tidal wave of war sweeping across Eastern Europe and North Africa, 1942 remained for Britain an *annus horribilis* that only those with faith in the possibility of Britain's ultimate redemption recognised to be the high tide of German ambitions and military achievement. In the meantime, planning for raids large and small, together with the escalating bomber offensive in the air, had to continue. It was via Churchill's 'hand of steel from the sea' that beleaguered Britain could demonstrate to its own people that the war was winnable, to the subject peoples of Europe that their nightmare would one day be over, and to its own planners that a succesful large-scale amphibious assault on the shores of France was possible.

THREE

Bordeaux

The capture of the French Atlantic coast was of considerable significance to Germany, the Kriegsmarine's submarine supremo, Admiral Dönitz, observing in June 1940 that it signalled an 'outstanding improvement in our strategic position in the war at sea' and allowed – to use his phrase – 'the Battle of the Atlantic' to begin. Whereas Bordeaux boasted neither a deep-water port nor complex repair and maintenance facilities, and was too shallow for the battleships and cruisers which needed the deep-water ports in Brittany (such as Brest, St Nazaire and Lorient), the city was nevertheless ideally suited for subsurface raiders and fast surface freighters, which could scuttle out on their nefarious business to hide themselves in the vast reaches of the neighbouring oceans.

It was also a relatively safe harbour for the receipt of the transshipped crews captured by raiders before they were sent to prison camps in Germany. The first of these arrived on 29 April 1941 when the Canadian SS *Canadolite*, captured by the raider *Kormoran*, docked with prize crew, along with the 7,000-ton SS *British Advocate*, captured by the heavy cruiser *Admiral Scheer* off the Seychelles in February. On 12 May the SS *Speybank*, captured by the German raider *Atlantis* in the Indian Ocean in January, arrived at Bordeaux with prize crew, followed on 23 August by the German raider *Orion* after a patrol of 510 days, seeking the sanctuary of the Garonne after its long journey.

The fact that the port of Bordeaux lay some sixty-two miles *inland* inside the Gironde estuary meant it was considered safe from anything but aerial attack. The Garonne nevertheless was a notoriously fickle waterway, especially for small craft, with ever-shifting sandbanks and dangerous, contrary tides. Bordeaux boasted three sets of dock installations in 1940. A range of ancient customs quays lay at the heart of the city running up to the old Stone Bridge, originally commissioned by Napoleon, with deeper docks at Bassens two miles downriver. Near the customs quays lay the lock at Bacalan, which was quickly developed in 1940/41 as a submarine base. The Italians placed a number of their submarines here when they entered the war on 10 June 1940, as it provided unequalled access to the rich pickings of the Atlantic shipping lanes and an opportunity for the Regia Marina Italiana (the Royal Italian Navy) to reap some glory from Hitler's war. The first three (of twenty-three) submarines of the 11th Gruppo Italiano del Fero Subaequeo in Atlantico skulked into Bordeaux in September 1940, the first to then depart (the *Malaspina*) leaving on anti-convoy patrol on 9 October.*

For these and other reasons Bordeaux was also of interest to Britain. In an attempt to starve Germany of supplies from abroad that would assist its war economy, the British government formally instituted a blockade of French ports, effectively closing them to neutral shipping, on 4 September 1940. This would not be a close physical blockade of the kind that characterised the pre-submarine era: rather, neutral merchant ships providing succour to the enemy were to be identified and intercepted on the high seas. As early as November 1940 the submarine HMS *Talisman*, with Dick Raikes as its First Lieutenant, captured the French fishing vessel *Le Clipper* in the Bay of Biscay near Lorient, thereafter for a period using the forty-ton vessel to observe U-boat movements off the Gironde estuary.

* In September 1941 the Germans began constructing massive U-boat pens at Bacalan, which started operating in January 1943. The pens remain, indestructible, to this day.

The port installations and fuel storage facilities in Bordeaux were intermittently targeted by the RAF as early as October and November 1940, as were the approaches to the mouth of the estuary sixty-two miles to the north-west. In February 1941 aerial mines were laid by the RAF in the Gironde estuary as a hindrance to shipping, and in April a series of bombing raids destroyed an estimated 100,000 tons of oil at Bec d'Ambès (which splits the Garonne and Dordogne rivers) and at Pauillac (fourteen miles north, on the Gironde), which constituted a substantial proportion of French fuel reserves (the Ministry of Economic Warfare estimated these in mid-1941 to amount to some 500,000 tons).

Then in October that year the RAF bombed the docks at Bassens for the first time, although the danger of bombs inadvertently hitting innocent targets meant that attack from the air was the least favoured option of the British planners. Likewise the Royal Navy attempted to prevent merchant ships entering the estuary, but with the considerable pressures placed on it by the Battle of the Atlantic many ships slipped through their net. In May 1941 RAF reconnaissance photography confirmed the arrival in the port of the 7,000-ton SS *Portland*, which had arrived from Talcahuano in Chile. In the same month the modern Italian ship MV *Fusijama* (6,244 tons), last reported in Yokohama, also broke through the flimsy blockade to dock in Bordeaux.*

Ships were coast-hugging from Spain, too, carrying vast quantities of iron ore from Spanish mines. British intelligence reports estimated that for the year up to the end of February 1942 nearly 250,000 tons of ore had been shipped from Spain to occupied France, much of it through Bordeaux. Six 'comparatively large ships totalling rather more than 21,000 tons and a considerable number of small coasters [were] engaged in this trade', the weekly Cabinet War Summary noted. That March, about 37,000 tons of iron ore was carried by the larger ships and a further 35,000 tons

* The *Fusijama* was scuttled in the Gironde on 12 August 1944.

by the coasters. In March 1943 a British intelligence report from Bordeaux noted that 'there are four small cargo ships of about 1,000 to 2,000 tons, and several small French fishing boats carrying fuel from Spain'.

Bordeaux was also the centre of a significant industrial region, the hub of a railway network that stretched east into central France and thence Germany, and south towards Spain. The harbour and docks, together with a wide area of occupied and unoccupied France, were supplied with power by a large transformer station at Pessac in the suburbs of south-west Bordeaux (situated on the railway line to Spain) which provided power to, among other strategic locations, the U-boat pens at Bacalan.

SOE targeted Pessac in an operation codenamed Josephine 'B' in 1941. On the night of 10 May a party of three French servicemen of de Gaulle's Bureau Central de Renseignements et d'Action (BCRA, Central Bureau of Intelligence and Operations), loaned to SOE for the operation and under the command of Adjutant Forman MC,* parachuted into Bordeaux to reconnoitre the transformer station. Once the attack was over they were to be collected off the coast by a submarine on 20 May. The first examination of the target left the party disheartened, as the site was closely guarded and surrounded by electric fencing. This led to delays, the party missing its planned rendezvous with the submarine. Dejected, the men made their way to Paris, where they managed to make contact with Sergeant Joel Letac, a fellow BCRA operative seconded to SOE, whom Adjutant Forman had been forced to leave behind following a reconnaissance of Brittany the previous March. The four men conducted a further evaluation of the target before launching a spectacularly successful attack on the night of 7 June. Six of the eight transformers were destroyed and the party escaped.

Later reports suggested that the Germans blamed local saboteurs.

* Adjutant is a warrant officer rank.

Two hundred and fifty people were imprisoned, a million-franc fine was imposed on the area, and twelve German soldiers were reportedly shot for dereliction of duty. London heard the news on 19 June via the first of SOE's secret radio transmitters in France,* Hugh Dalton passing the good news to Churchill on the 25th. 'We may therefore take it as practically certain that three [sic] trained men, dropped from an aeroplane, have succeeded in destroying an important industrial target,' Dalton wrote exultantly of SOE's first operational success in occupied France. 'This strongly suggests that many industrial targets, especially if they cover only a very small area, are more effectively attacked by SOE methods than by air bombardment.'

The sabotage party, having now literally missed the boat, were forced to find their own way back to Britain. Travelling south, Forman, Letac and one other man managed to cross into Spain, were spirited by British consular staff to Gibraltar, and were back in Britain by August. They had the advantage of being Frenchmen, and thus of merging unobtrusively into the local population. It was much more difficult for non-native escapers and evaders to do this.

Well before Japan entered the war in December 1941, the Tripartite Agreement† allowed for the exchange of strategic materials and manufactured goods between Europe and the Far East in a trade known to the Japanese as *Yanagi*. The advent of war in 1939 had automatically closed off many markets for the belligerents, a situation made worse by Germany's attack on the Soviet Union in June 1941 and, six months later, the arrival in the increasingly global conflict of the United States following the attacks on US territories in the Pacific and South China Sea in early December

* The radio, and its operator (Georges Bégué), had arrived by parachute at Châteauroux in the *Zone Libre* on 5 May 1941.

† Signed in Berlin on 27 September 1940 between Germany, Italy and Japan.

1941. Germany's particular needs encompassed raw materials such as rubber, tin, tungsten (wolfram), molybdenum, hemp, hides and vegetable (such as coconut) oils. These were all possessed in abundance by Japan and her newly conquered territories. By contrast, Japan was poor in certain essential metals, manufactured articles and technical processes, which Germany and, to a lesser degree, Italy possessed.

The programme was originally conceived in Berlin. This trade used both the trans-Siberian railway and the sea route around the Cape of Good Hope, until the invasion of the Soviet Union denied to Germany the former. Between 1939 and June 1941 some 452,735 tons of raw materials had been transported from the Far East across the Soviet Union by rail into Germany, including 28,542 tons of rubber. All this now had no choice but to go by sea. In time, twenty-four ships were involved in the *Yanagi* trade, either German-owned or taken as prizes; even the few Italian ships on the run were under German control. The Japanese, at the outset at least, were reluctant partners, as intercepted diplomatic radio traffic demonstrated.

In September 1942 a Japanese diplomatic message stated that the German commercial attaché in Tokyo had complained to the Japanese that (1) because Japan was slow in concluding a pact to supply Germany with rubber, loading of *Yanagi* ships would probably be delayed; (2) Japan did not permit the presence of Germans at the loading of *Yanagi* ships at Singapore; (3) Japan's offer to supply fuel oil to the ships was not working out smoothly; and (4) Japan had proposed the substitution of copra in place of the coconut oil which was originally promised, and which German tankers had been expressly sent to load. Despite this, the Japanese were quick to make demands of their new Nazi friends, although the nature of the first request – for 1,000,000 tons of steel as well as an unspecified amount of aluminium – shocked Berlin by its unreasonableness. If the steel had been available (and it was not), this amount would have entailed at least 160 journeys, given the size of the ships available. In any case, Berlin considered that copra for steel was an unfair exchange.

The arrival on 4 April 1941 of the 6,528-ton Hamburg–Amerika Line freighter SS *Ermland*,* commanded by Kapitän Krage, which had left Kobe in December 1940, saw the first use of Bordeaux as the European terminus for the *Yanagi* trade. Six weeks later, on 20 May, the SS *Dresden* arrived, carrying prisoners captured by the raider *Atlantis*, and on 27 June the *Regensburg* reached Bordeaux from Manchukuo. A fallow period then followed until the first of a spate of blockade-runners reached the Gironde after their long voyage from the Far East, with the arrival of the *Himalaya* and *Africana* on 29 August.

On 10 September 1941 the *Anneliese Essberger* dashed across the Bay of Biscay at the end of her long journey from the South China Sea, her crews anxiously scanning the skies for RAF reconnaissance planes or for the telltale smoke on the horizon that warned of a skulking destroyer. She safely reached the sanctuary of the Gironde. Later in the month the *Rio Grande* departed Bordeaux for Japan and in the next two months a further two freighters, the *Kulmerland* and the *Burgenland*, arrived from Japan. So between late August and November Bordeaux saw five arrivals and two departures. This excited the interest of watching spies in the networks quietly and independently observing the river, who immediately passed on the information to London†. In addition to the *Yanagi* traffic the German raider *Thor* arrived on 17 December and left on its second patrol on 14 January 1942, the raider *Michel* departing the Gironde for patrol on 20 March 1942. In the thirteen months following the arrival of the *Ermland* in April 1941 an estimated 75,000 tons of material (including 25,000 tons of crude rubber) passed through the Custom House Quay and the Bassens docks, carried by twelve ships (of the sixteen that left

* The *Ermland* was renamed the *Weserland*. She set out for Japan but was lost on the return journey in 1944.

† See Chapter 4

Japanese waters, four were lost to enemy action en route), together with large quantities of tin and tungsten. Six vessels carrying 32,540 tons of supplies, including engines and chemicals, successfully made the journey in the opposite direction.

Details of the blockade-runner programme reaching London were confirmed by both aerial photography and signals intelligence. Photographic reconnaissance by the RAF became particularly effective during the autumn of 1942, revealing not just the numbers of ships and submarines in the Gironde and Garonne but their size, together with the movement of vessels along the west coast of France and in the Bay of Biscay. A report dated 22 June 1942 counted twenty-two submarines in Bacalan, all identified by aerial reconnaissance. The United States had broken the Japanese diplomatic radio traffic in 1940, and this information was shared with Britain at the outset of war in the Far East and Pacific in December 1941. Baron Hiroshi Ōshima, Japan's ambassador to Berlin, visited Bordeaux a number of times, and although it seems unlikely that any of the spy networks across the Gironde ever knew of this, these visits were the subject of detailed signals traffic between Berlin and Tokyo that quickly found its way to the Government Code and Cypher School (GC&CS) at Bletchley Park.* Then, late in 1942, Britain managed to decrypt the German naval Enigma cipher, providing accurate information on, among other subjects, the blockade-runners, revealing a patchwork of information about the movements of ships and cargoes.

The intelligence reports from Bordeaux made an immediate impact on the head of the Ministry of Economic Warfare, Lord Selborne. The opportunity to deny the use of the Gironde to the blockade-runners was obvious. Selborne initially reported the trade to the chiefs of staff in a memorandum on 21 March 1942, developing the matter further with the Prime Minister in a letter

* Virtually all of Ōshima's dispatches were intercepted by the Americans: approximately 75 during the eleven months of 1941, some hundred in 1942 and all the way through to the end of the war.

on 9 May, urging action against the fast merchant ships running the thin blockade the Royal Navy had attempted to place against the Atlantic coast. From evidence provided by a number of secret organisations lurking in Bordeaux at the time (of which more later) together with aerial RAF reconnaissance photography between September and December 1941, it was clear that these ships were bringing to Europe rubber and tin from Singapore and Saigon, courtesy of the new owners of Britain's former colonies (lost in February 1942). The prospect of an unfettered trade relationship building up between these two countries, bringing in much needed war goods to Germany and potentially exporting German technology by return, was alarming to London. 'Among Germany's principal deficiencies,' Selborne wrote,

> [are] rubber, wolfram, tin, hemp, hides and vegetable oils . . . A total of 100,000 tons (say, 15 ships) would cover essential needs of the first three and make a valuable contribution towards the others. Japanese needs from Europe consist primarily of high grade types of specialised machinery (some of which has been awaiting shipment since June 1941); ball bearings; prototypes of naval, military and air material; small quantities of special chemicals; blue prints and working instructions for plants and processes; and expert technicians.

As the months passed a fuller picture was built up, demonstrating that the trade between Bordeaux and the Far East was probably sufficient to meet all of Germany's wartime needs of rubber, as well as supplying other materials such as tungsten. In fact Selborne's letters became as strident as they were regular, the Prime Minister being reminded of the Bordeaux blockade-runners on 22 June, 5 August and 9 September.

Selborne also raised the matter with Anthony Eden, the Foreign Secretary, on 15 July 1942, voicing the same concerns and asking that authorisation be given for a 'large-scale attack by the R.A.F.

on the terminal port' as a priority. He observed that the blockade-runners would 'obviously be given to cargoes which are most urgently required by Germany and Japan'. The assumption was that Germany would have no compunction in trading technical secrets, such as those for the new air defence Freya or Würzburg radars, as well as for raw materials of various kinds. While acknowledging the strength of these arguments Eden nevertheless demurred, observing in his response the following day: 'I am not sufficiently well acquainted with the lay-out of the harbour and the factories to be able to form any estimate of the loss of life among the civilian population which would be involved.'

This was clearly a task demanding a military response, and the government set the problem in front of the chiefs of staff. Accordingly the secretary of the Chiefs of Staff Committee prepared notes on the subject on two occasions, 9 May and 22 June, concluding that this was a job for Combined Operations HQ. A full-scale operation against Bordeaux would clearly require considerable force, perhaps as much as three full divisions, and consume resources even then being earmarked for the amphibious assault on North Africa. The task could, it was thought, be more usefully conducted as a raid. Accordingly the Examination Committee looked at the requirement in early July, but considered that the task was probably too difficult for the tools at hand.

One benefit of the now shelved consideration of launching a full-scale operation against Bordeaux of the type that would be launched in August against Dieppe was the extensive reconnaissance of the Gironde and Garonne that had taken place during the preceding months. The planning team in COHQ had in fact been looking at the estuary and the river for some time, producing a detailed typographical analysis of the river to support potential land operations against the region as early as 3 March 1942. With a large-scale operation now put on hold, a range of alternative options was briefly examined on 27 July in a paper by Commander Unwin RN to the Search Committee of Combined

Operations HQ. These included the bombing of the port by the RAF, aerial mining of the river, and the landing of commandos by submarine or canoe. The resources to launch anything larger simply did not exist in Britain's arsenal at the time. The Search Committee's response to this report, however, was lacklustre. Bombing would endanger innocent civilians; RAF mining was notoriously inaccurate and had not resulted 'in any noticeable decrease in any ships . . . using the river'; there were not enough submarines available to make a large-scale raid worthwhile and a Folbot raid was considered practicable only in conjunction with an air raid.

There seemed to be no easy answer to the problem of Bordeaux.

Because the solution was not immediately obvious, Combined Operations did not act immediately on Unwin's report, although this was not to suggest that the problem of the Bordeaux blockade-runners was ever forgotten. This was in major part because of Selborne's persistence. He prepared a further paper for the committee on 7 August in which the options for dealing with the blockade-runners were examined. 'Hardly a day passes without my seeing convincing proof of the determination of both countries [Germany and Italy] to execute their [blockade-running] programme,' he wrote in a letter signed two days earlier. Attacking the ships from the air in the South Atlantic was impracticable because of the lack of suitable aircraft for the task (either American or British), although Unwin urged consideration of the airborne anti-submarine patrols flying out over the Atlantic to combine with anti-ship operations as well. 'If immediate action could be taken,' he concluded, 'it should not be too late.'

Unknown to Combined Operations, however, one organisation did begin work on a solution to the 'Bordeaux problem', but in secret and without informing their colleagues in Richmond Terrace: that organisation was SOE. A Mauritian of French descent, Claude de Baissac (of whom more later), was within days of Unwin's report being readied for a mission to Bordeaux to replace an SOE agent already there, Robert Leroy, with explicit instructions to target the blockade-runners.

One of the only practical solutions to the problem posed by the presence of both raiders and blockade-runners in Bordeaux was the air-dropping of sea mines by the RAF. The RAF began to lay aerial mines off Brest, Lorient and St Nazaire in April 1941 to counter the major threat posed by the potential arrival of the Kriegsmarine's battleships, but also off the Gironde. On 7 March 1942 RAF Bomber Command sent 17 aircraft on mine-laying operations overnight against the Atlantic coast, 17 on 23 March and launched a further attack on the 25th. Mine-laying was thereafter repeated twice in April (45 aircraft), once in May (48), followed by a heavy effort in June and July when in seven operations 210 aircraft were active. While most of these operations were mounted further north, a number involved Hampden, Whitley, Stirling, Wellington and Lancaster aircraft sowing mines in the mouth of the Gironde. There seemed little immediate return for this effort, however, in terms of the ability of the blockade-runners and raiders to traverse the Garonne and Gironde in safety.*

Removing mines was a nuisance, but the navigable channel within the Gironde was relatively narrow, allowing it to be cleared speedily. On the nights of 14 July and 5 August 1942 Halifax bombers of 83 Squadron RAF again dropped mines along the Gironde – the local newspaper *La Petite Gironde* was effusive in its anger at this threat to the French civilian population. Nevertheless, the practice proved a constant irritant to the defenders. The Germans were forced to sweep the estuary mouth and the main river channel daily. Claude de Baissac reported in early 1943 that the threat of mines was a significant one for the Germans: the

* As an offensive weapon the air-dropped sea mine was nevertheless very successful during the Second World War. The RAF laid 48,158 mines in enemy waters, sinking 545 merchant ships and 217 assorted warships. Over 20,000 additional mines were laid by surface ships and submarines.

estuary was constantly being searched, the responsibility of at least two corvettes. 'One blew up recently.'

A new dimension to the *Yanagi* trade was the arrival in Lorient (between Brest and St Nazaire in Brittany) of the Japanese submarine *I30* ('Cherry Blossom') for a nineteen-day stay on 5 August 1942, following a successful patrol through the Indian and Atlantic oceans. Crewed by Commander Endo and 108 men she carried 3,300 pounds of mica (used in the production of electrical capacitors) and 1,452 pounds of shellac (likewise used in electrical applications). While the vessel was prepared for its return journey Endo and his crew travelled to Berlin where they met Hitler, returning to Paris for some sightseeing at the Eiffel Tower and the Champs-Elysées. On her departure on 22 August the *I30* carried a Würzburg air defence radar (the same type that the Bruneval raid had captured in February 1942), the latest aerial torpedoes, electric torpedoes, torpedo data computers, 240 Bold sonar countermeasure munitions, rocket and glider bombs, anti-tank guns, Zeiss anti-aircraft artillery directors, 20-mm AA guns, industrial diamonds valued at one million yen and fifty top-secret 'T-Enigma' coding machines. A month later, with the *I30* safely round the Cape of Good Hope, German news agencies announced jubilantly that a Japanese submarine had joined their U-boats operating in the Atlantic Ocean.*

All the while British aerial reconnaissance of the Gironde was being undertaken weekly, the shipping movements section at RAF Medmenham's Central Interpretation Unit near Marlow in Buckinghamshire building a comprehensive stereoscopic record of all German merchantmen over 2,500 tons. The phenomenally fast, unarmed all-wooden Mosquito fighter bombers converted to the photographic reconnaissance role, swept across France at over thirty thousand feet to take accurate photographs of the changes to the river and its traffic. With a top speed of 425 miles per hour

* However, the *I30* sank off Singapore on 13 October 1942 after striking a British mine. The Würzburg radar was lost.

they were too quick even for the fastest Luftwaffe fighter, the ME109, and deployed aerial photography techniques perfected by the Australian pilot and aerial photography pioneer, Sidney Cotton.

This regular high-level reconnaissance persuaded the Germans to provide motor torpedo boat escorts for the merchant ships as they attempted to dart out of the estuary and lose themselves in the broad expanse of the Bay of Biscay. Despite the fact that both the Royal Navy and the RAF were severely stretched in 1941/42, the successful sighting of a merchantman at sea by an RAF reconnaissance aircraft did not augur well for a vessel's successful transit into the sea lanes the Kriegsmarine had allocated to the blockade-runners in the deep Atlantic. When Kapitän von Zatorski's 10,697-ton *Uckermark** left the Gironde on 9 August 1942 it was escorted by three torpedo boats, but sighting by an RAF aircraft persuaded von Zatorski that he had little chance of making it through the Bay of Biscay intact, so he turned back. A similar problem affected the *Ermland* two days later.

After a number of these false starts a major spate of departures for Japan took place in September, with nine ships making the dash across the Bay of Biscay and running the gauntlet of mines, Royal Navy and USN ships and RAF aircraft, into the Atlantic. For these anti-shipping attacks the RAF's Coastal Command 'borrowed' Halifaxes, Stirlings and Lancasters from Bomber Command, diverting them from their usual task of night-time attacks on the Reich.

The Allied blockade of the French Atlantic ports was thin, however, and German caution in returning to sanctuary in Bordeaux, if they believed their ship had been sighted by hostile eyes, preserved the vessels for a second chance. Many were successful. The *Uckermark* made good her escape on 9 September on her fourth attempt (reaching Yokohama on 24 November), the *Rio Grande* left on 28 September followed by the *Pietro Orseolo* on 1

* The renamed raider *Altmark*, employed as a U-boat refuelling tanker.

October, the *Belgrano* and *Spichern* (2 October), *Irene* (3 October), *Brake* (7 October), *Weserland* (ex-*Ermland*), *Karin* (11 October) and the *Anneliese Essberger* (12 October).

Although apparently unworried by the failure of their previous mine-laying efforts, the RAF attempted this stratagem again, on the basis that there was little else that could be done at the time. During the six weeks between 16 October and 28 November 1942 RAF Bomber Command launched 158 aircraft on seven missions laying mines over the Bay of Biscay. There were no immediate results, however, and on 3 November the *Dresden* successfully arrived in Bordeaux (having left Yokohama on 20 August), followed five days later by the *Tannenfels*, which had left Yokohama on 8 August with a cargo of rubber, edible oils, fats, wolfram, titanium, copper, wood oil, opium and quinine. Some small success was gained by the Allies when on 21 November the *Anneliese Essberger* was scuttled by her crew near the Equator in the narrows between Brazil and West Africa, and on 1 December the *Cortellazzo*, en route for Japan, was sunk by the destroyer HMS *Redoubt*. On the 12th, the very night on which a British canoe-borne raid would launch a limpet-mine attack on Bordeaux, the *Germania* slipped her moorings on the Garonne for the Far East. She did not last long. Encountering a destroyer from a north-bound British convoy in the Bay of Biscay three days later, she was torpedoed and shelled. The last sight of her was as a drifting, burning wreck slowly settling in the water.

FOUR

The Intelligence War

One of Adjutant Forman's post-operation recommendations from June 1941 was that an SOE representative be dispatched to Bordeaux to provide a permanent pair of eyes on the ground, scouting for targets and energising like-minded potential saboteurs in the region. SOE obliged, and Lieutenant Robert Yves Marie Leroy (codenamed variously Louis, Dominic Kelly, Levy and Robert Jackson) was dropped into southern France by sea at Barcarès near Perpignan on the night of 19 September that year. He was transported on the armed merchantman HMS *Fidelity*, a 2,400-ton freighter formerly known as *Le Rhin*, in an operation codenamed 'Autogiro'.

Included in her crew as First Lieutenant was a Belgian Army doctor by the name of Albert-Marie Guérisse, who had adopted the nom-de-plume of Patrick Albert O'Leary (after a Canadian friend) and of whom more will be heard later. Arriving in Bordeaux the thirty-year-old Leroy, a seaman by background and vocation, settled immediately into the port environment, making friends and establishing contacts that were to provide the basis of an enduring intelligence relationship with Britain. The first SOE historian, its planning officer and peacetime solicitor Major Robert Bourne-Paterson, wrote a secret account in June 1944 of F (French) Section's operations in France, as an aid to diplomats, officials and war crimes investigators seeking to trace individuals associated with these groups. Bourne-Patterson explained that Leroy, who was born in Brest in 1911, 'worked as a tractor driver for the Todt* organisation and on ship repair work in the docks. He had established certain contacts, which were later to prove useful and brought back information concerning the river and docks. One of the most important things Leroy acquired was a pass to the naval base, which was to be used by agents in Bordeaux after him. While the base itself had men of various nationalities working in it, only French workers were allowed within the precincts of the U-boat pens at Bacalan in the heart of Bordeaux.

SOE had been established not to compete with the existing intelligence organisation (the Foreign Office's Secret Intelligence Service (SIS), better known as MI6) but to undertake tasks that were not part of the latter's mandate, particularly acts of sabotage. In the early months of SOE's existence its principal task was to create networks, gather intelligence and build up an understanding of potential targets in a given area, all tasks already being undertaken, albeit without sabotage as their rationale, by SIS. This made sense. Although SOE was not interested in intelligence per se, it was of course essential to build up information about potential targets in order to better inform the target-selection process in Britain. It was not unexpected, however, that friction and competition existed between both organisations from the outset, as SIS saw the brash newcomers of SOE upsetting its intelligence applecart.

The purpose of SOE was to fight an irregular or partisan-type war from inside enemy territory, operating as a dangerous cancer raging against the enemy's vitals. It was described by Churchill as 'the Ministry of Ungentlemanly Warfare', which summed up its ambition well. It aimed to sow discord amongst subject peoples abroad, to commit sabotage and acts of murder against the Nazi armies of occupation across Europe and, according to Dalton's

* Named after the German Minister for Armaments and Munitions who established a massive labour organisation that undertook large-scale civil engineering projects across Germany and occupied territories during the Second World War.

memoirs, to 'set Europe ablaze'. According to Major Maurice Buckmaster, who joined SOE in March 1941 and who went on in September to become head of F Section, the objective of SOE was to do the Germans harm:

> Our role at Special Operations Headquarters was not that of spy-masters, but of active and belligerent planners of operations to be carried out in advance of the Allied landings. The usual picture of an agent is of a man lying up and watching enemy movements and reporting them back to his home base, in short an essentially passive under-cover man. The agents of SOE were essentially active.

SOE's chief in 1942 was Sir Charles Hambro, a merchant banker in peacetime, who was replaced in 1943 by Major-General Colin Gubbins. At its height in the summer of 1944 SOE employed about thirteen thousand personnel, about five thousand of whom were agents deployed, or in training for, active service in the field. Many were female.

The purposes of MI6, SOE and Combined Operations were very distinct, therefore, although the truth was that they also had much in common, not least that they were secret, operated in enemy-occupied territory, and were often interested in the same targets, albeit for different reasons. The primary task of MI6 was to procure intelligence on behalf of the three armed services and government departments, upon which the services would then act. It *produced* intelligence, leaving it largely to the consuming agencies to evaluate and then use that intelligence to launch military action as it felt appropriate or necessary. The target intelligence relating to Bordeaux from MI6 was then sent to departmental *consumers*, which included the Ministry of Economic Warfare of which SOE was a part. The source of the intelligence was well hidden under the cloak of SIS secrecy, so its origin could not be independently determined.

These different perspectives, together with each organisation's understandable reluctance to share secrets (the 'need to know' principle was important among friends and allies), meant that practical cooperation was often poor, or non-existent. It meant, in particular, that the *sources* of intelligence were never, or very rarely, shared: in MI6's view any consumer of its intelligence, such as the Admiralty, Ministry of Economic Warfare, SOE or Combined Operations, was welcome to use the information gathered for it, but it did not need to know whence it came. This was right and proper, but led to situations where without careful demarcation competing agencies could quite easily have sources in the same place, reporting on the same targets. 'To some extent we were hampered,' recalled Buckmaster, 'by the uncommunicativeness of other arms of the Intelligence and Secret Service. Each little organization treasured its special nuggets of information with the zeal of prefects hanging on to their privileges. We could get nothing out of them.'

In Bordeaux during 1942 it was clear that both SOE and MI6 had agents operating in the region without each other's knowledge. There may well have been other organisations doing likewise (such as the Free French BCRA, for instance), as will be seen later. It also meant that different *consuming* agencies, provided with intelligence from different sources, could well end up unwittingly presiding over plans to attack the same targets. In Bordeaux in the later summer and early autumn of 1942 SOE, unbeknown to Combined Operations, was in the early stages of plans to attack the blockade-runners, under the auspices of Claude de Baissac. Using MI6 and partly SOE intelligence, Combined Operations launched their own attack on exactly the same target, oblivious of SOE's intentions.

It was not as though decision-makers were unaware of this potential problem. In March 1940 Lord Hankey delivered a secret report on the workings of MI6 in which he recommended the introduction of regular high-level meetings between the permanent

Under-Secretary at the Foreign Office (of which SIS was a part), the Directors of Intelligence in each of the three armed services, the Chief of SIS and the Ministry of Economic Warfare. Liaison at a working level between each of these departments also needed to be improved.

Likewise, demarcation was required between Combined Operations and SOE in respect of sabotage operations: as this was the *raison d'être* of SOE in occupied countries there was some resistance to the idea that Combined Operations should be undertaking this function. It was only in early 1942, when Mountbatten and Hugh Dalton agreed to treat each operation on its own merits and to cooperate (with an SOE staff officer, Major David Wyatt RE, attending meetings of the Search and Examination committees in COHQ), that something approaching a modus vivendi was established. Relationships between SIS and SOE, by contrast, started badly and struggled to improve. MI6 wanted to understand targets so as to gather useful intelligence, whereas SOE wanted to coordinate local resistance to facilitate their destruction. The former needed calm, even relatively benign local conditions to generate its information, whereas with SOE agents running about blowing up railway lines and sabotaging factories local security conditions were inevitably more turbulent and less suitable for intelligence-gathering.

The information SOE required related directly to suitable targets for sabotage, rather than the perhaps more esoteric intelligence sought by MI6 relating to wider political or economic objectives. This led SOE quite naturally into the business of securing its own target-specific intelligence, which served to compete directly with MI6 – in the words of Sir Stewart Menzies (the head of SIS), in respect of 'priorities, competition for agents, transport, passages, etc.'. At one stage, SIS actively hindered SOE's attempts to infiltrate agents into enemy-occupied France because it feared that the latter would tread on what it regarded as its turf, and in truth it resented SOE's success in deploying agents.

The historian of MI6, Professor Keith Jeffery, perhaps reveals no secrets when he states that despite the agreement between MI6 and SOE in September 1941, 'all of SOE's cypher communications would run through SIS, that intelligence collected by SOE would be passed on to SIS and that SIS's approval would be sought when engaging agents', it was precisely these areas that provided the basis for friction between the two organisations as the war progressed. Jealousy undoubtedly played a part. The fact that SOE proved to be more successful than MI6 in mounting operations could not have helped, especially when the 'cuckoo in the clandestine agency nest', to use Jeffery's phrase, dropped *amateur* agents into occupied Europe in contrast to the self-styled professionals in the SIS.

When Major Maurice Buckmaster joined SOE at its offices at 64 Baker Street on 17 March 1941 the organisation was, his new commanding officer Lieutenant Colonel Dick Barry, SOE's Chief of Staff, explained to him, 'highly embryonic'. When, at his introductory interview, he asked what sort of information was available, the response was: 'Very little. There's hardly anything to go on.' 'What about Secret Service reports?' Buckmaster asked. 'Oh no,' came the reply, 'we don't get those. Can't get hold of them.' By September, when Buckmaster took over responsibility for F Section, he reviewed the 'immense amount of work with which I was faced'. He had a staff of eight, including Major Lewis Gielgud, the recruiting officer, responsible for recruiting bilingual British agents, and Major Robert Bourne-Paterson, the Planning Officer:

> As yet we had no organisation, few means of having our agents received by friendly patriots or of accepting messages from them once they had landed. France was without means of speaking to us. So far we had landed only three or four agents whose job it was to make contact but also to obtain information; they were much more 'spies' than were our later agents.

Through to the end of 1941 SOE increased the number of its agents in France to ten, landing men from Q ships (such as HMS *Fidelity*), feluccas, MTBs, parachutes and Lysander aircraft.* 'The missions of these men,' recalled Buckmaster, 'were strictly exploratory: they were not to make any bangs until we gave the word. For our part, however, we were co-operating with the Ministry of Economic Warfare in an endeavour to plot the right targets to attack when the moment came.' SOE did not want to encourage premature action by the French before the time was right, as this would only induce repressive measures by the Germans and get people shot for no appreciable gain, and have a negative impact on French morale.

In addition to SOE, de Gaulle's Free French Secret Service (the BCRA) under Major André Dewavrin (codenamed Colonel 'Passy' after one of the Paris Métro stations) competed for influence, equipment, attention and targets. Within SOE itself an entire section (R/F Section) was given over to supporting, exclusively, the Free French (that is, de Gaulle's) resistance 'circuits' in a France that was so bitterly divided politically that several different shades of *résistants* took years to trust each other and work together. Some never did. 'General de Gaulle tended to discourage contact between his officers and mine,' recalled Buckmaster, 'and he never lost his dislike of the fact that our agents were working in France.' The number of F Section agents deployed across France increased from seven by the end of 1941 'to fifty by the middle of 1942 and one hundred and twenty by June 1943'. It was only at this stage that 'destructive raids against the German supply machine' were considered.†

There was much more in common between SOE and Combined Operations, however, particularly in the period through to 1942 when both organisations were involved in mounting small raids.

* Q ships were vessels that disguised their genuine purpose.

† By D-Day, in June 1944, there were over 250 agents in the field. In total, 480 active agents were employed by the French Section of SOE.

The raids on the Channel Islands and the Calvados coastline in 1942 were carried out by SOE, for instance, whereas the limpet-mine attack on Boulogne was by 101 Troop of the Special Boat Section (SBS), part of the Special Service Brigade (the 'Commandos') and thus part of the Combined Operations organisation. SOE possessed a technical production capability that proved useful to Combined Operations (Section IX of SOE designed the limpet mine and time fuses, for instance), while SOE relied on Combined Operations for small-boat support.

As well as technical and logistical cooperation at a practical level, SOE and Combined Operations attempted to communicate on operational matters, although here, ultimately, they proved to be less successful than they had first hoped. In order to reduce the potential for duplication, SOE staff officer Major Wyatt sat on the Combined Operations Examinations Committee, which assessed and graded potential targets for raids and sabotage missions. Major Wyatt, however, joined the Dieppe raid in August 1942 and did not return. His role as the SOE interlocutor at the Examinations Committee was not replaced. When that Committee considered the proposal for a second time in October 1942, for a raid against Bordeaux later that year, it is apparent that there was no informed SOE participation in the decision. If there had been, a different judgement might well have been taken, to allow SOE sabotage plans in the Bordeaux docks to develop rather than to risk any other form of action.

'The Bordeaux area was one especially suited to our purposes,' remarked Maurice Buckmaster. 'Just inside the occupied zone, a group operating from there could have ready access both to the north and to the unoccupied zone.' In September 1941 SOE launched Operation Barter to attempt to identify suitable targets for economic sabotage in the Bordeaux region. At the time, without the trained manpower to undertake the attack, Colonel Dick Barry of SOE had again asked Colonel Passy for the Free French to provide suitable men for the task. The two agents appointed were Lieutenant Roger Donnadieu and Pierre Laurent (the radio operator), both soldiers in the Free French forces. Their orders were to elicit the number of persons from whom they might get support, the locations of secret depots for the storage of weapons and equipment, the ideal locations of parachute drops, and the possibility of an attack on Mérignac airfield as well as on other identified targets.*

Mérignac was the base from which small numbers of the four-engined Focke-Wulf C200 Condor anti-shipping bombers of *Kampfgeschwader* 40 (KG40) began their long flights across the Bay of Biscay to Britain and then on to Norway.† In late 1940 and early 1941 these aircraft caused considerable havoc to British shipping, flying three or four sorties a day despite the notorious unreliability of their engines. The squadron, for the loss of a single aircraft, had sunk 108,000 tons of shipping by the end of 1940, and in the first two months of 1941 alone had sunk a further forty-seven ships and damaged nineteen.

By March 1941 Churchill decreed that the removal of the threat from KG40 was as important as the defeat of the U-boat. The RAF had launched an attack on Mérignac on 2 November the previous year by thirty-two Hampdens and Blenheims, destroying four hangars and six aircraft including two of the almost mythical Condors. Subsequent raids on 26 and 27 December 1940, the latter involving seventy aircraft, caught no Condors on the ground, although eleven Wellington bombers on 10 April 1942 managed to destroy a further two hangars and two Condors, alongside three other aircraft, for the loss of one RAF bomber. Donnadieu and Laurent were dropped by parachute as planned, but the SOE operation quickly fizzled out, with Donnadieu forced on the run.

* The SOE files (NA/HS 6/418) have lost the appendix detailing the nature of these 'other' targets.

† The C3, which appeared in Bordeaux in the summer of 1941, had a flying range of 2,210 miles.

At the same time letters were passing between British diplomats in Spain and SOE about the possibility of using Spanish Republicans living in the south of France to undertake sabotage operations against the Germans. One potential target was the Bloch precision aircraft works which had recently been transferred from Paris.

Meanwhile, between September 1941 and January 1942 Robert Leroy worked under cover in the Bordeaux docks, watching ships arrive and depart, observing cargoes being loaded and unloaded, developing a small network of informers and helpers and identifying opportunities for sabotage according to his instructions.* Leroy's direct role in this secret war should not, however, be exaggerated. His SOE file, opened at the National Archives on 15 March 2011, reveals that he was an alcoholic Walter Mitty type prone to 'drunken phantasy [sic]'.

The truth is that a plethora of agents were working largely independently against the Germans across Bordeaux and even inside the docks from as early as the autumn of 1940. In January 1941 a small group of as many as thirty-six informants working with two demobilised French naval officers, Commanders Léo Paillière and Jean Duboué, began building up their own intelligence organisation based in the heart of the Bordeaux docks at Quai de Chartrons. Indeed, from the outset the group had offensive ideas in mind, storing a small quantity of rifles and ammunition for the time when active resistance against the invaders would be necessary.† It is possible that Leroy had ties with this group from

* Leroy was absent from Bordeaux between January and June 1942 when he was on his way to London, making his way to Gibraltar through neutral Spain and arriving in London in May 1942, then returning to Bordeaux in June, which he reached in August. He remained in Bordeaux before handing over to de Baissac in September and October, returning to Britain in June 1943. Reports arriving in London during his periods of absence must, therefore, have come from the other resistance networks.

† Commander Léo Paillière was imprisoned by the Germans between June and September 1942 and during this time was replaced as leader by André Grandclément ('Bernard'), who eventually betrayed the resistance organisation to the Germans. Grandclément was executed by Roger Landes (of whom more soon) in July 1944.

his arrival in September 1941, but it is equally possible that he did not. What is certain is that other eyes were also carefully observing everything going up and down the Garonne into the quays at the heart of Bordeaux, enabling accurate intelligence from the docks to be sent directly to London. In fact, both MI6 and the BCRA were already in regular receipt of high-quality intelligence from Bordeaux, courtesy of as many as five separate resistance sources in the Bordeaux region.

For example, two experienced water pilots working for the Port of Bordeaux, Jean Fleuret and Marie-Ange Gaudin (formerly the radio officer of the ship *Colbert*), worked as *résistants* from the moment the Germans arrived. They provided information about shipping activity in the Gironde via letters that were smuggled to Spain or into the unoccupied zone by a twenty-seven-year-old female courier, Laure Gatete, and thence to London.* In February 1941 this dangerous journey – in which Laure was strip-searched each time she travelled from Perpignan across the demarcation line at Sainte Foy la Grande, hiding the letters she carried in bottles of caustic soda – was replaced by a radio transmitter built by Gaudin himself. The men operated within the Confrérie Notre Dame (CND) Castille *réseau* based at the Château La Roque, where the transmitter was hidden. One of the originators of the CND *réseau* was Louis de la Bardonnie, who recalled: 'When our radio links were established with London, I went every week to Bordeaux and returned each time with a richer harvest.' The men knew the tiniest movement along the river between Bordeaux and Le Verdon:

> Not only did they serve as pilots for many cargo ships, submarines and submarine support vessels, but they kept London fully informed of troop movements, the establishment of fortifications on the coast, the activities of aerodromes, those factories and

* Laure Gatete was betrayed to the Germans, and died at Auschwitz on 25 February 1943.

> construction sites working for the enemy: nothing escaped their vigilance.
>
> It is absolutely no exaggeration to say that nothing of what was worthwhile remained unreported to the Allies. To achieve these results, Gaudin had recruited his son, Mark, together with a number of local agents, particularly young people, mad with audacity, who penetrated everywhere, saw everything and found out everything.

The antenna of Gaudin's radio was betrayed to the Germans in June 1942. He and his son escaped arrest but Fleuret was caught and deported to Buchenwald.* Louis de la Bardonnie had been arrested in December 1941 and held at a camp near Mérignac, but was released in early 1942 for lack of evidence.

Likewise, a cell of the Polish F2 network was active in Bordeaux from as early as July 1940 and operated during the first six months of 1942 when Leroy was absent from the city. This vigorous and effective group was led by a Polish Army officer, Tadeusz Jekiel (codenamed 'Doctor'), who had escaped to Britain and was based out of Bordeaux, reporting to Wincenty Zarembski (codenamed 'Tudor') who worked in Marseille. Other parts of this network operated from Lyon, Toulouse and Paris.

The Paris-based group was sent information couriered by *wagon-lit* (sleeper) attendants on the Paris to Marseille express, which was then transmitted to MI6 via agents working for the one-time MI6 agent in Paris, Wilfred ('Biffy') Dunderdale, using a radio set that had arrived from London in August 1940. Maurice Buckmaster was to note that throughout 'the history of the Resistance the railwaymen were, almost 100 per cent, the keenest and most resolute resisters'. In Bordeaux, Tadeusz Jekiel led a strong group that concentrated primarily on sending London information about shipping and submarine traffic in and out of the

* He survived the war.

Gironde: in mid-1941 'Doctor' had managed to set up equally successful 'Marine' cells in Le Havre and Brest. By early 1941 the network comprised 210 French operatives and forty Poles. Elements of the F2 network were broken up by the Gestapo in late 1942 but the Marine cell continued under Jekiel's deputy, Leon Sliwinski (codenamed 'Jean-Bol').

One of the routes by which reports on naval activity were sent through to London was via the US ambassador to Vichy, who placed them in the American diplomatic bag which then made its way to the US Embassy in Bern, whence they were transmitted by MI6 to London. The French members of F2 in Bordeaux operating in 1942 included two Bordeaux doctors (Dr Henri Cathary and Dr Louis Mancourier, the former working at the Naval Institute of Health), together with eight others.

In addition to the CND and F2 there were at least three other resistance groups working in the region in late 1942, one reporting to the Free French BCRA and the others to SIS. There were two French sections in SIS, one specifically for supporters of de Gaulle (A5) and the other recruiting from sources that were not the natural bedfellows of the Free French, such as Vichyites and monarchists (A4): the latter section was the responsibility of Biffy Dunderdale. By 1941 A5 had established loose networks of spies across the French Atlantic ports, many utilising connections between First World War veterans. According to Keith Jeffery, good coverage of the French Atlantic ports had been established by the end of 1941. Likewise, Dunderdale had been instructed by Sir Stewart Menzies to concentrate the efforts of A4 on securing intelligence from these ports, especially about U-boats and commerce raiders, and it was the F2 network that provided Dunderdale and A4 with much valuable information.

As the SIS records remain closed, the only information about these groups comes from French veterans themselves, not the least of which was provided by one of the *résistants*, Pierre Moniot, in 1946. One of them was the Phalanx-Phidias network created by

Christian Pineau, and another the Jade-Amicol network established in October 1940 by Captain Claude Arnould, a renegade Vichy officer (one of whose nom-de-plumes was Colonel Olivier), and Father Anthony Dieuzayde, the Jesuit chaplain general of the Catholic Association of French Youth.

The Phalanx-Phidias cell was part of the Free French BCRA network (not the British SIS), and although there was considerable dialogue between SOE and BCRA in 1942 (BCRA providing SOE's early saboteurs, for instance) there is no evidence that much, if any, intelligence traffic moved between the BCRA and the SIS. The Phalanx-Phidias cell in Bordeaux was built on the ranks of the *pompiers* (firemen) in the docks, although the offensive capabilities of this group in December 1942 are unlikely to have been great. It was led by Raymond Brard, Head of Security at the port, whose codename was 'Colonel Raymond'. Jade-Amicol was a different story, however, the members of the network reporting directly to an MI6 officer who worked under the pseudonym of Captain Philip Keun (codenamed variously 'Admiral', 'Friend' and 'Deux'), a Dutchman raised in Britain and thus able to pass himself off as an Englishman.* Of the nineteen men and women listed as members of this group one was an expatriate Englishman in Bayonne (Armstrong) and another, Raymond Gal, was a police inspector in Pau. The main agent in Bordeaux was Pierre Moniot, a tram engineer since 1939 who was Director of the Bordeaux tramways. His resistance group was formed principally of tram crewmen, and the network operated with the active support of Moniot's wife, Marie-Suzanne. The task of the network was to 'listen, watch and forward' information from four main areas: the tram network, the port, the railways and the aerodromes. Rather fantastically, Moniot's tramway offices were in the same building as the German Propaganda Directorate in the city: he was able to operate unhindered and

* Keun was captured in June 1944 and transported to Buchenwald, where he was executed three months later.

unsuspected until 15 September 1943, when he and his wife were forced into hiding.*

Intelligence sent to London included the results of aerial bombardment; detailed inventories of equipment and supplies sent by rail to Germany; details of work undertaken in the Bacalan submarine base; detailed maps of the Pointe de Grave and the Cap Ferrat–Soulac peninsula; detailed movements in Bordeaux harbour, including the berthing plan and information about the departure of submarines and cargo ships; and detailed summaries of ammunition stocks and locations of aircraft across the region.

All in all, the various receivers of intelligence in London were extremely well served in late 1942 by the secret organisations all working independently in the Charente Maritime, Aquitaine and Landes regions of south-west France. Leroy undoubtedly played a part in the acquisition of the intelligence about the blockade-runner's activities, but the truth is that he provided only part of the picture. Jean Fleuret and Marie-Ange Gaudin, the Marine cell of the Polish F2 network, the Jade-Amicol and possibly also the Phalanx-Phidias networks also contributed to the jigsaw by supplying MI6 and the Naval Intelligence Department of the Admiralty with consistent, accurate and timely information about enemy activities in the French Atlantic ports.

This does not mean, of course, that any of this additional intelligence was ever directly shared with SOE. No evidence exists that SOE ever knew that a number of spy networks had already spun their webs across the Bordeaux region, each priding itself on reporting every single ship and submarine movement into and out of the Gironde. Nor is there any evidence that the intelligence provided to MI6 ever made its way to SOE. The different groups in Bordeaux fed information to London, where it was carefully pieced together. It did not matter that the groups were unaware

* They survived the war. His notes record that there were 1,200 *résistants* in the twenty-eight resistance groups across the Gironde, of whom 68 were arrested, 42 deported to Germany and 20 shot, hanged or beheaded.

of each other's presence, nor that information was often patchy and incomplete. What one group might have missed, it was possible that others had picked up, leading to a remarkably accurate picture of German activity in and out of the Gironde in 1942.

But from whatever angle the problem was examined, the practical difficulties of successful action against the blockade traffic were immense. It appears that the information provided by Robert Leroy during his first few months in Bordeaux convinced Maurice Buckmaster and the planners at SOE that the facilities at Bassens and Bordeaux were an ideal target for sabotage from *inside* the docks. This was not as farfetched as it might seem. As the information upon which Selborne was basing his letters came directly from agents (both SIS and SOE) within the docks workforce, it was logical to conclude that anti-freighter operations might be considered from inside the dock organisation itself. But the biggest issue had to do with scale: in order to cause the greatest damage to the largest number of ships, considerable numbers of agents and quantities of explosives would be required to ensure that the ships were put permanently out of action.

SOE's capabilities in mid-1942 in Bordeaux remained nascent, however, and Selborne undoubtedly believed that somewhat bigger guns would be required. But no option was ruled out at this stage, and Combined Operations HQ carried out its own investigation of the possibilities for action while SOE did the same. It is improbable that at the level of the Examinations Committee and above both COHQ and SOE were entirely unaware of each other's aspirations, at least insofar as planning was concerned. They carried on independently, however, with no cross-fertilisation of ideas. This was a natural extension of the 'need to know' principle. Until a plan had been prepared for execution, its contents remained the closest of secrets and only those very few with an absolute need to know, were informed. This could, of course, lead to a situation where two entirely separate parties ended up planning an operation on the same target, wholly ignorant of each other.

Still blind to the fact that MI6 had already deeply penetrated the Bordeaux docks – it remains a moot point whether Selborne knew where his information was coming from – SOE decided, after Leroy's month-long return to Britain in May 1942, to build an entire network of agents (known as a 'circuit') in that city. The name of the group was 'Scientist', and its first two new agents were dispatched to the region by parachute in July. The first of these was the son of a wealthy Mauritian landowner, Claude Marc de Boucherville Baissac (codenamed 'David'), and a young French-speaking British soldier called Henry Peulevé ('Jean').

By way of preparation de Baissac read all of Leroy's reports, alerting him to the blockade-running traffic. However, through a series of mishaps de Baissac did not reach Bordeaux until September that year. Peulevé, his original radio operator, had been dropped with de Baissac near Nîmes, but far too low by the inexperienced RAF dispatcher (a common problem at the time, complained SOE), and he suffered a dangerous compound fracture of the right leg on landing. Also, de Baissac suffered a sprained ankle. He and Peulevé, in accordance with their training, had split up after the accident, Peulevé to crawl off to find what help he could from local sympathisers, and de Baissac to find his way to Bordeaux alone by way of a contact, one Monsieur Hèche, in Cannes. Peulevé's place in 'Scientist' was taken by Major Roger Landes (codenamed 'Aristide'),* who joined de Baissac in Bordeaux in November 1942. At the same time de Baissac received an assistant: Captain Charles Hayes (codenamed 'Printer'), a specialist in electrical matters and sabotage, to help him in his work.†

The 35-year-old de Baissac had joined SOE on 6 March 1942. Educated at the Lycée Henri-IV in Paris, his entire family were

* The name of his circuit was 'Actor'.

† Captain Charles Hayes (field name 'Yves') arrived in France for his second period of duty on 26 November 1942. He was arrested and badly injured during a shoot-out on 13 October 1943 and was executed at the Gross-Rosen concentration camp in Poland on 1 August 1944.

passionate believers in *la gloire de la France* and were accordingly humiliated by their country's political and military collapse in 1940. All three siblings joined the British forces rather than the Free French. Claude and his sister Lise joined SOE and their elder brother joined the British Army. De Baissac escaped from France on foot across the Pyrenees in a journey that took seven months and included a long and uncomfortable confinement in a Spanish internment camp. He had held a variety of jobs in Paris before the war and had visited Bordeaux several times. Volatile and emotional, he was also stubborn and single-minded as well as physically and mentally tough – characteristics that would stand him in good stead when operating as a secret agent and saboteur.

The report on his training at Special Training School No. 5 at Arisaig in the Scottish Highlands, dated 15 April 1942, described him as having '[e]xcessive though not obnoxious self-confidence, leading to an impetuous approach to subjects of which his knowledge is only limited. Extremely French and volatile. Plenty of courage and guts and should be an acquisition: from conversation seems to possess a really good grasp of French affairs and from a reasonably placed angle.' A month later he completed training at STS No. 27, where he impressed the staff. His report stated that he was 'a first rate man. He has a very firm intention of causing a lot of damage operationally, with the ability to do it and take care of himself. A great love of his Country and keenness to do his part should prove him to be of great value.'

The purpose of the Scientist network was sabotage, especially against economic targets. De Baissac's objectives (described in his orders as 'for immediate action') were

1 rubber and other cargoes from the Far East entering the port of Bordeaux. In order of priority he was ordered to plan attacks on
   (a) the ships
   (b) cargo in the ships

(c) cargo on the wharf
(d) cargo on rail.

2 dredgers
3 the lock gate at Bacalan (the U-Boat pens), but only if Leroy failed in this objective.

Robert Leroy returned to Bordeaux from London in August 1942 in order to hand over his contacts to de Baissac, and had been there for several weeks before the latter was able to make his belated appearance in September. On Leroy's advice, de Baissac based himself in the docks and lived above a café on the waterfront called La Coquille: the owner was a *résistant*, and became a member of de Baissac's *réseau*. Buckmaster described Scientist as a model of its kind: 'The whole thing was arranged in the manner which was supposed to be standard practice: there were a large number of separate knots of resisters who knew, of course, of the existence of others, but knew nothing either of names, identities or areas.'

Leroy introduced de Baissac to the small group of people recruited to the cause of resistance in the docks, but de Baissac was not initially impressed, forgetting perhaps that Leroy had enjoyed a mere three months in the city the previous autumn and had been absent for the previous six. De Baissac told London by radio on 19 September 1942: 'Louis (i.e. Leroy) did not seem to have a cut and dried organisation. He had only got in touch with a few people who seemed willing to follow him.' De Baissac, hungry for action, was himself soon to recognise that it was still too early in Bordeaux to be able to set up a fully functioning resistance organisation in an area of France with notoriously 'soft morale'. What was necessary was the gradual evolution from an indigenous organisation able to recruit and organise itself to one that could procure intelligence, receive weapons and equipment from the air and plan attacks. Only then would successful sabotage operations be possible. He was pleased to report, nevertheless, that Leroy's enthusiasm for his mission remained undiminished. He recorded that Leroy's chief collaborator was a man named Bourrière, who had found a reception ground near the village of Cadillac-en-Fronsadais, a few miles north-east of Bordeaux, for the delivery of parachute supplies, and had already organised a reception committee.

De Baissac began flooding London with information about the blockade-runners. It was the start of a series of reports that in 1943 SOE described as the 'outstanding series of intelligence reports that came out of Bordeaux'. He was aided considerably in November 1942 by the arrival from Britain of a female courier, Mary Herbert ('Jeweller'), who in time was to become de Baissac's lover and bore him a child in 1943. They were married in England in 1944. De Baissac was described by Major Bourne-Paterson as 'an excellent officer', 'one of the most capable organisers we ever sent to France', and M.R.D. Foot placed him as 'probably the most forceful and one of the most efficient' among SOE organisers. The SOE war diary captured the essence of de Baissac's first messages back to London:

> Only two or three blockade-runners have come into Bordeaux since August. He thinks that two of these contained rubber and a third discharged a complete cargo of oil of all kinds, including vegetable oil, olive oil and peanut oil as well as fuel oil. Nobody has any idea where this vessel came from. He hadn't seen a tanker in Bordeaux – all the oil is transported in barrels. The vessels appeared to be moved regularly by the port authorities in order to deceive and confuse any watchers. He reported the name of one ship, the *Kalanga*, of 8–10,000 tons. He reported that the crews were all German. He gave us information a week or two ago that the PORTLAND was ready to sail. This ship was loaded with machine tools and spare parts and left once but returned later to VERDON. It carried rations for nine months. Six ships were currently loaded and ready to sail. In addition there were three or four 'fair sized ships' and very many small ones carrying

food to Spain and bringing pyrites from Spain. He believed that mercury was part of the blockade-runner's trade.

Leroy's idea, with which de Baissac agreed and developed further (Leroy continued to work in Bordeaux until late 1943, but also supported the Buckthorn circuit in Lyon), was to use trusted workers in the dockyards to smuggle explosives into the ships when they were being repaired or prepared for their sea voyages. Painters preparing the inside of the holds for their new cargoes could take the plastic explosive parachuted in from Britain into the dock area and on to the ships in their knapsacks. In London, Buckmaster's team at SOE believed that the scheme was feasible and encouraged de Baissac to continue his planning. A small number of explosive charges, placed at strategic points on the inside of the hull (such as the edge of external bulkheads and the bow area), could be timed to explode when the vessel was at sea. If the ship was travelling at speed, even relatively small holes under the waterline would increase the potential for the vessel to sink, due to the rapid ingress of large quantities of water.

The major problem, as de Baissac made clear in his detailed report in March 1943, lay in providing Scientist with sufficient quantities of explosive. 'Louis is only waiting for the necessary material in order to get on with the job,' he wrote. 'He can do the work on the painting of the boats down in the hold, he has already informed you how he needed the goods (small packages which could easily go into a workman's haversack).' Yet repeated efforts to drop supplies to the Scientist group were unsuccessful. Only one, on 20 November 1942, got through, four containers being dropped to Scientist at a forested and hilly drop site near the remote village of Sauveterre la Lémance, one hundred and five miles south-west of Bordeaux, which contained 60 pounds of plastic explosive, 12 Sten guns, 12 revolvers, 66 grenades and 15 'clams' (small explosive devices). The clams could be attached to any large metal targets, including ships.

Clearly, considerably more explosives would be required before de Baissac would be in a position to carry out a successful and simultaneous attack on more than a single ship. In March 1943 he told London that this was the major hurdle preventing him from undertaking sabotage: '[O]wing to the complete lack of supplies he [de Baissac] has been forced to confine himself almost entirely to the organisation, as opposed to the active side, of his mission.'

But the situation did improve later in the year. In the seven months that followed, de Baissac built up his organisation, receiving supplies from the air and moving from the intelligence-gathering to the execution phase of his sabotage campaign. His connections with the developing French underground, together with his own formidable organisational and leadership skills, led to no fewer than 121 successful dropping operations being made to the Scientist circuit between November 1942 and August 1943. In these, 1,600 containers and 350 packages were delivered, including, among other things, 18,400 pounds of high explosive, 7,500 Sten guns, 300 Bren guns, 1,500 rifles and 17,200 grenades.

De Baissac's success in Bordeaux mirrored the gradual transition of F Section SOE from fledgling to full flight. In Sir Charles Hambro's quarterly report to the Prime Minister in October 1942 relating to the period between July and September, written in an excited, Churchillian manner – perhaps unconsciously mimicking the style of the reader – the Director of SOE reported that occupied Europe was 'seething with the spirit of revolt and revolution'. In his next report, in January 1943, he described the spirit of resistance as growing daily stronger, and SOE as continuing 'to stoke the furnace'. In the anti-German turmoil he described across occupied Europe, in which he listed 226 attacks on Axis or collaborationist premises and personnel, 104 train derailments and acts of railways sabotage, 155 general acts of incendiarism, 53 acts of sabotage in factories or against public services, he claimed that 'S.O.E. have been the moving spirit'.

This was clearly hyperbole (much of his information was gleaned from reading newspapers published in the occupied territories), but SOE's capacity to strike was nevertheless developing rapidly. In the earlier quarter Hambro recorded that fifty-two agents had been dropped into enemy territory, along with 298 containers carrying 300 pounds each of arms and explosives, together with six 50-pound packages of stores and 137 radio transmitter sets. By the start of October 1942 SOE had sent into the field 458 agents; 643 were fully trained and awaiting assignment, and a further 734 men and women were undergoing training. By January 1943 he was able to report that the number of agents in the field had risen threefold (to 150), and 347 containers of arms and explosives had been dropped together with a further 187 radio transmitters.

This growth was impressive. Nevertheless, in Bordeaux in December 1942 Scientist's capabilities in terms of delivering sabotage *effect* remained nascent. An attack could have been mounted only after several more months of planning and supply drops of explosives. Using the pattern of supply drops to Scientist as a guide, it appears unlikely that de Baissac could have launched an attack of any substance against the blockade-runners much before Easter 1943.

FIVE

'Blondie' Hasler

The success of raiding in the early years of the war owed much to the perseverance and commitment of a small number of unconventional individuals. All who found themselves involved in encouraging the raiding agenda were, like those across the armed services who pioneered the development of Special Forces (such as the Commandos and the Special Air Service), unique characters imbued with outstanding energy and conviction, as well as physical and moral courage of the highest order.

George Courtney, who joined his brother Roger in the Special Boat Section, described him as 'a wild man [who] should have been an Elizabethan free-booter'. The same could be said for the remarkable trio of adventurers who formed No. 62 Commando, Gus March-Phillips, Geoffrey Appleyard and Graham Hayes. March-Phillips set up the SSRF almost single-handedly, forcing the authorities to formalise what was little more than a group of men of action determined to do what they could to take the war directly to the enemy. Lieutenant Brooks Richards, one of the naval officers supporting the SSRF raids, recalled of him: 'Before the war he'd had expensive tastes and slender means. He loved fox hunting and he liked driving fast cars and he indulged these two tastes by becoming someone's kennel huntsman and then by becoming a racing driver.' He had 'all the dash and flair and the outward signs of a commando', recollected his SSRF comrade Lieutenant Freddie Bourne.

On the night he died they had considerable trouble identifying the site off the coast of Sainte-Honorine-des-Pertes that had been determined as the landing place, because a sea mist had enveloped the coastline. The *Little Pisser* throttled down a mile or so off the coast, the commandos quietly scanning the coastline to see if there was a way through. Bourne recalled that March-Phillips then broke the silence: 'What do you think, chaps? Shall we have a bash?' They did so, and went to their deaths fighting, unwilling to turn down the chance to fight in favour of returning home, tails between their legs.

A man made in the same adventurer's mould was a stocky, six-foot-two-inch Royal Marine officer with an intense passion for small boats and the open sea, who had been awarded the Croix de Guerre and the OBE as a member of the Royal Marine Fortress Unit (RMFU) during the abortive Norway campaign in the spring of 1940. The twenty-eight-year-old Captain 'Blondie' Hasler, so nicknamed by his peers not so much for his magnificent and carefully tended moustache as for the swathe of golden curls that swept around the back of his head and poked out above his ears, was already a well-known figure in the Royal Marines before the war, joining as a regular officer in September 1932. Those who knew him best described him as an inspirational leader, in part because he was the complete master of his trade, always did first what he asked his men to do afterwards, and contained not an ounce of pomposity. The thoroughness of his preparation in advance of a task, together with his phenomenal attention to detail, surprised even those unwilling to do something on the fly, but it was precisely his determination to understand the minutiae of a piece of equipment, or of a procedure or problem, that gave his men confidence in this man who had considered every angle. They knew that, with Blondie, every inch of an assignment would have been examined, and every practical option or alternative turned over in his febrile mind, and that Blondie himself would have practised it first. His methodical unflappability was an inspiration to those who served with him.

He was also good fun to be with; he had a ready wit and a deep sense of humour able to penetrate even the bleakest of situations. As a young officer he was regularly in trouble for his impish practical jokes. The fact that he preferred small groups of friends to large crowds led some to believe that he was antisocial: aloof, cold or distant. This is far from the truth. Despite being naturally reserved he enjoyed company, and took pleasure in building people up, rather than belittling them. But he also loved being alone. In a letter to Mountbatten (then the First Sea Lord) on 2 May 1956 David Astor, at that time editor of the *Observer* but who had been on Mountbatten's staff in COHQ during the war, described Hasler as having 'the solitary and highly independent type of "explorer" nature' which made it difficult for him to settle down into any sort of uninspiring routine. For relaxation he liked nothing better than a long walk with friends, a quiet drink in his local, mowing his mother Annie's extensive lawns with a push-mower (cited frequently in his diaries, it was an important form of exercise for him), or a solitary blow on his saxophone.

An intensely practical man, he loved tinkering around with bits of wood or machinery. He loved making things work. In this he demonstrated in abundance the defining characteristics of the meticulous man: a hatred of wasted time, and obsessive attention to detail. Creative, he was never happier than when designing a better sail or rudder, or solving a difficulty that had flummoxed other men. He then secured the greatest satisfaction by building or *doing* whatever he had designed or planned on paper. He always had a dozen things on the go.

Blondie was also supremely fit. Few knew that he suffered from ankylosing spondylitis, a type of arthritis that affects the spine, especially the lower back. Causing stiffness and reduced movement in later life, it often leads to some of the bones of the spine fusing together. As a result Blondie struggled to run. Yet he remained superbly athletic, compensating for his lack of running with long daily walks – between four and eight miles every day – and swimming, which his condition never seemed to impede.

A small measure of the man is provided by regular diary entries, which catch something of the excitement of solo adventure. On Monday 29 June 1942, for instance, he records that he went alone deep into the Solent in a MkII carrying with him portable diving apparatus: 'Calm, dead LWS [Low Water at Spring tide]. Marvellous. Diving from the canoe.' A month later his diary recorded a similar story. Out in a tempestuous sea he was in his element: 'Wind strong easterly. Sea rough. Great fun.' After the war he was to pioneer the science of single-handed ocean yacht racing, skills he had begun honing from the days when, as a teenager at Wellington College in Crowthorne,* he became obsessed to distraction by the freedom and challenge provided by the open sea. With a friend he built his first seaworthy canoe at the age of twelve, and an equally seaworthy sailing dinghy (a ten-foot 'flat-bottomed punt') at fourteen. Many happy, solitary hours were spent exploring the waters of the Solent, camping out on mudflats and beaches at night. His mother must have fretted, but claimed that she 'knew he would always turn up'. His defining characteristics were well captured by his 1945 Confidential Report:

> Thinks clearly and expresses himself well, particularly on technical subjects, and has a lively imagination and a leaning towards development or invention . . . He is in the centre of work which borders on a hobby for him and works exceptionally hard and long, and also at routine and some administrative work with interest and thoroughness, despite this being at the expense of work which he finds more interesting. He has a well developed sense of humour, is a good practical seaman and keeps himself fit. A strong character with the ability to inspire enthusiasm. Popular.

* He was a member of the Lynedoch (one of the school's houses), and became Head of House.

There is almost a sense of annoyance in his commanding officer's tone that Hasler was doing something he enjoyed.

Hasler's meticulous diary records that he joined the Combined Operations Development Centre (CODC), based at Eastney Barracks in Southsea near Portsmouth, at precisely 10.30 a.m. on Monday 26 January 1942. He was now an acting major. Previously known as the Inter-Services Training and Development Centre (ISTDC), which had first opened its doors in May 1938, the CODC (an intimate part of COHQ) was responsible for designing and delivering practical solutions for amphibious raiding and assault. In short, the CODC was Combined Operations' amphibious workshop.

Dramatic successes by the Italian Navy against the Mediterranean Fleet in 1941 had proved beyond doubt the ability of tenacious, well trained men to breach the defences of even the most heavily protected harbour, and COHQ began the search for a man to lead the British effort to emulate these successes. Hasler's deep and practical knowledge of the sea through his years of single-handed sailing, his battlefield experience and his inventiveness, made him the ideal man for the task. He had been well aware of Courtney's canoe raids in the Mediterranean in 1941 and had, that year, submitted a paper to COHQ suggesting the use of underwater swimmers, employing the portable Davis Submarine Escape Apparatus (DSEA) to gain access to enemy harbours with a view to sabotage. He and friends had used it for sporting purposes in Egypt as early as 1935. His ideas had been rejected at the time, but Blondie had not been forgotten.

His principal task at the CODC was to improve the techniques and equipment used by Combined Operations for amphibious operations, raids and sabotage against enemy harbours. He was to spend a considerable amount of time at 1a Richmond Terrace. Indeed, his first visit to the COHQ took place on his second day in post, his diary recording a pattern that was to repeat itself many times in the coming months. The night before, he sketched out the terms of reference for his new appointment, which included the need to identify ways of inserting small groups of trained men into enemy territory:

> 0830. Train from Havant to Waterloo with Captain [T.A.] Hussey [RN].*
> 1045. Met CCO [Commodore, Combined Operations (Mountbatten)] and Rear Admiral [H.E.] Horan [DSC]. Terms of reference approved. CCO rang up ADNI [Assistant Director Naval Intelligence] to fix access to information.
> 1130. Visited ADNI, then NIDVII [Section 7 of the Naval Intelligence Department] up to 1815.
> 1815–2200. With NID 3/Xi (Interrogation Reports). Stayed at Charing Cross Hotel.

In addition to approving immediately Hasler's terms of reference, Mountbatten instructed him to concentrate on developing methods for attacking ships in harbour. Foremost in Mountbatten's mind was the need to develop a British equivalent to the devastating Italian explosive motor boat, which entailed an extraordinarily brave man driving a motor boat packed with explosives at speed against a ship, like a manned surface torpedo, the driver ejecting himself from the back and into the sea moments before the weapon struck its target. Six of these kamikaze-type craft had attacked and sunk the cruiser HMS *York* in Suda Bay on 26 May 1941.

In the months that followed this remained Hasler's primary task, and he worked closely with shipbuilders to build for the Royal Navy a vessel akin to the Italian. It was given the cover

* Captain Thomas ('Tom') Hussey was the Commandant of the CODC and therefore Hasler's immediate superior. In April 1942 he became Coordinator of Experiments and Developments at COHQ (a title that became, in August, Director of Experiments and Staff Requirements, or DXSR) and was replaced at CODC by Lieutenant Colonel H.F.G. Langley, Royal Artillery.

name 'Boom Patrol Boat' (BPB), reflecting the requirement for such craft to somehow get over or through the antisubmarine nets that protected harbours from underwater or small-vessel attack. In time a lethal machine, powered by a V12 Lagonda engine and packed with enough explosives in the bows to blast open the thick armour-plating of a battleship at the waterline, was designed and tested.

But fast boats, though great fun, were not Hasler's key obsession. His diary reveals that within days of beginning at Eastney, Hussey had introduced him to the handful of men then involved in the development of military canoeing. Getting the BPB over the protective boom guarding an enemy harbour was one thing: cutting through the boom, as well as rescuing the BPB's driver from the sea once the boat was making its way, at speed, towards the enemy ship, were tasks which Hasler believed could be best done by accompanying canoeists.

On the afternoon of Thursday 29 January 1942, in Eastney, he was visited by Captain Gerald Montanaro of 101 Troop based at Dover (which was in the process of being merged into the 2nd Special Boat Section (SBS) of the Special Service Brigade), and a few days later he was at HMS *Vernon* to 'discuss the accommodation of Gerald Montanaro's boys'.* Montanaro was able to brief Hasler on the current status of Army canoeing, and invited him to visit his tiny base in Dover harbour to try his hand at the equipment then in use. The canoes Montanaro was using were essentially unchanged civilian Folbots, poorly constructed craft made of rubberised canvas stretched over a rigid sixteen-foot plywood frame that broke into three parts for carriage. It had an open cockpit and was not designed well for rough water or prolonged exposure to conditions in the open sea.

Hasler hated it from the moment he set eyes upon it. Its canvas

* HMS *Vernon* was a shore establishment, the home of the Royal Navy's Torpedo Branch, responsible for mine disposal and the development of mine countermeasures.

covering tore easily, it was delicate (it could not, for example, be dragged across a shingle beach without being ripped to shreds), and its three separate parts demanded it be constructed on the surfaced deck of a submarine before being deployed. The collapsible version of the canoe had been made to solve this problem, but the task of erecting it on the submarine's deck was a difficult one and took considerably more time than Hasler believed safe, not merely for the crew but more importantly for the surfaced submarine.

The Admiralty had arbitrarily given the Folbot the designation 'Cockle', the standard civilian version made for military use being the Cockle MkI, although a range of different modifications were made to various canoes that all came under the same 'MkI' label. Hasler hated the name, believing it to be frivolous, writing an indignant letter to the Admiralty to complain. The letter was ignored. Slight improvements to the original produced the Cockle MkI* and, in 1943, the MkI**.

The poor quality of the first boats ordered by the Admiralty from Folbot Ltd in London forced Tom Hussey to look elsewhere for an alternative supplier.* His search took him to Mr Fred Goatley of Saro Laminated Wood Products Ltd on the Isle of Wight, and to the Tyne Folding Boat Company in Richmond. Fred Goatley had already produced a collapsible twelve-man assault boat which was in use among the raiding forces. Without the firm promise of an order, he nevertheless turned his hands to the development of a suitable folding canoe, designing on paper a two-seat fifteen-footer in September 1941. Hussey told him that there was not yet the demand for such a vessel, but Goatley persevered in his own time and at his own expense to improve the design. On 10 March 1942 he wrote to Hussey with the news that he had designed a two-person folding canoe capable of being passed through a

* Folbot Folding Boats Ltd in East London were blitzed into liquidation, shortly thereafter resurrecting themselves as Folboats Ltd of Cambridge. The quality of their canoes remained poor.

24-inch circular hatch, which was the diameter of the torpedo-loading hatch of a submarine. For Hasler's purposes, the fruits of Goatley's initiative could not have been better timed.

One of the organisations that maintained a permanent and active presence at Richmond Terrace was SOE. Indeed, from his earliest visits Hasler included the SOE representative, Major David Wyatt, in his discussions, and CODC directly benefited from the technical developments that SOE were making in the field of subversive warfare. It is clear from Hasler's diary that COHQ had a close relationship with SOE, principally through Wyatt: indeed, Hasler was to have many discussions with SOE about the best methods of inserting saboteurs into enemy territory undetected. One of Wyatt's early reports, dated 19 January 1942, noted: 'I have obtained permission . . . to arrange a meeting between an officer from Station XII and Major Hasler of CODC to discuss attacks on warships in harbour.'* A typical diary entry for Hasler, for 25 June 1942, is 'Met a party from SOE [at Lump's Fort, Southsea]. Discussed "Dover Sole".'†

As yet, however, CODC had no canoes with which Hasler could develop his ideas. On 20 February he went to Sparke's Yard, Hayling Island, to enquire about buying a canoe: the advice he received was to try the marine outlets in Worthing. That evening he spent time 'writing letters re canoes', seeking authority to purchase a small number of civilian vessels for testing. The following Sunday found him at home and 'considering canoe technique', a subject he then pursued all afternoon on Monday 23 February with Major Roger Courtney at Eastney. On Monday 9 March he was back in London with Hussey to meet with Courtney and Montanaro at 2.15 p.m. 'to discuss MKII Tadpole staff requirements'. It proved

* Aston House in Stevenage, Hertfordshire, designed and manufactured explosive devices for clandestine use.

† Presumably an exercise or operation, the details of which have not survived in the SOE archives.

to be a crucial meeting, for all were agreed that Hasler be given responsibility for developing an improved version of an operational military canoe for universal use across the services. The three men agreed that the Cockle Mark II (Hasler's attempt to call it the 'Tadpole' instead did not stick) should have the following design characteristics:

1 to be of decked canoe type propelled by two men using double paddles
2 maximum load to be two 13-stone men plus 1 cwt of cargo – total 480 lbs
3 weight of boat to be, ideally, less than 70 lbs . . . but in any case less than 100 lbs
4 to be easily driven for long periods at 3 knots fully loaded with a maximum speed of 5 knots in a light condition
5 to be able to stand up to a force 4 wind blowing in the open sea and able to be beached through surf
6 strength of skin to be such as to withstand indefinitely grounding on shingle and working alongside other vessels
7 length to be about 16 feet
8 beam: sufficient stability to satisfy (1) above must be achieved without prejudice to the ability to get out of the forward torpedo hatch of a small submarine. This demanded that the width of the collapsed canoe had to be at least ½ inch less than the 28½-inch diameter of the torpedo-loading hatch of a T Class submarine.

Hasler also stipulated that the new canoe had to be assembled by its crew in no more than thirty seconds in the dark.

The deployment of military canoes in successful military operations began gradually to devour more and more of Blondie's time and interest. It struck him increasingly that there were was more than one way to penetrate an enemy harbour. The first was the Italian way: plenty of noise, speed, smoke and large doses of heart-stopping courage. His V12 Lagonda-powered BPB would achieve that. There were more subtle alternatives, however, in which the Italians had already demonstrated considerable expertise. These included underwater swimming and the use of tiny two-man submarines which could slip through boom nets that would be impossible for conventional submarines to penetrate. The underwater saboteurs would then lay delayed-charge magnetic mines against the hulls, and depart well before the resulting explosions and inevitable hue and cry.

The one approach not yet adopted by the otherwise intrepid and innovative Italians entailed the use of military canoes that could slip over, rather than under, the boom. Canoes could be launched at close range from submarines (which the BPB could not do) and enter a harbour by stealth. Indeed, the effort to get a BPB even close to an enemy harbour for it to be of use was considerable; by comparison, the effort required to insert a small number of canoes over an enemy boom and into the defended sanctuary of an enemy harbour was much less. Getting to the enemy target was the major difficulty – the options were boat, aircraft or submarine. MTBs could carry commando raiders from England to northern France, but no further. Nor was there a mechanism for carrying BPBs or canoes by aircraft, or dropping them by parachute. The other option, practised during 1941 in the Mediterranean, was by submarine. There were not many of these available in RN service, however. Britain started the war with sixty submarines, together with nine in the process of building, only twenty-five of which were in home waters and the Atlantic.* These numbers were eroded by enemy action, one being lost in 1939, 24 in 1940, 11 in 1941 and 19 in 1942.

Now that Montanaro and Courtney had recognised the role CODC could play in developing an idea that all three men had originally pursued independently, Blondie began work with added

* A total of 178 were commissioned during the war.

enthusiasm. His diary demonstrates his growing obsession with the potential offered by this means of infiltration into enemy harbours. The first thing he needed to do was to create the perfect military canoe. To do this he needed to see what types, in addition to the Folbot, were available on the civilian market and which could, perhaps, be modified for military use.

On Thursday 12 March he took a car for Worthing with Sergeant Pennicott, one of two Royal Marines assigned to Hasler to help him conduct tests and experiments (the other was Corporal Wallis), known collectively as the 'Experimental Party'. Blondie ordered two of the boats they found, which were delivered to him in Eastney the following Monday. He named them *Cranthorpe* and *Blondin* respectively. He had already asked Courtney to send him two Folbots from existing stocks: these arrived in Eastney barracks on Tuesday 24 March. Blondie spent the ensuing days teaching Pennicott to canoe in *Cranthorpe*, although the latter proved not a very successful seaman and the canoe was badly damaged on its first outing at sea. He found *Blondin* almost impossible to manoeuvre, and wrote exasperatedly in his diary: '*Blondin* tried for the first (and almost the last) time. The boat is only to be used as a joke.'

As the weeks went by, in between visits to COHQ in Richmond Terrace, developing the BPB, and underwater swimming experiments with the Davis escape apparatus, Hasler spent every spare moment he could at sea. As soon as the Folbots arrived, he took out one of them single-handedly for the first time, repeating this two days later, 'testing forward and after positions' in a south-east wind while the remainder of the Experimental Party spent the day with two-seater Folbots. As with *Cranthorpe*, *Blondin* and the Cockle MkI ('Folbot'), Hasler became quickly convinced that no existing boat met the requirements for a robust, submarine-launched vessel able to cope with the demands of the open sea and shingle beaches, not to mention the requirement to carry a heavy load of anti-ship mines. He would have to design, and perhaps build, his own. Hussey had helpfully passed on to him Fred Goatley's letter of 10 March, and urged him to visit the boat designer on the Isle of Wight. The two men got on well from the outset. Hasler described to Goatley what he wanted, and asked him to prepare some drawings that they could develop together. Goatley agreed, assuring Hasler that he could see no difficulty in producing a vessel of the type required.

On his return from the Isle of Wight to Southsea that afternoon, Hasler had another visitor: Major Gus March-Phillips of No. 62 Commando. Hasler took him to see *Cranthorpe* under repair and described to him the work Fred Goatley was undertaking for him regarding the MkII. March-Phillips became a regular visitor to Southsea, but it is clear from Hasler's diary that insofar as the design of military canoes was concerned, he learned little from his friends in the SSRF.

It was not until Tuesday 31 March that Hasler was finally able to take the train from London to Dover to take up Montanaro's offer to look over 101 Troop. He spent the afternoon examining its equipment; saw a demonstration with Cockles MkI and I*, including the placing of a Type R mine (limpet) on the hulls of vessels by means of a 'placing rod' designed by Montanaro. The canoe would come alongside the target, and while one of the crewmen held on to the hull with a magnetic holder to keep the canoe steady, the second crewman would lower the limpet by means of the long metal rod.

Once the magnets in the limpet had allowed it successfully to attach to the vessel five or six feet below the waterline, the rod would be disconnected and placed on another limpet. The hulls of large ocean-going vessels were divided into a number of compartments, necessitating the use of several mines at different parts of each ship to guarantee that it would sink. The fuse mechanism enabled varying times to be set before the device exploded. The first limpet mine had been designed by Stuart Macrae (editor of

Armchair Science magazine) and Major C.V. Clarke in 1939.* The SOE further developed the idea, which was first conceived of as a dinner-plate design, able to be attached to a ship by a series of magnets. Rubber bushes on the contact side allowed for the curvature of the hull, while six strong magnets ensured that the device remained attached. The mine contained 4½ pounds of explosive and measured 9½ by 5½ by 5½ inches.

For two hours that night Hasler joined a routine exercise with the Mark I* Cockles in Dover harbour, in a fresh south-west wind. Fired up by his visit to Montanaro but still convinced that 101 Troop's Folbots were simply not suited for the raiding task demanded by Combined Operations, Blondie returned to Southsea determined to translate his emerging design ideas into a prototype for what he was now calling the MkII. The following day he sat at his desk to sketch out his initial designs, which he shared with Fred Goatley at 3.15 p.m. on 2 April. Goatley promised that he would have a fully built prototype ready by the end of the month.

In his diary for 11 April Hasler noted as an aside: 'Boulogne raid, Montanaro'. The near-disaster to Operation J.V., when the rubberised canvas on Montanaro's MkI ripped on an underwater obstruction in Boulogne harbour, proved conclusively to Hasler the inadequacy of the Folbot for combat tasks. This had been the fate, in fact, of the first offensive use of Folbots in the war. In May 1941 Sergeant Allen and Marine Miles had entered Benghazi harbour in a Folbot and sunk an enemy ship by attaching limpets to it. Unfortunately, coming away the craft struck a piece of unseen underwater masonry and sank, the two men being taken prisoner. On another occasion a Folbot broke up in heavy seas after embarking from its mother submarine, and the operation was aborted. The original Folbots, and even those that had been modified, were simply not robust enough for military use.

* The story of the invention of the limpet is told brilliantly by the inventor, Stuart Macrae, in *Winston Churchill's Toyshop* (Kineton: Roundwood Press, 1971).

Hasler pushed himself, and the Experimental Party, hard. He was, subconsciously perhaps, rehearsing his training methodology for the time when he would have his own small unit to prepare for war. He wanted to know what was important, and what was not; what needed training, and what required persistent application. Ewen Southby-Tailyour, Blondie's biographer, explains the relentless nature of Hasler's experiments: 'Trial followed trial and all the time they canoed to improve upper arm strength, techniques for embarking and disembarking while at sea, paddling with double paddles for speed and with one, thus lowering the silhouette. For hours on end he would make his crews sit, crouched and motionless while the canoe drifted as a log.'

At 10.15 p.m. on the evening of Sunday 31 May, Hasler took the Experimental Party out on their first night patrol. The so-called Margate patrols were designed to exercise the Experimental Party in genuine boom-defence activities at night, while at the same time conducting further testing of the boats. Whenever the weather was suitable the Experimental Party found itself at sea, in the dark, exercising off and around the boom. At 6.30 p.m. on a hot 2 June he went out in a Cockle MkII with Corporal Wallis: 'Visited patrol vessel. Then over to [HMS] *Dolphin*,* swung both [adapted aircraft] P8 compasses on magnetic N and E bearings and got them pretty good. Expended 20 rounds in single shot aiming practice.'

Two days later another 'Margate' exercise was undertaken, starting at 9.30 p.m. on Southsea beach for the patrol vessel. At 10.00 p.m. they had Colt 45 revolver practice. It was flat calm. The patrol returned inshore unchallenged by either the Boom Patrol or military sentries along the coast, Hasler getting to bed by 4 a.m. Ten days later they carried out another Margate, with both MkIs and

* At the time, the home of the Royal Navy Submarine Service at Fort Blockhouse, Gosport, and location of the Royal Navy Submarine School. It was here that the men of the RMBPD learned to use the Davis Submerged Escape Apparatus (DSEA), diving in the submarine escape training tower (SETT), a 30-metre-deep tank of water used to instruct all RN submariners in pressurised escape.

MkIIs. Each time the boats went out, new lessons were learned. On this occasion Hasler recorded: 'Wind moderate easterly . . . Small lop coming into boat under edge of cover. Evolved attack drill (single paddles) versus human torpedoes, using Tommy gun and charges. 0200 beached and stowed away unchallenged. Slept at office.' The lop problem needed to be dealt with, so the morning of 16 June found Hasler in his office at Eastney Barracks designing new cockpit covers.

Lying in the bath on the morning of 21 April, Hasler's thoughts had turned to the organisation that would use them in operations against the enemy. 'Birth of embryo idea for more active service role for yours truly,' he wrote. A man of action, he certainly did not want to remain in a staff job, interesting and practical though it was, for the remainder of the war. In conjunction with developing a combat canoe, why not at the same time create a small raiding organisation specifically commissioned for the protection of friendly harbours and attacks on enemy ones? When not doing either of these, they could be used to expand the hopelessly inadequate – in terms of size – Experimental Party and take part in operational trials for new ideas and equipment. He could lead them. Two days later he suggested the idea to Tom Hussey, who immediately agreed, suggesting that what was required was an all-Royal Marine boat unit.

Thereafter events moved unusually fast. The following day, 24 April, he talked over the idea 'of the Royal Marines Harbour Patrol party' in London with Colonel Godfrey Wildman-Lushington, the COHQ Chief of Staff and a fellow Royal Marine. Hasler wisely did not press the potential for this 'harbour patrol detachment' to become yet another raiding organisation: there were probably already more than were needed, with the Commandos (the SBS) and SOE's own SSRF, to carry out all the raids Combined Operations required, and there was no room for any more private armies of the type that had proliferated across the services during the previous eighteen months. The plan was not to 'specialize in small scale raids on coastal positions, demolitions ashore, reconnaissance of beaches, routine patrols in submarines or the landing and re-embarkation of agents', as these functions were 'adequately covered by others'. Instead, the Royal Marine Boom Patrol Detachment (RMBPD)* would concentrate on evolving 'new methods of attacking ships in harbour'.

This was not really true, of course. Hasler was itching to get back into useful combat service. From the outset, his intention was that the new outfit would be a combatant organisation whose purpose was to seek out and to *execute* innovative ways of breaching enemy harbours. Hasler had his sights set on taking the war to the enemy and never had any doubt as to what he hoped to achieve with the RMBPD: remaining off Southsea beach, or hanging about the boom in a training or experimental role, was certainly not part of it. Nevertheless, the title 'Boom Patrol' gave the unit a suitably defensive and reasonable cover name to satisfy even the most persistent of enquirers.

Hasler took every opportunity to badger COHQ to be allowed to convert the Experimental Party into an operational unit. His persistence was rewarded. Mountbatten forwarded his proposal to form the Royal Marine Boom Patrol Detachment to the Admiralty for final sanction on 26 May. The Admiralty agreed Mountbatten's proposal and granted authority to build an establishment of about thirty officers and men, with effect from 6 July 1942. Hasler was appointed the first Officer Commanding, whose purpose was the trial, testing and operational delivery of methods to protect friendly, and breach enemy, harbours.

From the time the RMBPD was formed, Hasler lost no opportunity to pester COHQ for a suitable operation for his little unit to undertake. He was far from gung-ho: rather, he understood that a military organisation without a role would be an easy

* Mountbatten, when authorising the new unit, changed its original name from 'Harbour' to 'Boom'.

target for amalgamation or disbandment. And he was right to be worried. Despite the speed and apparent ease with which his organisation was formed, powerful forces gathered quickly against any so-called private armies, urging their amalgamation. On the afternoon of 17 August Hasler found himself in Richmond Terrace in conference 'with [Major General Sir Robert] Laycock, [Tom] Hussey, [Gus] March-Phillips and [Colonel Geoffrey Courtney]* re amalgamating the three units. Managed to stave it off for the present, but I fear CCO will overrule it.' Clearly, there was some thought of bringing these raiding units together but Hasler naturally wanted to preserve the distinctiveness of his creation. This undoubtedly led him to find an operation that would demonstrate its competence and usefulness.

On 25 April Hussey had authorised Hasler's request for an order to be placed with Fred Goatley for the production of six prototypes of the Cockle MkII (when the Admiralty letter arrived at Saro Ltd, Goatley was bemused to find it describing them as 'punts'). Hasler's plan was that he would retain two for the Experimental Party, while 2 Special Boat Section, the submariners at HMS *Forth* (the support ship for the Third Submarine Flotilla based in Holy Loch) and the SSRF would be allocated the remainder.

When in Southsea, Hasler spent much of his free time at sea, testing and measuring, educating himself to the fullest possible extent in the canoeist's art. Not content merely with testing the canoes, he sought to read widely into the subject. He was fast approaching the status of lead authority in Britain on seagoing canoeing: the only source for answers to the questions he raised seemed to be his own experiments.

* Not to be confused with Roger Courtney, his brother. Geoffrey Courtney was the first Commanding Officer of COXE (Combined Operations Experimental Establishment), a spin-off from the CODC at Portsmouth. He was an MI5 officer who had been head of the Eastern Mediterranean Special Intelligence Bureau from 1921 to 1938, before becoming head of station for MI6 in Paris until the fall of France in June 1940.

He and the Experimental Party began to spend time in their eclectic collection of unsuitable canoes along the boom that stretched from Lumps Fort above Southsea beach across to Horse Sands Fort, testing the various craft for both their seaworthiness and their suitability for boom-breaching operations. Hasler was a well known character in the waters of the Solent, but it remained a heavily guarded and deeply sensitive locale for the naval defence of southern England, and in particular the massive and strategically critical naval base at Portsmouth. A naval vessel was on permanent patrol along the boom.

It was strictly closed to all leisure sailing, but that never bothered Hasler, who liked nothing better than to take out his successive girlfriends for runs along the boom in his little skiff, *Mandy*. Whenever the Naval Police launch would bear in on *Mandy* the young lady in question would have a WREN's cap placed very firmly on her head to provide some pretence that this was a duty trip. Even when clearly on duty or testing a canoe, Blondie rarely bothered with the formality of asking permission for his forays out and along the boom, although he always did so on night exercises, as the sentries of the local Army defence brigade were always itching to fire off their live ammunition at suspected intruders (they did so at Hasler's men at least once). His diary for 25 April contained a typical description of one of these sorties, when he had not bothered to tell Harbour Control of his plans: 'Out in *Cranthorpe* – boom dodging, warping off in smart SE wind. Got arrested on arrival back. Home by staff car.'

On 30 April he spent the whole afternoon at Saro's, testing the half-completed pilot model of Cockle MkII and settling finer points of design with Goatley. Goatley had been as good as his word. What he showed Hasler met virtually every aspect of Blondie's requirement. The vessel was fifteen feet long and 28½ inches wide, able to be flat-packed from a height of 11¼ inches to just six, with a flat bottom made of tough 1/8th-inch marine plywood, with two parallel runner strips, and covered with thick rubberised canvas. Hasler asked for a breakwater to face the stern for beach landings and the cockpit coaming to be flared all round, to enable it to accept an extra innovation: a waterproof jacket that fitted over the coaming when the crew were on board – an early example of the modern spray deck.*

On 13 May, back at Saro's yard on the Isle of Wight, Blondie saw a Cockle being developed for SOE (the SSRF) and in the afternoon tested for the first time a Cockle MkII in the Medina River next to the boatyard. He was determined not to accept a second-class design for the MkII, and insisted on a robust process of testing and improvement. This found him talking through each new iteration of the design with Goatley, before taking the revised prototype out to sea for testing. His diary for May to July demonstrates the degree of care he took over this process. The day after receiving the first prototype MkII single-seater from Goatley he took it out to sea off Southsea beach with 150 pounds of ballast, racing it against a MkI in the afternoon before undertaking maximum loading tests. At 6 p.m. he took out the MkII again, with 500 pounds of ballast. His efforts proved too strenuous for the canoes, the Experimental Party flooding and breaking the forward deck beam of a MkII.

Fred Goatley visited Southsea on 20 May to discuss the modifications these breakages demanded, and on 28 May Hasler found himself back at Saro's to check the work under way. He was very pleased with the results, taking delivery two days later of the rebuilt prototype, taking it out into the Solent singlehandedly on Sunday the 31st for what his diary describes as 'successful trials equipped with a Tommy gun and [five-pound] depth charges'. The charges were designed to be dropped from canoes to attack mini-submersibles of the type the Italians had deployed successfully against British ships at harbour in the Mediterranean. The new prototype

* The final version delivered to Holy Loch for Operation Frankton in late November 1942, according to the Admiralty orders to Lieutenant Dick Raikes RN, captain of HMS *Tuna*, described the vessel as 15 feet 8 inches in length.

required lengthening, the final version being 15 feet 8 inches long, 24 inches beam and 11¼ high. Empty, the canoe weighed about 105 pounds; while fully loaded, with her two crew, it weighed some 480. Fifty MkIIs were then finished by Goatley, ten going to Hasler at CODC and forty to Courtney's 2 Special Boat Section, based at Ardrossan in Ayrshire.

Courtney and Hasler did not see eye to eye on the final design of the MkII. The minutes pages of the COHQ's file notes almost apologetically that Courtney and the SBS 'think that the Cockle MkII is an unsatisfactory boat and not seaworthy [possibly because of its inability – once fully loaded, and because of its flat bottom – to right itself if it capsized]. RMBPD think Cockle MkI is unsatisfactory.' George Courtney wrote of his brother that 'Roger and Blondie did not see eye to eye over equipment to be carried in canoes. Roger felt that Blondie was far too gadget-minded and that a frail canoe bobbing up and down on a choppy sea off an enemy coast was no place for non-magnetic anchors and masses of signalling gear and wiring within which the operative could strangle himself.'

The testing continued, however, minor niggles being identified and overcome, and improvements being made to the design throughout June and July. On 6 June Hasler took out a flooded MkII, keeping it afloat by means of buoyancy bags. It was still usable although it rode up at the ends, he recorded, and 'paddling [was] very strenuous'. Two days later found him sitting at the drawing board at Saro's with Fred Goatley designing a bilge pump for the vessel, and on 9 June he carried out towing tests for fully loaded MkI and MkII craft, before seeing whether the prototype MkII could be inserted into the forward torpedo hatch of a U Class submarine, HMS *Unbeaten*: 'MkII slowed up rather badly, except at low speeds, but did at least tow straight. 1230. Tried MkII down hatch of HM Submarine *Unbeaten* and decided we could add 1½ inch of gunwale.'

On the afternoon of 12 June he took out a Cockle MkII, trying to work out a way of improving its sitting comfort, a telltale sign of the effects of his ankylosing spondylitis, which remained a secret to all but his mother. On the 17th he recorded his verdict that the MkII canoes were not stiff enough in the water, being too springy and fragile, especially in a heavy sea. Once again discussions with Fred Goatley led to further modifications. The design and testing work was relentless, but the ideal assault craft was emerging from the chrysalis, thanks to the productive partnership of Goatley and Hasler.

SIX

The Boom Patrol

Hasler was now looking to recruit a full complement of officers and men for the RMBPD, an establishment of four officers and thirty NCOs and Marines being agreed by COHQ on 27 June 1942. A notice had been sent out across the Royal Marines asking for volunteers for 'hazardous service'.

As it was now relatively late in the war, and these trawls had already been conducted across the three services for the Commandos, Hasler was unsure what response he might get. He was certain from the outset, however, that he did not want daredevil types. Rather, he sought fit, strong, motivated young men who were 'eager to engage the enemy; indifferent to personal safety; intelligent; nimble; free of strong family ties or dependants; able to swim and of good physique'. Experience was not required: Hasler wanted the opportunity to mould his new recruits without having to undo bad habits learned elsewhere. All else would be forgiven if they demonstrated a determination to learn and a commitment to the unknown.

Taking the recruits directly from the ranks of the Royal Marines was perceived to have two advantages. The first, laid out in the proposal submitted by Lieutenant Colonel H.F.G. Langley to the CODC on 12 May that year (but written by Hasler), was that 'the execution of such attacks is a typical RM role, calling for close cooperation with the Royal Navy, ability in the commando type of fighting, and a good deal of "sea sense"'. The second reason touched on the fact that the RM recruits would come with a certain amount of loyalty and commitment 'ready made'. 'The success of the operation rests entirely on the individual morale of the men concerned,' Langley wrote. 'It is felt that the highest standard of individual morale could best be achieved by starting with a strong foundation of Esprit de Corps.'

Initially Hasler needed three good young officers, the first to be his second-in-command and the other two to command each of the sections in the detachment. For the first job he had his eye on one particular candidate, and on 19 June he arranged to have dinner with Lieutenant J.S. ('Jock') Stewart, with whom he had worked during the Norwegian campaign. Stewart sounded interested and, following a visit to the CODC at Southsea the following day, agreed to Hasler's proposition. It was an inspired choice. Despite being only twenty-eight, Stewart's calm good sense and self-evident maturity led to him being given the nickname 'Old Man' by the men. During the planning stages of Operation Frankton Hasler was to trust its secrets only to Jock Stewart.

Then, on 25 June, he had the opportunity to select two second lieutenants from the ten who presented themselves at the Royal Marine Small Arms School at Browndown, choosing Jack Mackinnon and William ('Bill') Pritchard-Gordon. Both were young, eager and physically strong, Mackinnon being an exceptional swimmer and Pritchard-Gordon an experienced athlete. Mackinnon was given command of No. 1 Section, and Pritchard-Gordon No. 2. From a working-class background (his father had been a groundsman), Mackinnon had been a clerk in a Glasgow coal merchant's office before joining the Royal Marines as a soldier. He had then been selected for officer training. He was a natural leader, decisive and well liked by his men, and Hasler held him in high regard.

Whatever his two subalterns lacked in experience Hasler was certain they would make up for in enthusiasm and a willingness to learn. Both men arrived at Lumps Fort at Southsea, the RMBPD's new home, on 4 July 1942.

Three days earlier Hasler travelled by train to Plymouth to interview all the NCOs and Marines for the BPD, from which he chose one sergeant (Sammy Wallace), one corporal (Bert Laver) and four marines as suitable for training to be instructors. Colour Sergeant 'Bungy' Edwards, the detachment sergeant major, and Sergeant King, the physical training instructor, joined the small band. Hasler need not have feared that he was scraping the bottom of the volunteer barrel. The men who were eventually to undertake Operation Frankton were a snapshot of fit, intelligent and eager young soldiers from across the Royal Marines.

The man destined to share a canoe as his No. 2 was the twenty-year-old Bill Sparks (known as 'Ned' to his mates), described as 'a tough, wiry, witty cockney, slim to the point of emaciation, but his inveterate grumbling was leavened by all the wit and wisdom of the cockney'. Sparks had been recuperating from a bout of bronchial pneumonia after two years on HMS *Renown* when he saw the notice asking for volunteers for hazardous service. Tired of seeming to be doing little in the war, and wishing to avenge the loss of his elder brother Benny, killed when HMS *Naiad* was sunk in March 1942 by the German submarine U-565 south of Crete, his action in signing up for the RMBPD was an instinctive one. He had no idea what the task entailed.

The only two career soldiers in the party were Sergeant Sammy Wallace, who hailed originally from Dublin and retained his strong native brogue, and Corporal Albert (Bert) Laver, twenty-two, a reserved but dependable north Londoner. Corporal Laver was a quiet, intelligent man who had joined the Royal Marines shortly before the war and whom Sparks described as 'fair haired and round-faced'. He was an accomplished sportsman. Wallace has been described as 'a cheerful extrovert. If a canoe capsized in training he would immediately capsize his own so as to be in the water alongside his men.' Sparks described him as 'full of so much cheerful determination that even when we felt exhausted he inspired us to keep going'. Marine Robert ('Bob') Ewart was a twenty-year-old farmer's son from Glasgow, and was enthusiastic and brave. Sparks described him as 'quiet, tall and bony' and commented on his physical toughness. Marine William (Bill) Mills was 'a spirited, altruistic and likeable chap' from Northamptonshire who had worked in a sports shop in Kettering before joining up. Fit and strong, he was always making light of difficult situations and became known as the section comedian. He too was just twenty years old.

Corporal George Jellico Sheard (known as 'Jan' to his mates), was a small, tough Devonian. He was described by his nephew as having been 'a much-loved and much regretted brother among ten siblings. As the youngest he had been the most spoiled and everyone was amazed when he joined the Royal Marines.' Unusually, for Hasler had at first insisted on accepting only unmarried volunteers, Sheard married in August 1942, and his new wife would soon be expecting their first child.* Then there was Marine David Moffatt, a big, strong, lively, enthusiastic character, born in Belfast but with a family home in Halifax, West Yorkshire. Sparks noted that, unlike his peers, he rarely used bad language and hardly drank alcohol.

Marine Jim Conway was a strong, quiet, quick-witted young man who loved horses, from Stockport in Cheshire. He too was twenty years old, and had been a milk roundsman before joining up. Marine Bill Ellery, a reliable man who was also a fine swimmer, hailed from London. In fact he was a good all-round sportsman who Sparks thought might have undertaken trials for Chelsea. Marine Fisher was 'a fine young man, a non-swimmer but with plenty of guts, from West Bromwich'. He had, according to Sparks, a tendency to awkwardness. Sergeant Wallace struggled to teach him to swim, and failed, but whereas he demonstrated no penchant for surface swimming, he was later to become an

* Mrs Sheard and her unborn child were killed in a German air raid on Plymouth on 17 December 1942, only days after her husband had died in the cold seas off the Gironde and the day on which Bob Ewart's body was found.

expert at underwater swimming with the DSEA apparatus. At thirty, he was an old man in comparison to his peers.

From the morning of their arrival from Plymouth at 9 p.m. on Monday 6 July Hasler began to instruct the vanguard of his new organisation in the art of canoe-based warfare. His then girlfriend Val, who was staying at his mother's house in Catherington for a few days, conspicuously played second fiddle to his new charges. He made it up to her that evening, as his diary records:

> a.m. Instructing up 'til 11.50 a.m.
> p.m. Instructing swimming. Feeling grand.
> 6 p.m. – 1 a.m. Val to ballet and dinner.

But so as to ensure that he did not miss the following day's early-morning parade, he slept that night on a camp bed in his office. Thereafter each day was packed full, including intense periods of instruction. His diary for 11 July, for instance, is very typical:

> a.m. Instructing most of morning.
> p.m. Swimming, and testing new type of Mae West. Office work 'til 9 p.m.
> Home.

In the weeks leading up to 6 July Hasler put considerable thought into the training regime he would need for his tiny army. The list was extensive, starting with boatmanship and swimming lessons: none of the men who volunteered had ever handled a boat, and few could swim well. The new recruits spent much time at sea, in various small craft, learning watermanship and navigation. The programme involved canoeing and small-boat techniques in all weathers with oars and paddles, shallow-water diving, navigation by day and night using both stars and compass, the construction of camouflaged hides; escape, evasion and survival in enemy territory, and military parachuting.

On at least one occasion the men were left without rations in the countryside and forced to fend for themselves, which they did to the detriment of the poultry on a local farm. On others they were dropped off from trucks a day's march from home, and ordered to return to Southsea without being caught by the constabulary. The men needed to be thoroughly conversant with the behaviour of their canoes, and many hours were spent at sea in them. Capsize drills were practised routinely, and on land the men learned how to do running repairs. Training, recalled Bill Sparks, entailed 'many, many hours of canoeing'. Navigation was the most important skill the recruits had to learn, he judged. Not only did you 'have to plot your course, you have to know the strength of tide, strength of winds, all these can throw you off, and a few degrees out at sea and you can be miles away from your target'. Every aspect of what was required of a skilled military canoeist was formulated by Hasler, drawing on the experience of Courtney and Montanaro, and codified for the first time. His lesson plans sketched out the detail of what had to be learned:

> Lesson 1: Double paddles fastest and least tiring for our types of craft. Always used when noise and visibility can be accepted. Paddles always feathered. To reduce silhouette change to single paddles. Always feathered with paddle horizontal. If challenged by sentry or searchlight 'freeze up' and turn directly towards or away, preferably the former. If possible allow pause for observer to lose interest, then paddle gently away, keeping end-on. If fired at from a stationary position, paddle away, diagonally at full speed, formation scattering. If approached by patrol boat 'freeze up' with faces turned away, prepare grenades and pistols below cockpit cover.
>
> Lesson 2: Lying up. Aim at arriving at beach one hour before morning nautical twilight. Thorough recce up to 100 yards radius. Beware coastal footpaths. Lie up several hundred yards inland if

necessary. Carry up equipment first, boat last. Sleep in canoe for extra warmth and shelter or when in mud.

Hasler pushed the men right to the limits of exhaustion. The canoes in use were the MkIs. The RMBPD war diary recounts how on 10 August No. 1 Section (Mackinnon) attempted to reach the Isle of Wight in rough weather: 'The attempt failed, owing to a strong wind and high seas swamping three of the boats. The crews climbed onto the Boom, from which they were rescued some time later by the Dolphin Patrol Yacht. All boats were salvaged the same day.'

'Even in the calmest sea, propelling these canoes throughout the night, as we often did, was exhausting,' Sparks recalled. The men would sometimes badger him to ask Hasler (when, later in training, Sparks was Hasler's No. 2) to call off the training, when the men had had enough. He only tried it once. 'Getting a bit late in the day, sir,' he said to Blondie (they never called him that to his face) late one afternoon after several hours in the water. 'Oh plenty of time yet,' replied Hasler. 'Twenty-four hours in a day. Right, let's get on with it.' Once he had his mind fixed on something, noted Sparks, he was impossible to budge.

One of Blondie's exercises was for the men to run barefoot along the rough shingle of Southsea beach in order to toughen up their feet, followed by a swim in the sea, whatever the weather. This became part of their daily routine. Bill Sparks was struck by Bob Ewart's fitness on these occasions: 'While the rest of us groaned and moaned as the pebbles pummelled our feet, he skimmed across them as though he had feet of leather. He was first home; in fact, he beat us all every time.' An important consequence of their training was the binding of the men into a single team, driven by a common object. Without exception, all developed a pride in their new unit and a trust in each other that would, before long, help them through the obstacles they would encounter when at last they found themselves fighting the enemy.

'We were by and large,' Sparks recalled, 'a happy unit and there was a real spirit of comradeship among us. We took great pride in ourselves.' Langley and Hasler's initial hope that the RMBPD would enjoy high morale was in fact borne out by the men relishing the friendship and camaraderie of their newly formed team. They learned fast, and quickly became proficient canoeists. Training was even enjoyable on occasions. Hasler recognised the need to treat his citizen volunteers in a way different from the professional soldiers of peacetime service. One example that illustrates his approach was his discovery that his junior officers were drinking with the men in their favourite Southsea pub, the Granada: 'The lounge of the Granada had been appropriated by officers under *droit de seigneur*, and they let everyone know that they resented the presence of other ranks in their "club". Going into the lounge one evening, Hasler took in the situation at a glance and called up a pint for each of his men. Everyone knew Blondie Hasler, and from then on his men were accepted.'

For all his approachableness, Hasler was nonetheless a strict disciplinarian, aware of the critical importance of creating a coherent and effective military team rather than simply a group of individuals willing only to do their own thing, as was often the charge levied against the other so-called private armies. Despite their differences Hasler worked in close coordination with the canoeist commandos of 2SBS (Montanaro and Courtney) as well as the SSRF (Gus March-Phillips). His diary for 1942 contains records of several meetings at Southsea and London with Roger Courtney, and several visits by March-Phillips to the RMBPD. Indeed, shortly before the SSRF's ill fated attack on Sainte-Honorine, the three units held what Hasler described light-heartedly in his diary as a 'Cockle rally', comparing the effectiveness and handling characteristics of four different types of canoe.* After photographs

* The Cockle MkI, the Cockle MkII, the 'Foldflat' canoe produced by Cavender and Clark Ltd (they also built the Cockle MkI) and a rigid canoe by Camper and Nicholson.

and demonstrations on Eastney beach in the morning of 26 August 1942 the massed canoes left at noon, reaching Seaview on the Isle of Wight ninety-five minutes later. It took two hours against the current to complete the return journey, the men beaching at Eastney at 5 p.m.

The fact that the three units served the same master (COHQ), used the same tools (military canoes) and served the same purpose (offensive raiding) had not escaped the notice of the military authorities, who periodically threatened them with amalgamation, a worry that appears several times in Hasler's diaries. The way in which he could best demonstrate the uniqueness of his force, as he well knew, was to allow it to take part in its own raid.

As the Cockle MkII was intended to be carried in a submarine and designed to be delivered on to the deck through the angled forward torpedo hatch, Hasler was keen to ensure that the Submarine Service was comfortable with the design he had agreed with Goatley. He therefore arranged to travel north to Holy Loch to meet Captain Hugh Ionides, Commander of the 3rd Submarine Flotilla, to talk through these and related issues. To help him, Fred Goatley built a five-foot replica of the Cockle MkII which Hasler took with him on the overnight sleeper service (third-class, his diary records) from London to Glasgow. From there he travelled by boat to HMS *Forth* for a conference with both Courtney and Captain Ionides.

Hasler needed to resolve a number of practical issues, such as storage of the Cockles and their associated equipment in the submarine, plus the most effective means of launching the boats as well as the training that would enable his men to be fully conversant with operations from a T Class submarine. Nicknamed 'Tinsides' by his colleagues, Ionides was a practically minded man who was only too happy to help, and that night Hasler was back on the sleeper for the return journey to London. He arrived at Euston at 7.15 the following morning and went directly to COHQ to write up what he described as a 'rough report for Hussey'.

The remainder of his new recruits arrived at Lumps Fort for their first parade at 8.15 a.m. on 24 July. Hasler's little army was now complete, and all he now needed to do was prepare them for war. The men had in fact arrived the previous day, going to their billets (as was customary with commando troops) in residential guesthouses in Eastney and Southsea. The two sections were spread between Mrs Powell's guesthouse, The White Heather (27 Worthing Road), and Mrs Montague's at 35 St Rownan's Road. The officers were billeted at 9 Spencer Road, although Hasler remained at his mother's house thirteen miles north in the village of Catherington before moving into Spencer Road on 7 September. That first morning, he introduced himself to the men on the parade ground, welcomed them to the RMBPD, and then threw them in the deep end – quite literally. He marched them to the shingle beach where the Experimental Party, and the now part-trained vanguard of NCOs, awaited with a selection of canoes and twelve-man assault boats. The men were going to be introduced to the practical work of the RMBPD without any formalities. The theory would follow later.

How Hasler must have chuckled. After a day on the water every man had spent time struggling to regain his boat after repeated capsizes. They were wet and exhausted. His diary records: 'New troops almost drowned themselves. pm. Salvaging boats, and continue training.' The pattern repeated itself the following day: 'Troops doing MkI revision and finishing by sinking one MkI and one 12 man Assault Boat.' It was what he had anticipated, but it was almost certainly not what the new recruits expected. They were all, Bill Sparks declared, 'desperately keen to make the grade'. Each man had volunteered from within the ranks of the Royal Marines, knowing nothing about their future duties except that they entailed hazardous service. They were without exception ordinary young men, from ordinary streets, in ordinary towns across industrial Britain, given the most extraordinary task of their short lives. Hasler described them in August 1942 as 'a good cross section of average young fellows'. Once begun, the operation had to continue, even if only one canoe remained. Carrying on alone, having experienced the loss of one's comrades, would require outstanding reserves of determination, moral fortitude and physical energy. 'Morale was terrific,' affirmed Sparks:

> The men worked very, very closely together. They were very, very friendly and it was just a little unit that were wrapped up in one another. Everybody helped each other. Many a time when we first started training, someone would tip over in the canoe, and immediately all hands were there to help them back to shore. Morale was very, very high.

The more Hasler became mentally and emotionally engaged with his tiny army, the more the issues associated with the CODC development agenda began to play second fiddle in his busy life. Nevertheless, his preparations for the RMBPD necessitated a significant number of conversations with experts on various facets of the raiding business. On 22 June he spent time in London with Professor J.D. Bernal* discussing explosive charges. How many of the newly designed limpet mines were required to sink a ship and where, precisely, were they to be placed? On 3 September he drove to Welwyn for a conference with Bernal and others on underwater charges and submerged propulsion. Professor Solly Zuckerman, seconded from Oxford University to COHQ as Mountbatten's scientific adviser, used Hasler and one of his men as guinea-pigs in a trial to assess the effectiveness of drugs designed to extend physical endurance and night vision:

> *Tuesday 16 August*
>
> 4 p.m. Zuckerman arrived re organising night vision and endurance tests. Paredrene [sic] inserted into eyes [in an attempt to

* Professor J.D. Bernal of London University was, along with Solly Zuckerman, one of Mountbatten's private scientific advisers.

improve night vision – Paredrine dilates the pupils]. 10.30 p.m. Paredrene test. Not very convincing. 11.25 p.m.–6.30 a.m. Corporal Birch and myself on endurance test.

Wednesday 17 August

7.30 a.m. Swimming. 9.20 a.m.–1.15 p.m. in Cockle MkII to IOW and back. 2–4 p.m. being tested before and after Dipthal [a chemical designed to boost energy and reduce tiredness for men on prolonged operations]. Fairly convincing.

Throughout the summer months Hasler continued to meet regularly with Goatley and his team of designers and builders, going through a cycle of testing, development and acceptance into service of a range of modifications to the MkII. On 27 July he went out in the Cockles with the entire detachment. 'Full moon, calm. Wetness is the only problem,' his diary noted. They remained out until 5 a.m. the following morning. He then spent over two hours with Goatley 'testing new seats, backrest [and especially the need for a new, watertight] cockpit cover for MkII' to deal with the problem of water ingress during heavy seas. 'The end is actually in sight, I think,' he noted, optimistically. The cockpit cover was indeed waterproof when the canoe was upright, but a death trap if it capsized. When it was tested on 28 July during capsize drills the men had trouble extricating themselves underwater from the upturned vessel. A solution was quickly needed. By the following day, in fact, after a brief visit to Saro's Hasler was back in the office at Eastney Barracks designing a new quick-release cover for the cockpit. Fred Goatley produced it. His diary records that on 4 August he 'saw Goatley, tested new cockpit cover'.

Constant testing and modifications to the MkII and to operational procedures were undertaken as the summer months drew to a close. Hasler tested each new adjustment and modification, no matter how minor, personally. His diary records tests for the new cockpit cover, magnetic holders for the limpets, dummy limpet mines, a new bottom-line assembly, compass deviation on the P8 compasses, and a prototype Goatley had modified 'with extra beam, seats 1-inch higher, also zipper cockpit covers'. Hasler was not impressed with the waterproof clothing used by the SBS, so he designed his own, as well as testing a cardboard model of a wind and tide calculator ('the system shows promise'), a MkII 'with fin and without, to test for windage effects', the MkII Sten gun and 'kicky' fins, an innovation newly arrived from the United States.*

As training developed, Hasler introduced the men to night exercises of the Margate type, which gradually got longer and more demanding. These he called 'Exercise Grundy'. Not all exercises were completed successfully. On 10 September the RMBPD war diary recorded: 'No. 2 Section left Southsea to attack Thorney Island in canoes. No boats reached objective.'

Three days later slightly better news was reported. Five of the seven boats of No. 1 Section dispatched on the exercise to Thorney Island made the trip successfully.

It was clear to Hasler that it would be Mackinnon's section that would form the core of any future small-group operation.

* The tide calculator was important in determining the times of the four stages of the tide, a critical factor in getting the traverse of any tidal river right. First, the *flood tide* occurs when the sea level rises over several hours. The water then rises to its highest level, reaching *high tide*. Immediately following this comes the *ebb tide*, when the sea level falls over several hours. Finally, when the water stops falling it reaches *low tide*. The moment the tidal current ceases is called 'slack water'. The tide then reverses direction and is said to be turning. Slack water usually occurs near high water and low water.

SEVEN

Decision

Hasler's persistent badgering of the planners at COHQ for a raid for the RMBPD finally bore fruit. On Friday 18 September 1942 Lieutenant Colonel Robert Neville, the Royal Marines adviser at COHQ, had mentioned in passing Hasler's search for an appropriate operation for his men to Lieutenant Colonel Cyril Horton, one of COHQ's planners. Horton thought immediately of Frankton, a dossier in COHQ relating to the Bordeaux blockade-runners. Could the RMBPD prove to be the hitherto elusive solution to the problem of Bordeaux? This type of raid was, after all, as Hasler never tired of reminding anyone who would listen, the entire *raison d'être* of the unit. It would not, in the minds of the planners in COHQ, have a high probability of success, but at least a trained unit was soon to be available. 'Tell him to come back and see me after the weekend,' Horton told Neville.

So on the following Monday Hasler travelled to London to look for the first time at the Operation Frankton file. His train departed from Havant at 10.24 a.m., smoking and rattling its way slowly into London's Waterloo station. 'Tell me what you think the possibilities might be for the RMBPD to take on this task,' Horton said when he handed over the dossier some twenty minutes later, after Hasler had arrived at Richmond Terrace following the short walk over Waterloo Bridge and along the Embankment.

Intrigued, Hasler sat at a desk, locked away from the world, and began to read. He spent the entire afternoon reading, rereading, examining aerial photographs and maps, and jotting down notes. The dossier contained detailed reports on the Gironde and Garonne prepared by the Inter-Services Topographical Department (ISTD), the earliest ones dated 3 and 8 March 1942, together with the letters Lord Selborne had sent to the chiefs of staff advocating military action against the blockade-runners, as well as summaries of the intelligence reports gathered by SIS and SOE.

The ISTD report in the National Archives is a remarkably detailed survey of the Gironde, encompassing a mass of aerial photographs, with extensive information on the river, the state of the tides and currents, as well as vegetation and habitation along the bank. Hasler was immediately taken by what he was reading. This was an operation which the RMBPD could undertake. He made a number of notes, and then spent the evening talking to Neville. He stayed that night at the Royal Ocean Racing Club at 7 St James's Place, an increasingly popular haunt of Hasler's as it offered far more convivial accommodation than the rather austere and faded charms of the old Charing Cross Hotel, which had thus far provided him with overnight accommodation in London. The following morning, sitting in the comfort of the Club, he prepared a short summary addressed to the Combined Operations Central Planning Committee, of how an operation against Bordeaux might be conducted, then discussed it again (in draft) with Neville. It was, he admitted, 'produced without close study of the natural features of the locality or of the defence measures which might be encountered', but it was unequivocally supportive of the idea that the RMBPD could successfully mount and execute a canoe-borne operation to attack the blockade-runners in the Garonne.

At this stage it is clear that Hasler's views as to the best way to proceed were far from finalised. The outline plan entailed dropping off no more than three Cockles MkII from 'a carrying ship' (a submarine or surface vessel such as a Q ship) five miles off the coast and in the dark. Six Royal Marines in the three Cockles would then travel up the river into Bordeaux, carrying limpet mines, aiming to destroy 'between 10 and 20 of the cargo vessels' in the harbour. As if the Combined Operations staff were in any doubt about his keenness to undertake a canoe raid, he added: 'At first examination, the Cockle side of the operation appears to have a good chance of success, and it is hoped that RMBPD may be allowed to carry it out.' The timetable Hasler proposed entailed a three-day journey up the Gironde, ignoring for a moment the unknown detail about the tides, which would determine the exact timings of each day's travel:

D[ay]1	Not later than 2300	Carrying ship drops Attacking Force not more than 5 miles from the mouth of the Estuary
D2	Approx 0600	Attacking Force lands and goes into concealment
	Approx 2000	Attacking Force resumes passage
D3	Approx 0600	Attacking Force lies up
	Approx 2000	Attacking Force resumes passage
D4	Approx 0600	Force lies up at advanced base (within 10 miles of targets)
	Approx 2000	Final approach commences
D5	Not later than 0230	Commence withdrawal to advanced base
	0600	Limpets explode

After the successful detonation of the limpets, how would the raiding force return home? At this very early stage there seemed to be two options available to Hasler. The first, and perhaps most obvious, was to return whence they had come. All that was needed was for the saboteurs to rendezvous with the carrying ship 'not earlier than 0300 on D8 at position not more than 8 miles from mouth of Estuary', Hasler wrote. This, after all, had been the standard practice for operations across the Mediterranean. However, it was notoriously difficult to ensure a precise rendezvous location and time for this sort of pick-up, especially as any prolonged waiting by the collection vessel put it, and her crew, at considerable risk.

The German coastal defences around the mouth of the Gironde estuary were formidable, and enough was known about German radar capabilities to recognise that a surfacing submarine or arriving surface vessel would be quickly spotted and attacked from sea, land and air. The problem with Operation Frankton was that it would take several days to execute: identifying the exact date by which the raiders would be ready to return – they would not, for instance, be carrying any radio transmission equipment in their canoes to get messages back to any waiting craft – would be almost impossible. Other raids that had relied on the use of submarines or surface vessels required them to wait in the vicinity of the drop-off, a risky practice. When daybreak arrived, any vessels remaining on the surface or close to a defended shore would be dangerously exposed. Even at night considerable risks were taken in allowing vessels to remain near the drop-off, as Operation Aquatint was to demonstrate that very month.

A complication at this point in the war was the scarcity of resources to extract the raiders from France. The Royal Navy was hard-pressed to undertake the range of operations to which it was ordinarily committed, without any added strain on its limited submarine fleet. It was theoretically possible for the RAF to evacuate them by Lysander, the tiny aircraft that nightly floated over the Channel or Atlantic coast to deposit and recover agents from landing sites scattered across the length and breadth of occupied France. But using this method was impractical. Lysanders could take only one passenger: an operation to evacuate any more than a handful of men would have exposed too many aircraft to the risk of discovery, not to mention the greatly increased risk to the groups of resistance workers on the ground responsible for keeping the landing sites from interception by alert German and Vichy authorities. Launching a fleet of such aircraft on a mission to recover a handful of British raiders was never a viable option. In any case, Bordeaux was out of range for Lysanders flying from Britain.

There was one final option. It might be possible for the raiders, assuming that there were any survivors, to be thrown on the mercy of local resistance workers willing to hide them from the occupiers and their Vichy collaborators, and to escort them to safety in neutral Spain. This, again, was a big ask. There was very little organised resistance in the Bordeaux area in late 1942. As has been seen, most resistance at this stage of the war was disparate and disorganised, and concerned with the gathering of intelligence. It took time, in France, for the shock and humiliation of defeat to wear away, before the equally bitter resentment and humiliation of occupation took its place – a disgrace gradually reinforced by food shortages. These were caused by the fact that in 1940 there were ten million displaced refugees, a quarter of France's population, and that 1.5 million members of her male population remained in captivity in Germany. Added to all this were the increasingly harsh laws, curfews and generally unpleasant and unused-to restrictions on liberty.

In some parts of the country resistance began with small-scale acts of rebellion, although the actual numbers involved in violence or sabotage against the occupiers during the war remained tiny, perhaps fewer than one in ten thousand of the total French population. The one-time Hamburg clerk turned secret policeman, Hugo Bleicher, was surprised to discover, when moved from the benign Caen in early 1941 to Cherbourg, the 'strong and instinctive opposition of the inhabitants to the invader'. He observed a distinct strengthening of the resistance movements the following year, as organisations that were previously disparate joined together, supported by drops of arms and the arrival of leaders, radio transmitters and equipment from Britain. It was difficult for the Germans to find loyal supporters from among the French population. Instead, they recruited from the fragments of the evader and resistance organisations they managed to break, promising prisoners freedom if they informed on their countrymen.

As the repression grew, so too did individual assassinations of Germans, which triggered vicious reprisals authorised from Berlin, Hitler insisting that a hundred Frenchmen be executed for every German killed by the Resistance. A senior member of the Wehrmacht's civilian staff was shot dead in Bordeaux on 20 October 1942, by young communists dispatched on their assassination task from Paris. The more shootings, the more savage became the reprisals, as the infuriated Germans lashed out with the disproportionate violence only available to tyrants. Fifty hostages were seized at random in Bordeaux and shot in retaliation for the death of Hans Reimers.

In the early days of the occupation opposition by the French to their new German overlords tended to be sporadic, spontaneous and small-scale. At the start it involved individual acts of protest such as anonymous graffiti, vandalism of German and Vichy posters, the cutting of telephone and electricity lines and the slashing of tyres on unguarded military vehicles. On 13 August 1940, barely two months after the occupation had begun, Heinrich Konrad a German sentry had been shot dead by an anonymous assassin outside the Hôtel Golf in Royan in Charente-Maritime, on the northern side of the Gironde estuary opposite Le Verdon. In reprisal, the enraged German authorities rounded up several prominent citizens and imprisoned them indefinitely. Any further acts of terror would entail the arbitrary execution of these prisoners. On 22 August, in Bordeaux, a thirty-two-year-old docker, Raoul Amat, allowed himself to be caught slashing the tyres of a German truck, and was sentenced by a military court to thirteen months' imprisonment. Others merely shook their fists – and lost their lives for it.

On Saturday 24 August, Leizer Karp, a Polish Jew, shouted abuse at German military musicians playing near the Saint-Jean railway station in Bordeaux. Taken into custody, he was transported to Sougez Camp and sentenced to death. German justice was as rapid as it was brutal. On the 26th the newspaper *La Petite Gironde* published the following announcement:

> By ruling of the military court, the *Israeli Jew** Karp was convicted of violence against members of the German Army and sentenced to death. Pursuant to this judgement, the prisoner was executed this morning.

The terror had begun. By 1944 French retaliation would have graduated to acts of armed resistance and sabotage, but in Bordeaux in 1942 the CND, the Polish F2 network, the Phalanx-Phidias and Scientist cells existed in only immature form, and the prospect of any of these being able to look after a dozen fleeing commandos, with the Germans hot on their tails, was remote. And with the Germans strongly in the ascendant at this early stage in the war, it remained uncertain to any but the most committed Frenchman whether anything other than resigned acquiescence to the new rulers of France was worthwhile.

While it was true that there were many Frenchmen willing to assist escaping raiders, as Operation Aquatint had demonstrated, it was equally true that for an evader or escaper to rely on meeting by chance a French man or woman willing to place their own lives, and those of their families, in peril for a stranger, was an

* My italics

impossible risk. But there was one option that might just work. In the months following the Fall of France a further clandestine activity emerged across the Low Countries and France, as many thousands of British troops, cut off from their units during the fighting, found themselves trying to evade the Germans in the occupied zone and the Vichy authorities in the French zone. Helping these men became the business of the escape line, a largely ad hoc and unorganised activity which in time developed its own structures, organisation, training and coordination.

Escape lines often emerged in unplanned and spontaneous ways as French civilians came forward to provide succour to men attempting to find their way back to Britain. A powerful means of resistance embraced by many French civilians – at considerable personal danger – was to assist the bedraggled men they found camping out in the woods near their home, begging for food or clothing at their doorstep, or walking (often still in uniform) down a country lane. In time whole 'lines' of civilian helpers – *passeurs* – were established in many different *réseau* to coordinate the escape of these men. Men, women and children became involved in various ways: in hiding evaders, arranging identity documents and work and travel permits, accompanying them on public transport, acting as lookouts for German patrols, securing food, clothing and shoes and providing medical care for the wounded. Food and clothing became increasingly scarce, as German sanctions and reparations hit the civilian population hard.

Offering young male evaders with voracious appetites a portion of their food ration was a substantial sacrifice for most French people, especially those in urban areas where access to home-produced or black-market food was far from easy. It was much harder for the escapers and evaders in winter, and the support of helpers was essential not just to avoid capture, but to survive.

Many escapers and evaders were prepared to walk the hundreds of miles to safety in Switzerland or Spain after bailing out of stricken aircraft, or escaping from prison camps, but had little chance of doing so successfully without guides, food, clothes and shelter. Couriers would collect escapers and evaders from outlying areas, then accompany them by road or train through enemy-patrolled territory to hubs or collection points, where they could be prepared in groups for the final assault on the Pyrenees. It was an exceptionally dangerous undertaking for the French *passeurs* who willingly engaged in this activity, often out of nothing more than patriotism or a sense of duty.

The most obvious (and therefore most popular) escape route was through neutral Spain, which entailed travelling long distances across France. Until November 1942 the Germans were content to occupy only part of France – the part that was most significant to them in strategic terms, namely the entire Atlantic coastline, and the north – while their puppets in Vichy were allowed to administer the remainder, the *Zone Libre*.

In the days following the evacuation from the Pas-de-Calais in late May and early June 1940, large numbers of unitless men made their way through both occupied and unoccupied France, congregating in the Mediterranean ports in the hope of finding their way home. As time went by the type of evader changed, as more and more airmen found themselves shot down and anxious to avoid a long period of imprisonment. Men also managed to escape from enemy captivity, and they too were intent on making their way to safety. Captain Airey Neave escaped from Colditz Castle on 5 January 1942 and made his way by train and foot to Switzerland four days later. He was then spirited out of France via an escape route established by the Belgian military doctor Albert-Marie Guérisse (Pat Albert O'Leary), who had moved on from HMS *Fidelity* to an escape line first begun in Marseille in 1940. The Pat O'Leary Line (often abbreviated to 'the Pat Line' or 'the PAO') was the first properly organised escape line in France, managing to carry over six hundred escapers and evaders to safety before Guérisse was betrayed and arrested on 2 March 1943. The Marie-Claire Line, run by the redoubtable Mary Lindell, the

Comtesse de Milleville, which cooperated closely with the Pat Line, was another.

The branch of the Secret Intelligence Service known as MI9 was given responsibility to assist the growth of escape lines across Europe, finding a home in Room 055A* of the War Office in London. Created on 23 December 1939, it was headed by Major (later Brigadier) Norman Crockatt DSO MC who, in time, was to run a secret army of *passeurs* across a wide range of *réseau* behind enemy lines. Where they could, MI9 attempted to support, train and sustain these operations, which often operated like birds in winter, with few resources and very little money, eking out a precarious existence amid the frozen wastes of Nazi occupation.

London helped provide cash, radio operators, agents and training, as well as leadership to give often isolated *passeurs* a firm sense of direction and a feeling that the risks they took were contributing to an eventual Allied victory. Nightly BBC radio programmes were used to send messages to agents in the field. MI9 routinely used SOE's F (France) Section's training school at Beaulieu in the New Forest, and its parachute and survival training schools to prepare servicemen for the rigours of evasion. It also collaborated effectively with SOE in the design and development of all sorts of useful material: silk maps, a range of tiny compasses, language cards, explosive devices and 'escape kits', which contained emergency rations, local currency and survival aids. By 1945 MI9 had helped over seven thousand men and women to escape from occupied Europe.

In 1942 MI9 was staffed by two successful escapers. One was Captain James ('Jimmy') Langley of the Coldstream Guards, who had lost an arm at Dunkirk and found his way home through Marseille, courtesy of the Pat Line. He was joined the following year by the Colditz escaper (and Pat Line 'parcel'), Captain Airey Neave. Neave's codename became 'Saturday', hence the title for

* For security reasons, mail was always posted to 'Room 900'. In due course the latter became the unofficial name of MI9.

his bestselling account of this work, *Saturday at MI9*. Within the SIS Langley was known as 'P15' and, in Madrid, the MI9 agent Michael Creswell was 'Monday'.

Neave's invaluable experience as an escaper, together with his real-life experience of the operation of an escape line, made him an ideal choice to join MI9's tiny room in the Metropole Hotel on Northumberland Avenue.* 'When one has been in the field with the workers of the escape lines,' he later observed, 'it is difficult to be anything less than enthusiastic about providing aid for them.' The south of France acted as a magnet to most of these evaders and escapers, as the entry point, across the Pyrenees, to safety. Donald Darling, MI6's man first in Lisbon and then in Gibraltar, and MI9's local escape coordinator (codenamed 'Sunday'), estimated that at any one time during the war at least five hundred escapers and evaders were at large across Europe, all making their way, individually or with help, towards the Pyrenees.

Many (but not all) of the *réseau* were coordinated by agents appointed and sustained by MI9 in London and supported by the apparatus of the SOE, becoming quite elaborate affairs. Airey Neave estimated that twelve thousand people across occupied Europe supported the escape lines. For those escapers and evaders captured or recaptured by the Vichy police or the Germans, a short stay in prison would, on the whole, be their lot until transported to a prisoner-of-war camp in Germany or further east. For a *résistant*, however, the penalty was death. If one was unlucky, death would be preceded by imprisonment and torture. For their family members, it often meant arrest as well, and deportation to a death camp.

Few *réseau*, however, survived intact for long, as the multifarious intelligence agencies of the Reich – the Gestapo, the Sicherheitsdienst (Himmler's Security Service, the SD), the Abwehr, the Secret Field Police and even the Luftwaffe security organisation – all sought

* Crockatt later moved operations from London to Wilton Park, Beaconsfield, Buckinghamshire, known as 'Camp 20'.

to eradicate this evidence of rebellion and destroy those involved. General Otto von Stülpnagel, the military governor of France, produced thousands of posters to be pasted across the occupied zone setting out the penalties for supporting escapers, and the financial benefits of collaborating:

> All men who aid directly or indirectly the crews of enemy aircraft shot down by parachute or having made a forced landing will be shot in the field. Women who render the same type of aid will be sent to concentration camps in Germany. People who capture crews . . . or who contribute, by their actions, to their capture will receive up to 10,000 francs. In certain cases this compensation will be increased.

The Germans proved remarkably successful in their efforts to capture or kill *passeurs*. James Langley estimated that three died for every escaper who successfully reached Spain. The Germans not only arrested and tortured those intimately involved in the escape lines, but also deported innocent members of a *passeur*'s wider family.

It was Lieutenant Commander G.P L'Estrange at COHQ who first investigated the possibility of the Royal Marine raiders being evacuated through an existing *réseau*. Captains Langley and Neave recognised immediately, when briefed by L'Estrange on the location of the target, that the best escape line was that run by Mary Lindell. Indeed, at the very moment L'Estrange was talking to Room 900 about Bordeaux, Lindell was also in London.

Nevertheless MI9 had to weigh up the pros and cons of placing one of their escape lines at risk. Providing support to planned operations was not the purpose of escape lines: indeed, using them for operational purposes placed them at considerable risk. Captured soldiers could easily reveal details of their French contacts under interrogation. Langley and Neave decided to make an exception for Operation Frankton, probably on the basis that Hasler and his men were organised raiders for whom MI9 represented their only chance of returning to Britain. An exception had also been made for the commandos preparing for the raid on Bruneval in February that year, although on that occasion the addresses of safe-houses were for emergency use only. With suitable instruction, Langley felt the risk was acceptable. 'Particular care,' he recalled, 'was taken to provide them with advice, including cover stories.'

Airey Neave's biographer hints that it was Neave who had briefed Hasler and offered him information about the Marie-Claire Line (based in the town of Ruffec, ninety miles north-east of Bordeaux and a mere six miles from the demarcation line), which would help them escape from France.* It seems more likely, however, that Neave and Langley briefed L'Estrange, who in turn explained the plan to Hasler a few days before the start of the operation. Given this was top-secret, Hasler had no trouble at all in agreeing to Neave's undoubted insistence, transmitted through L'Estrange, that the information not be divulged to the rest of the raiders until they were at sea. 'Neave was very anxious about giving the raiding party details of the escape line contacts, fearing that the commandos might reveal the secret under torture.'

With her teenage son Octave ('Oky') murdered at Mauthausen,† another son (Maurice) beaten up by the notorious sadist Klaus Barbie in Fort Montluc prison in Lyon, her daughter Mary Ghita (nicknamed Barbé by the family) deported to Germany‡ and herself a survivor of Ravensbrück concentration camp, Mary Lindell was one of the French Resistance and MI9's most remarkable characters. Married shortly after the First World War to the Comte de Milleville, who in 1940 was in South America pursuing

* Paul Routledge, *Public Servant, Secret Agent* (London: Fourth Estate, 2002).

† He had been deported to Germany in February 1942.

‡ She had been repatriated after a year.

his business interests,* Mary kept alive a spirit of passionate, unashamedly patriotic resistance to tyranny throughout the longest and darkest days of the occupation. Forty-five years old at the time the Germans entered Paris, she soon found herself swept into the whirlwind of resistance, through life first as a *passeur* and then as head of her own *réseau*.

At the onset of the First World War she had attempted to serve her country as a nurse in the Voluntary Aid Detachment but, unwilling to spend the war cleaning bedpans (with which she had once assaulted an overbearing matron), she travelled to France and joined the Secours aux Blessés Militaires, a division of the French Red Cross. Lindell was awarded the Croix de Guerre in 1916 for her selfless ministrations to wounded French soldiers, the youngest nurse (she was twenty-one) ever to receive this honour. Her heart now in France, but always fiercely British, Mary remained in Paris, marrying into French society to become the Comtesse de Milleville.

She fell into the business of the *réseau* by accident when in 1940 she happened upon British evaders in Paris attempting unsuccessfully to blend into the local environment. Very quickly she found herself finding, hiding, feeding and escorting these men across the demarcation line via the little town of Ruffec, north of Angoulême, to the relative safety of Vichy France and into the arms of one of the organisations of *passeurs* (such as the Pat O'Leary Line), who would guide the men across the Pyrenees. From the start her sons Maurice and Octave, together with her young daughter Mary Ghita, were all fully signed-up members of her *réseau*. Her methods were simple, if brazen. Wearing her French Red Cross uniform, with her First World War medal ribbons displayed prominently on her chest (her British decorations characteristically worn ahead of her French ones), Lindell would secure

* He returned to France in 1941, but then spent two years in prison until 1944 on account of his wife's activities.

permits and scarce fuel rations from the German authorities in Paris under the pretence of escorting children separated by the war across the demarcation line to be reunited with their desperate parents in the *Zone Libre*. The evader would often be the 'mechanic' accompanying her.

Relying on the upper-class courtesies practised by the overly polite Prussian officers in the Wehrmacht's Paris HQ, Lindell charmed and bullied them all (one of whom was Count von Bismarck, great-grandson of Germany's first Chancellor) into acceding willingly to the humanitarian demands of the forceful, elegant Anglo-French aristocrat, their patrician sensibilities blinding them to her deceit. A woman used to getting her own way, Lindell's aristocratic hauteur was nonetheless underpinned by great reserves of courage and resourcefulness. The fact that she was able to march determinedly into the Paris HQ of the German commander of France, General von Stülpnagel – who had already published orders threatening to shoot men who helped evaders and send women who did likewise to concentration camps – and walk out with permits and petrol coupons to take her car out of the occupied zone powered with German fuel, suggests some measure of her courage and nerve. 'My mother had a very narrow channel of interest,' Maurice later said. 'Her heart was in getting people out of France. There was no other thing.'

Mary's approach, while flattering the social sensibilities of the Wehrmacht, did not have the same effect on the Gestapo, however. Her strident Englishness (she always carried her British passport), high-profile campaigning in her Red Cross uniform and her loud, authoritarian approach ensured that she was soon in the sights of the counter-intelligence authorities in Paris. Arrested in 1941 on no more than suspicion of wrongdoing of one kind or another, she was held in solitary confinement in Fresnes prison, where she was repeatedly questioned about her activities by sceptical intelligence officers who suspected that she was up to no good but could not put their finger on it.* Perhaps with the intention of following her, she was released. Knowing that it was only a matter of time before she was rearrested, disguised as a governess Mary followed her own escape route to Ruffec before making her way over the Pyrenees to Spain. In Barcelona she so impressed Sir Henry Farquhar, the British consul in Barcelona, that he gave her a note that allowed her to contact MI9 when she arrived in London in July 1942.

So it was that Jimmy Langley and Airey Neave found themselves interviewing Mary in a flat over Overton's restaurant at the bottom of St James's Street. Mary's entire purpose was to return to France to run her escape line, but the more she told them the more the two men were convinced that it would be a mistake. She was too well known to the Gestapo to be able to survive for long without placing other people in danger as well. Claude Dansey, the brilliant but widely hated Deputy Director of MI6, was also initially strongly opposed to letting her return, principally because of concern about German infiltration of the escape lines, a significant problem that also affected SOE's circuits. Because Lindell had been an unwilling guest of the Gestapo for nine months, and because it was highly unusual to be released from this form of incarceration, he worried lest she, like so many others, had been 'turned' and released so as to inform on their fellows, using close members of their family as hostage. Mary Lindell's three teenage children were ideally placed for this form of coercion.

Even the redoubtable Lindell was not, in Dansey's view, incapable of being blackmailed by the Gestapo under fear of losing her children. He was right to be worried. The collapse of many *réseau* was due to the work of traitors. One of the causes of the eventual demise of the Pat Line was attributable to traitors (one of whom, Paul Cole, was a British evader himself who had done

* Fresnes, Val-de-Marne, Paris, was used by the Germans to hold captured British SOE agents and members of the French Resistance. Held in horrific conditions, prisoners were tortured and many were executed.

much good service before being subverted, for money, by the Gestapo). Indeed, the entire Dutch Section of the SOE in Holland was turned by the Abwehr in June 1942 and remained in German control for eighteen disastrous months, at great loss of life. The Germans even infiltrated agents into the escape lines.

One example of attempted subversion, as against many that succeeded, will suffice. A British expatriate in France, Stella Lonsdale, left Marseille for Britain on 27 October 1941 with the blessing of Albert Guérisse. She took the train to Barcelona and Madrid and then a Lufthansa flight to Lisbon, arriving on 4 November. There, James Langley interrogated the 'extremely attractive and intelligent woman in her late twenties, with more than her fair share of sex appeal'. In time it was revealed that she had been persuaded to 'work for England' by acting as a link between MI6 and German intelligence. The truth was revealed when a packet arrived, couriered across Spain from Guérisse. 'Pat' had rifled through Mrs Lonsdale's apartment in Marseille after she had left, and discovered a set of incriminating photographs that included one of a picnic with four German officers, all of whom were toasting the smiling woman with champagne. She spent the remainder of the war in Holloway Prison.

The slightest whiff of suspicion of her commitment to the cause of freedom, however, riled Lindell, whose loyalty and courage had already been amply demonstrated, in contrast to the desk-bound bureaucrats of MI6 and MI9. She insisted to Langley and Neave that she would return to France with or without their consent. Indeed, she came to regard Langley's reticence as a personal insult, and never forgave him, even many years after the war. Langley later described her as 'a woman who brooks no opposition but prefers to use a battle-axe rather than the more usual feminine charm when dealing with difficult males'.* He attended the meeting with Lindell at which Claude Dansey had planned to tell her that he

* J.M. Langley, *Fight Another Day* (London: Collins, 1974).

refused to sanction her return to France: 'He never got round to that as Mary took control of the interview and informed him of all his shortcomings as far as helping evaders was concerned. When he pointed out that he was only trying to save her life she replied that it was not her life he was interested in but his reputation.'

Beaten, Dansey relented, and Mary was prepared for her return. Unfortunately, her stubbornness prevented her from accepting the services of a young Australian radio operator, Tom Groome, whose mother was French and who spoke French like a native. MI9 failed in its duty to the entire Marie-Claire Line – and to the many men and women who would have to depend on it for their survival – by not insisting that Mary Lindell return with a fully trained radio operator and a properly functioning radio. She returned by Lysander to Limoges on 21 October 1942 without either, to take up the reins of the Marie-Claire *réseau*, based at the Hôtel de France at Ruffec, with no direct means of communicating with London. The only way she could get messages home was by giving them to Pat O'Leary, or travelling herself from Lyon to Geneva to hand them in person to the British consul (and MI9 agent), Victor Farrel. This was a serious error, and very nearly undermined Hasler's escape plans from the very beginning.

EIGHT

1a Richmond Terrace

Robert Neville had passed Hasler's two-page operational plan to Horton and others in the planning team. Aware that at long last they might have been presented with a solution to the problem of Bordeaux, they immediately asked that Hasler talk to Captain A.J. Herrington of the Royal Corps of Naval Constructors, seconded to COHQ, about the best type of parent vessel to use for the raid. Hasler's diary reveals that he was able to answer Herrington's questions quickly enough to catch the 6.45 p.m. train home from Waterloo that evening. Transport by submarine seemed to be the most sensible option.

Between Thursday 24 September and Thursday 1 October Hasler was ostensibly on leave, although his diary records that he spent most of it working. At 5.30 p.m. on Friday the 2nd, for instance, he was back at Saro's on the Isle of Wight to discuss modifications to the MkII. This was followed by a Margate exercise between 8 p.m. and 2 a.m. On 12 October he was back in Richmond Terrace. His first meeting that morning, which lasted two and a half hours, was with Lieutenant Commander L'Estrange, who had been given the responsibility at COHQ of developing the detailed plans for Operation Frankton. Hasler was later to write: 'L'Estrange undertook the bulk of the detailed planning, and personally prepared, with great thoroughness and accuracy, the actual charts, tide tables etc used by the attacking force.' Hasler's diary records that he spent two hours in the afternoon with Tom Hussey and Jock Stewart, agreeing further aspects of the plan.

At 5 p.m. he was interviewed by Captain Sidney Raw, the Chief Staff Officer (Submarines) at the Admiralty.* Grumpily, Raw said that he was loath to use one of his submarines for the job, arguing that the task of his vessels was 'to sink ships'. Quick as a flash, Blondie replied: 'Well, sir, that's precisely what I intend to do.' He got his submarine. That night he stayed over in the Royal Ocean Racing Club, a short walk from Whitehall and Richmond Terrace. The next day he spent several hours at the Admiralty with L'Estrange, discussing anti-ship mines before, at 11.45 a.m., presenting himself to the Examination Committee with his plan.

In the days that followed, Hasler found himself back in London finalising aspects of the operation before the completed plan was sent before the Examination Committee at the end of the month. The essentials were laid out as follows:

> NATURE OF OPERATION
> A small party, six strong, will be disembarked from a submarine approximately 9 miles from Cordouan Light. The party will paddle up the Gironde Estuary in Cockles MkII, lying up by day and paddling by night to the Bassens–Bordeaux area, where they will carry out a limpet attack on blockade-runners in the Port. The party will escape overland to Spain . . .
> INTENTION
> To sink between 6 [and] 12 of the cargo vessels in the Bassens–Bordeaux area . . .
> FORCES REQUIRED
> a. One submarine carrying three Cockles MkII
> b. Six all ranks, Royal Marines Boom Patrol Detachment
> METEOROLOGICAL CONDITIONS
> a. No moon is essential. It will only be possible for the Cockles to proceed on the flood tide or on slack water.

* Raw reported to the Rear Admiral (Submarines) at HMS *Dolphin*, the submarine depot at Gosport.

c. Wind force maximum force 3 . . .
COMMAND
a. Operation will be under command of Flag Officer, Submarines.
b. Naval Force Commander, Officer Commanding HM Submarine.
c. Military Force Commander, Major H.G. Hasler, OBE, RM . . .
EVACUATION
The party will escape overland through occupied France to Spain as per special instructions [from MI9] . . .

In the meantime there was more than enough to keep Hasler busy. His diary, and that of the RMBPD, records an endless flurry of meetings, visits to Fred Goatley to discuss modifications to the MkII, discussions with different agencies with regard to a test exercise he was planning in the Thames estuary (Exercise Blanket) and the testing of equipment.

The only man outside of COHQ in his full confidence was Jock Stewart, who took responsibility for training the men during Blondie's regular absences from Southsea. Activity was as demanding under Stewart's tutelage as it was under Hasler. During the day training was carried out across a myriad of activities, including daily strenuous physical fitness, canoeing, swimming (regardless of the water temperature), seamanship, navigational skills and combat drills. Each night involved Margate and Grundy exercises. the training was hard and relentless training, the best possible preparation for the trials to come. On 27 October an exhausted Jacky (as he was known to his family) Mackinnon wrote home to his parents in Glasgow: 'I'm sorry that I don't write oftener but for the last 5 days I have been working nearly 18 hours a day and I am only good for bed when I come home. As regards news, nothing ever happens down here that I can tell you about because as you know my work is secret.'

An insight into Hasler's character can be gleaned in part from the fastidious care he took with regard to listing, weighing, testing and collating equipment. As a self-taught sailor he understood just how important detail was when it came to achieving success in hazardous operations. Paying close attention to the minutiae was the only way he could gauge the risk of the plan he was developing, and therefore the chance that he, and his men, would come out alive. Instructions were written down with an immense regard to clarity and thus to the ease with which they could be used to train the men. Likewise, Hasler focused carefully on the kit list for his men. Everything on this list was designed for a purpose, and to be useful. It started with the obvious ('Cockle, Mk. II') but it extended to the obscure ('toilet paper, packets') and to the infinitesimal ('spare bulb' for the two reading torches the party would take). The item labelled 'Repair Bag' had in the 'Remarks' column the comment: 'Each containing Bostick cement, patching canvas, needle, waxed thread, Oil bottle, Waste, Tyre Patch, Rubber Solution, spare split pins and copper tacks.'

Nothing was left to chance. Nor was any allowance made for personal discretion, such as little comforts or personal items. All in all the equipment list included thirty-one items under the title 'Boats' Gear', seven items under 'Weapons and Explosives', fifteen under 'Food and Medical', twenty-six under 'On the Man' and fourteen under 'In the Bags'. The list under the latter extended from handkerchiefs (one each), to bird calls (on lanyards) [whistles that mimicked the call of sea gulls], to sheets of paper. Each piece of equipment was allocated to one of the five storage boxes in each canoe: two side by side in the stern compartment, one between the two cockpits and a further two in line in the bow. Each item was packed according to the planned time and frequency of its use. As the boats would get progressively lighter during the operation, the kit would need to be rearranged to maintain the correct balance in the canoe. The operation was not going to be allowed to suffer from any form of disorganisation.

Likewise, Hasler's written instructions for limpet training left no room for doubt or confusion. The process of arming each limpet was written down in eighteen steps on a single sheet of foolscap entitled 'Drill for Fusing Limpets'. Every minute procedure was included, to be learned by heart in the same way his men learned their personal weapon drills: in the dark, in the cold, and under pressure of time. The small magnetic limpets were to be the Royal Marines' assault weapon, and as with oil in a rifle and ammunition in a magazine, careful preparation was required to ensure that the weapon worked as planned. In the original, secret, copies of these instructions in the National Archives, Hasler's neat handwriting can be seen making observations in the margin: 'Examine to see if it is unbroken,' he notes against no. 9. The process was as follows (the underlinings are in the original):

1. Separate limpets. Put aside keep plate. Oil faces of magnets.
2. Take one limpet, remove wood plug <u>from blank end</u>.
3. Take one AC Delay. Unscrew cap, remove ampoule, examine for breakage or leakage. Replace ampoule <u>in tin</u>. Lute [lubricate] threads of cap. Replace cap but do not screw down too tightly. Secure safety pin in with thread attached after opening points. Scratch one line on the fuze body.
4. Lute both lower threads of fuze, making certain no luting enters the striker passage.
5. Attach burster.
6. Screw into limpet, tighten with spanner. Work any spare luting round the edge of the fuze.
7. Repeat operation with the second limpet.
8. Place two limpets carefully together, face to face. Square off the magnets.
9. Remove one wooden plug from filler cap end.
10. Take one sympathetic fuze. Examine to ensure rubber cap, small split pin . . . and washer are correctly in place.
11. Tie safety pin in with sailmaker, taking it round the bottom of the rubber cap, to help hold the latter in place.

12. Lute both lower threads of fuze.
13. Take one burster from the tin, and screw in place.
14. Screw fuze into limpet. Work any spare luting round the edge of the fuze and of the filter cap. Repeat for second sympathetic fuze. Mark each limpet with distinguishing mark [inserted by hand: 'of owner.']
15. Repeat the operation for a second pair of limpets.
16. Take one AC delay fin, and place two ampoule boxes in it. Fill them as follows: –

    One fuze chart
    4 red ampoules
    4 orange ampoules [9-hour-delay fuzes]
    2 full tins of luting
    4 soluble plugs

Seal tin with tape and varnish.

17. Paint all sympathetic fuzes black (very thin coat over everything).
18. Examine placing rods. Crease the joints. Fold and secure with twine.

On the evening of Thursday 29 October the plans for Operation Frankton were put before the Examination Committee, chaired by Mountbatten, for final consideration. Major General Charles Haydon, Captain Tom Hussey, Robert Neville and Cyril Horton were among those who found themselves sitting around the large oval table in the COHQ board room.

Hasler's paper was accepted with hardly a demur. When it came to the issue of command, however, the situation was different. Hasler had assumed from the outset that he would lead the operation. Mountbatten queried this assumption, especially given that there was little or, most probably, no chance of returning. Hasler had been, for many months, the driving force in the CODC. His inventiveness and personal dynamism marked him out from the crowd and, if the staff officers at COHQ were honest, the business of the RMBPD played to only some of his strengths. If he were sent with the RMBPD to Bordeaux and did not return, COHQ generally, and CODC in particular, would lose a valuable asset. Frankly, it was not necessary, Mountbatten thought, that Hasler go on the three-canoe raid. It was a job for a young officer: the officer commanding No 1. Section (Mackinnon) could do it admirably.

Tipped off a week before by Robert Neville of Mountbatten's attitude, which was widely shared in COHQ, Hasler prepared a letter to Lieutenant General Sir Alan Bourne in which he expressed his determination not to be left behind, arguing that only by virtue of his personal leadership could the raid have any hope of succeeding:

1. Operation is an important one, and appears to have good chance of success. Main difficulty is a question of small-boat seamanship and navigation on the part of the force commander. My second-in-command [Jock Stewart] has only been using small boats for about 4 months and chances of success would be materially reduced if the most experienced officer available were not sent.
2. A failure would prejudice all future operations of this type.
3. In a new unit, the OC can hardly gain respect if he avoids going on the first operation.
4. I am supposed to be no longer a member of the Development Organisation in general but simply the OC of an operational unit.
5. If I am not allowed to go on this operation, what type of operation will be permissible for me? The case of Major Stirling [founder of the Special Air Service] in Egypt is thought to be similar.

Helpfully, Horton had forwarded a copy of Hasler's plea to the Planning Committee in advance of the meeting. Mountbatten allowed Hasler to argue his case, which he did passionately, elaborating on the points made in his letter and asking, rhetorically, how he could possibly be expected to look his Marines in the eye when they returned, if he had not shared the same dangers as them in a live operation. In any case, if canoe-borne raids were to have any chance of success in the future it was important that he went on this first one, to enable learning points to be developed profitably for the next time.

But Hasler's arguments did not trump the single most important issue for the hard-nosed staff officers at COHQ: as Officer Commanding of the CODC and the RMBPD, he was simply too valuable to lose. At the end of the discussion Mountbatten asked those sitting around the table to give their verdicts. All, except his fellow Royal Marine Robert Neville, considered that Hasler should not go. His heart sank to his boots, but Mountbatten then surprised him. Perhaps the Chief of Combined Operations understood the truth that all operations, no matter how small, were dependent for their success on the quality of their leaders, and Operation Frankton stood a far better chance of success with Hasler than without him. Proving his willingness to be his own man, Mountbatten ignored the assembled advice of his staff, and with a slight smile said to Hasler: 'Much against my better judgement, I'm going to let you go.'

'Won after a ding dong battle,' a relieved Hasler wrote triumphantly that night, as he rattled north in his third-class sleeper en route to Glasgow. His reaction was not mere selfishness. Hasler knew his men better than anyone. He knew their state of training, confidence and competence, and realised that without him the remaining raiders would be little more than babes in the wood and their chances of capture or destruction much greater. The raid was on, and the RMBPD was to undertake it.

But it was clear to Mountbatten, after listening to the discussion on 29 October, that sending only three canoes into Bordeaux risked the failure of the enterprise, as it ignored the possibility that some would not survive the approach. It seemed inevitable to him that there would be casualties along the way. In agreeing the operation, Mountbatten ordered that Frankton should instead be carried out by six canoe teams instead of Hasler's original three. It proved to be a prescient decision. It was relatively easy, therefore, for Hasler to extend the planned number of participants from six men in Mackinnon's No. 1 Section to eleven: Mackinnon, Wallace, Laver, Sheard, Conway, Ellery, Ewart, Fisher, Mills, Moffatt and Sparks. Hasler would be the twelfth man, and a thirteenth, Norman Colley, would travel in the submarine as the reserve to replace anyone who was injured or fell ill during the journey.

So far as Mountbatten was concerned, in the aftermath of the massive losses at Dieppe on 19 August, a canoe raid on Bordeaux met all the requirements of simplicity and economy. Large resources in terms of men and equipment would not be required and if the RMBPD failed in its task, its loss, in the grand scheme of things, would not be overly significant to COHQ.* In terms of human capital, twelve lives were to be put at risk, similar in number to two fully manned Lancaster bombers (each of which had a crew of seven). The loss to the RAF's Bomber Command alone in 1942 was 9,440 men: of 35,050 sorties mounted that year 1,400 aircraft were to be lost.† If this number were divided across three hundred nights of operational flying, it represented the deaths of over thirty-one men every night. Likewise, the operation was to take

* Another Combined Operations raid taking place at the same time as Operation Frankton, (Operation Freshman) involved the launch of a 34-man team of airborne trained Royal Engineers by glider on 19 November to destroy the heavy-water plant at Vemork in Norway. The weather was poor and, together with the failure of navigational equipment, one of the two glider-towing Halifax bombers crashed into a mountain (after releasing its glider at a very high altitude); the two gliders carrying the men and equipment crashed badly on landing. Those who weren't killed outright were murdered by the Germans soon after capture, at least one by the injection of oxygen into his bloodstream, a procedure administered by a Gestapo doctor. But a second operation, carried out by a six-man team of the Norwegian SOE in February 1943, the basis of the Hollywood epic *The Heroes of Telemark*, was completely successful.

† Ten women also lost their lives, but in British skies, bringing the total to 9,450.

place six weeks after 3,000 Combined Operations casualties had been suffered at Dieppe. The wider context of the war as a whole in late 1942 needs to be appreciated. On 8 November 60,500 Anglo-American troops were to be launched into Algeria and Morocco in the invasion of North Africa to bring about the beginning of the end of Hitler's speculative ambitions in North Africa and the Near East.

During October the climactic battle for Egypt was being fought around the hamlet of El Alamein, which pitted 177,000 British and Allied troops against the 93,000 men of Rommel's experienced but outgunned Afrika Korps. The figures in the East surpassed even these in terms of scale. By 1 November 1942 the Wehrmacht High Command had estimated that 5,150,000 Soviet soldiers had been taken prisoner since the beginning of Operation Barbarossa seventeen months before. In the fighting for Stalingrad, which saw the obliteration of von Paulus's 6th Army, some 270,000 Germans were surrounded in the city by the start of the Soviet winter offensive on 22 November. In the first seven days of December, as HMS *Tuna* was making its way down the Irish Sea, into the Atlantic and then the Bay of Biscay, over three hundred members of the Royal Navy and Royal Australian Navy lost their lives at sea.

The country was at war, and with hundreds of British lives being lost every day in the West, not to mention thousands of Soviet lives in the East, together with the thousands of British and Commonwealth lives being slowly extinguished in prison camps scattered across the jungles of South-East Asia, it was no time to be sentimental. In the context of the rest of the war in general, therefore, as well as in the more specific orbit of Combined Operations, the risk of losing twelve lives in an operation against blockade-runners in the Gironde was one that the planners in Richmond Terrace were content to make. Even if they had known that a week earlier the seven surviving captives from Operation Musketoon had each been shot in the back of the head before being cremated in Sachsenhausen's ovens, and that a similar fate awaited any future member of Britain's raiding forces unfortunate enough to fall into the hands of the enemy, the operation would undoubtedly have continued.

So it was that on 30 October 1942, Mountbatten appended his signature to a memorandum sent to the Chiefs of Staff Committee, who duly approved the COHQ plan on 3 November:

1. Operation 'Frankton' has been planned to meet Lord Selborne's requirements . . . that steps should be taken to attack Axis ships which are known to be running the blockade between France and the Far East.
2. Both seaborne and airborne methods of attacking the ships have been carefully examined and the plan now proposed is the only one which offers a good chance of success.
3. On an average, between six and ten blockade runners are usually to be found alongside the quays at Bordeaux, in addition to other shipping. It is hoped to deal with at least six blockade runners.
4. Briefly, the plan is for one officer and five other ranks of the Royal Marine Boom Patrol Detachment to paddle up the River Gironde in cockles, moving during the hours of darkness only, and to place 'limpets' on the water line of the ships they find at Bordeaux. The cockles will be carried to within nine miles of the mouth of the River in a submarine which will be on passage to normal patrol duty and thus will not require to be specially detailed.
5. Twelve copies of the summary of this outline plan are attached.

The die was cast.

NINE

The Clyde and the Thames

At the Admiralty in London, following Hasler's request, Captain Raw had arranged for the men of Jack Mackinnon's No. 1 Section to undergo a week of intense training on submarines to prepare them for the forthcoming operation. The men as yet had no inkling of what lay in store for them. Hasler had assumed that he would win through at the Examination Committee in London, and so characteristically pressed ahead with all the arrangements for the training well in advance of the decision. After this short but intense bout of training he intended to bring the Section back to the Thames estuary for a five-day exercise that would serve as the final rehearsal for the raid, in terrain resembling that of the Gironde and Garonne. In Scotland the submarine allocated to the actual mission – the newly refurbished HMS *Tuna* – was at the time on patrol in the north Atlantic in weather that its captain, Lieutenant Dick Raikes, was to describe as 'truly appalling', so Hugh Ionides of the 3rd Submarine Flotilla assigned two other vessels – HMS *Taurus* and HMS *Sea Nymph* – to the task of assisting in the training of the RMBPD during this critical week.

HMS *Tuna* was a good choice. One of fifty-five T Class submarines built for the Royal Navy before and during the war, she had a length of 275 feet, a displacement of 1,325 tons, a complement of 59 and carried 16 torpedoes. With two diesel engines for surface work and two electric ones submerged, her fastest speed under water was nine knots and on the surface, fifteen. She knew the waters off the Gironde very well, having spent considerable periods of the war to date patrolling the Bay of Biscay. On 22 September 1940 she had torpedoed and sunk the 7,000-ton German merchantman *Tirranna* fifteen nautical miles south-west of the Gironde estuary, two days later sinking the seaplane tender *Ostmark*. At 4.30 a.m. on the morning of 18 December that same year she attacked, and probably damaged, the Italian submarine *Brin* with torpedoes and gunfire in the Bay of Biscay about fifty-five nautical miles west of the Gironde estuary, and later that night sank the French tug *Chassiron* with gunfire about twenty-five nautical miles wcst-south-west of the Gironde.

Nor was she new to commando operations, having supported the raid on the Lofoten islands in December 1941. Likewise, Dick Raikes had extensive knowledge of the target area when he took command of *Tuna* on 26 August 1942. In late 1940, when First Lieutenant on the submarine HMS *Talisman*, he had been responsible for landing two French agents off Bordeaux. It didn't go entirely to plan, as he later recalled:

> It was the first time that it had been done, I think. We landed these two chaps by frog boat, with a wireless set and they were on the end of a long line, so that when they got ashore we could pull the canoe back, so as not to leave any trace of them. But they'd insisted on a 'Vive La France' and saying goodbye to everybody. And so we virtually kicked them into this boat . . . And then, instead of pulling to the shore, they pulled out to the Atlantic . . .

Hasler arrived in Glasgow en route for Holy Loch at 7.45 a.m. on the morning of Friday 30 October, taking the opportunity of shaving in the gentlemen's lavatory at the railway station before catching the train to Gourock, then the steamer across the Clyde to Dunoon and the bus to Ardnadam, reaching HMS *Forth* in Holy Loch at 12.30 p.m. Fred Goatley had arranged for six of the brand-new MkIIs to be ready for Hasler's arrival. Each boat had been named after a fish – *Coalfish*, *Crayfish*, *Conger*, *Cachalot*, *Catfish* and *Cuttlefish* – the crews carefully painting the names in blue on the side of each vessel, over the camouflage scheme devised by Hasler. Once there he met Hugh Ionides to agree the best method of getting the canoes off the submarine. As Hasler's diary, written in long-hand at the time, states: 'Saw S3 [Ionides] re object of visit. Fixed details of hoisting in/out apparatus.'

There were two traditional methods for releasing canoes from a submarine. One was to assemble them on the casing, complete with stores and crews, and then float them off by trimming the submarine down by releasing air from the ballast tanks. The second was to lower the canoes to the surface by ropes. There were difficulties with both approaches, however. In the first the surface turbulence associated with releasing ballast threatened to capsize the heavily laden little craft, and in the second the lowered canoes could find themselves sideways on to the sea, stuck to the one of the bulbous edges of the submarine at an angle that was not always possible to right.

With Hasler's prompting, the ever practical Ionides came up with an inventive alternative. The T Class submarine had a 4-inch gun on the main deck, in front of the conning tower. Could not an apparatus of some kind be attached to the barrel of the gun to hoist the fully laden canoes out on to the surface of the sea? The solution was simple: a four-foot girder attached to the bottom of the barrel and a tackle array that allowed a suspended canoe to be gently lowered from the gun and swung out from the surfaced submarine. Hasler's diary demonstrates that within a day of the remainder of No. 1 Section arriving at Holy Loch they were practising with the new device:

Monday 2 November

a.m. Rigging port quarter davit for hoisting out. Hoisted all boats out.

p.m. Limpet attacks.

The hoist was then successfully deployed the next day, coincidentally the same day on which the Chiefs of Staff Committee authorised Operation Frankton:

> *Tuesday 3 November*
> a.m. Hoist out. 10 a.m. All boats leave ship in formation for long day trip up Loch Long. Two boats fully ballasted. 4.30 p.m. returned to ship, very exhausted. Total distance approximately 13 miles.

Ionides had also made available a six-year-old 460-ton Dutch naval minesweeper, the *Jan Van Gelder*, for their training. Because of its unkempt appearance the men nicknamed her 'Scumbag'. Travelling at a speed of two knots, the minesweeper mimicked the effect of the tidal stream, allowing the canoe teams to practise laying dummy limpets on a ship's hull while paddling hard to counter the effect of an ebbing tide. This was invaluable, as in Southsea the only practice the men had had was against sheets of metal placed at an angle in the water.

A profitable twenty-three hours of training was subsequently undertaken in HMS *Taurus* in the Inchmarnock area. Commanded by Lieutenant Commander Mervyn Wingfield, *Taurus* was brand-new, having been commissioned only three days earlier. Hasler's diary for the last two days of training in Scotland, before the group travelled back south by train, captures the busyness of the period:

> *Friday 6 November*
> 7.40 a.m. Embarked all ranks in P339 [HMS *Taurus*]. Wind fresh SE, getting up.
> 12.00 noon. Experimental hoist out under lee of Arran in heavy squalls. Successful except for bending of guides.
> p.m. Diving and action trials on P339. Very interesting. Evening. Blowing Force 6–7. Programme for hoisting out abandoned.

Jan Van Gelder with [Jock] Stewart on board weather bound at Rothesay.

Saturday 7 November

10. a.m. RV [rendezvous] with *Jan Van Gelder* at Rothesay. Hoist out under lee of land all six boats successfully, including one on the end of the gun barrel with P339 listed to starboard. Hoist into *Jan Van Gelder* [using derricks] by ropes end. Arrive back at Forth at 12.30 p.m. Pick up all gear and leave at 2.30 p.m. for Gourock. Stewart and self went on ahead to Glasgow. Caught 9.30 p.m. train south with two first class sleepers.

The training in Scotland over, the next task was an exercise that mimicked in as much detail as possible the distance that the Royal Marines would need to travel into the Gironde. This was Exercise Blanket. As yet, of course, only Hasler and Jock Stewart had any inkling of what lay before the RMBPD.

On 9 November the exercise got under way on the south-east coast as the tide ebbed later that night. The weather was calm, but a mist hung low over the sea. It proved to be, in Hasler's own words, 'a complete failure'. The aim was to canoe the nearly seventy nautical miles from Margate to Deptford up the Thames. Part of the problem may well have been hinted at by Bill Sparks's account of the evening of the launch. After a week of rigorous training and abstinence in Scotland, the men were billeted in a pub on the Margate sea front:

> Seeing that we were all blacked up with camouflage cream, the locals were convinced that we were going on a real raid, and they insisted on buying us rounds of drinks . . . At midnight we left the pub and made our way to the jetty where our canoes had been unloaded. Light-headed with beer, we launched our canoes and climbed in, ready for five full days of paddling.

But alcohol probably played no more than a small part in the fiasco that followed. Certainly, bad luck and the alertness of the riverside patrols did much to undo the best intentions of the Royal Marines. The local defences had been alerted, passwords issued and eager Home Guard volunteers ordered to scour the banks of the River Swale skirting the underbelly of the Isle of Sheppey and the approaches to the Thames estuary. Six canoes duly set out as planned. At 3.30 a.m., the coastline wrapped in darkness, all the boats landed successfully on the Isle of Sheppey, where the crews pulled the boats across the mud on to dry land and harboured up under camouflage. With a sentry on duty, the men slept and lay undisturbed while the tide ebbed. At 1 p.m. the tide was back, allowing the boats to venture up the River Swale where they again camped that night. So far, so good. The sea remained kind to them, and the low sea mist hid them from observers on the shore. It was then that things started to go wrong. Hasler's diary records:

> *Thursday 12 November*
> Pleasant morning. Camp routine. Colt 45 instruction.
> p.m. Mackinnon and remaining boats arrive. 8 p.m. leave in single convoy. Wind NNW Force 3. Lost all remainder after a short time. 4 a.m. landed at Broad Ness [on Friday 13 November].

From then until *Catfish* reached Blackwall Point opposite the Isle of Dogs, deep in the Thames, at 6 a.m. on Saturday the 14th Hasler and Sparks saw no other members of No. 1 Section. In fact, they were far behind, Mackinnon and three boats getting only as far as Greenhithe. It was only now that the full story of the expedition became clear. Leaving the Swale on 12 November, Mackinnon's boat had grounded on mudflats. In the confusion all sense of direction had been lost, and the canoe returned in the direction whence it had come. Sheard also ended up lost. Most of the crews were then challenged by Home Guard patrols at least once, and some were seen twice. When the exhausted men were finally herded together and extricated from the water on Saturday morning, Hasler gave vent to his frustration at what he regarded as an incompetent performance. According to Sparks he 'spared no breath in telling us exactly what he thought of us. Despite all the training we had let him down . . . We obviously were not ready for operations.'

That night, though, never one to say no to an invitation and wanting perhaps to drown his sorrows, Hasler dragged Mackinnon to a party thrown by some Wrens he knew in London. By his own admission he was 'weary', but a dance with some pretty Wrens was never something to be lightly dismissed by Blondie. It was nevertheless a depressed and grumpy OC RMBPD who found himself accosted in the canteen at Richmond Terrace the following day (widely regarded by military staff as one of the best eating places in London) by no less than the Chief of Combined Operations himself. 'How did it go?' asked Mountbatten in his typically breezy fashion. 'Disastrously, Sir,' replied a dispirited Hasler. He explained the shortcomings identified, and the fact that halfway through the exercise every canoe had lost contact with the others, and many had become hopelessly lost. 'Oh well,' Mountbatten replied, refusing to be discouraged. 'At least you won't make those mistakes again.'

Hasler's fear that the failure of the exercise might lead to the cancellation of the operation was immediately dispelled. Operation Frankton was still on. Exercise Blanket might well have been a disaster, but Mountbatten was right: it was only a practice run. The errors made merely concentrated the attention of all involved to an unusual degree, such that none was willing to make the same mistakes again. The men knew that if they did, the consequence could be fatal. Hasler's view came to reflect Mountbatten's: he noted in his summary to Frankton's post-operation report, submitted in April 1943, that Blanket had in fact proved to be a very 'useful exercise'. One of his decisions was to split the Section into two separate 'divisions', A and B. If one division were compromised by the enemy, the other had a chance of getting through. Both divisions would therefore need to split up on the approach to the estuary, then operate independently of each other. A Division was to be led by Hasler and B Division by Mackinnon.

The chastened members of No. 1 Section now enjoyed a short spell of leave (except for Hasler, who busied himself in Southsea and London) before returning to Gourock on Thursday 19 November for the last, intense period of training and preparation, in advance of the mission that all knew was imminent but the detail of which only Hasler and Stewart were privy. The men could meanwhile only speculate, still knowing nothing about either the target or the timing. Most money was on an operation against the *Tirpitz*, hidden behind anti-torpedo netting deep in a north Norwegian fjord. The prospect of creeping up to this fearsome leviathan in their canvas canoes to place limpet mines against her foot-thick hull seemed not to depress the men one bit. Hasler did nothing to dispel these rumours. 'When the Major heard that we had figured out we were going to Norway,' recalled Bill Sparks, 'he warned us that rumours had a very nasty habit of being true.' 'There, you see,' Sparks and his mates reasoned, 'it's true. We are going to Norway.'

Time was spent preparing and packing stores, testing the hoisting gear under full load (with two crew, 480 pounds), swinging compasses, field training ashore, fusing limpets, testing and preparing uniforms, and painting the canoes in camouflage pattern. The men continued to swim each day in the freezing waters of Holy Loch, conducted weapons practice with silenced Sten guns (two of which were being taken on the operation) and American Colt 45 automatic pistols.

When not on the water improving their canoeing technique and practising laying limpets on the hull of the *Jan Van Gelder* by day and by night, they spent their time marching across the bleak and windswept hills, climbing cliffs and maintaining their fitness levels.

Hasler had expended considerable thought on the men's gear and uniforms, and after several months of experimentation had designed a waterproof and camouflaged combat smock with an elasticated skirt that could fit around the cockpit cowling of the canoe to form a watertight seal. On the smock were hand-sewn a range of distinguishing badges, including the Combined Operations emblem with anchor, tommy gun and vigilant eagle that left no room for doubt that the men were members of a bona fide military organisation. The title 'Royal Marines' in red on a blue background was carefully sewn on to each shoulder. The remainder of the uniform was nothing but practical. In addition to more standard items such as khaki battledress trousers, woollen socks and long woollen underpants, Hasler insisted on silk gloves covered by blue woollen mittens, plimsolls worn under thigh-length waders, a roll-neck sweater, blue scarf and blue balaclava, together with an inflatable lifejacket.

During this time L'Estrange travelled up from London, giving Hasler final intelligence on the Gironde, on the blockade-runners that were expected to be at anchor in Bordeaux, as well as on German defences; and supplied him with updated maps, charts and photographs of the estuary and riverbanks, which would enable Hasler to determine the best places to lie up during the day. He was also able to provide further information from MI9 about the withdrawal to Spain following the attack, which he could discuss with the men only once the submarine had set sail. But there was not much to be told. Neave and Langley had described to L'Estrange a range of methods for evading capture, for reducing the risk of endangering any would-be helpers and resisting interrogation. But secrecy was such that Hasler did not know *who* would be his escape-line contact in the town of Ruffec, about ninety miles north-east of Bordeaux, or *where* he might go in the town to find help.

Ruffec was the centre of the Marie-Claire escape line especially chosen by its creator after the German invasion of France in 1940, because it straddled the demarcation line between German-occupied and Vichy-occupied France. Escapers could be brought to the vicinity of Ruffec from across the occupied zone, before being smuggled into Vichy territory from remote farms across a relatively permeable (at the time) frontier. It also had the advantage of putting any would-be German pursuers off the scent. Spain, and safety, were towards the south, and it was assumed that no self-respecting German pursuit would think of looking anywhere else.

However, in a serious blow to the viability of the entire escape plan, the view in Room 900 was that it was too dangerous for the security of the *réseau* for detailed information to be given to the Royal Marines as to where the escapers should go to receive sanctuary. If Hasler or any of his men were to be captured, so the reasoning went, the Gestapo had effective methods for prising crucial information from even the most unwilling prisoners, and the entire Marie-Claire operation could be placed in jeopardy as a result. Without providing him with any other details, therefore, Hasler was instructed simply to make for Ruffec. There he was told that he would find people waiting who would then guide them to safety, again without being given any more than the vaguest of details. It was 'the worst of both worlds', concluded Airey Neave. 'I did not see how those of the party who escaped could be certain of making contact with Mary or her friends in the Ruffec area. Nor had she been warned that the Commando raid in the river Gironde was taking place.'

The plan was indeed foolhardy, and represented a distinct departure from Blondie's normally diligent modus operandi. But he could only trust MI9 to do their best for him and his men, and he went into the field uncomplaining. To be instructed to find a *secret* resistance cell in the midst of a major market town in France without any specific detail about people or locations was grievously deficient in terms of planning, and placed the lives of the men at great risk. When they arrived at the outskirts of the town the Royal Marines, on the run from the authorities for several days and undoubtedly looking like tramps, would have stuck out like sore thumbs. As Airey Neave was later to admit, Hasler and

Sparks made contact with Mary Lindell's organisation only by 'an extraordinary chance'; and by its poor planning and preparation 'Room 900 did not especially distinguish themselves on this occasion'.

In addition to the limited information available to them about Ruffec, both Hasler and Mackinnon were introduced to the special code they were to use to communicate with London during the recovery phase, assuming that they would be able to make contact with the Marie-Claire Line. What they were not to know was that the escape line had neither radio nor operator. There is no evidence that in the flurry of activity to prepare for the raid anyone gave any thought to the possibility of SOE helping the escapers, not least of all because Combined Operations had no idea that SOE had a nascent operation in place in the port itself. It was conceivable that Claude de Baissac and his contacts could have provided aid to the escapers (such as safe-houses and onwards transport), but the dangers to the SOE operation would have been precisely those that faced MI9. Either way, the plans for the escape were poorly considered, and placed Hasler and his men in extreme danger.

Hasler's diary captures something of the intense activity during this last stage of preparation, during which for want of space on HMS *Forth* the men were accommodated on the supply ship HMS *Al Rawdah*, anchored in Holy Loch:

Friday 20 November

a.m. Building and examining boats on deck of [HMS] *Forth*. Arranging for repairs. Unpacking stores in *Al Rawdah*.

p.m. Short forced march over hills with interludes for instruction on Colt 45 and Silent Sten.

Evening. Cleaning guns and short talk on Cockle Suit and Escape Box.

Saturday 21 November

a.m. In HMS *Forth* fixing repairs to boats and getting all stores. Troops doing cross country march.

p.m. Lecture troops on fitting of Colt 45 holsters and fighting knives and on fusing of limpets.

Evening. Fuse live practice limpets. Write detailed orders for fuzing operational limpets.

Sunday 22 November

a.m. To HMS *Forth* to chase up repairs. Troops fuzing remaining limpets. Borrowed lifeboat from *Al Rawdah*. 11 a.m. started fuzes and dropped limpets on sea bed up Holy Loch.

p.m. Practised single paddles drill. Watched 3 out of 4 limpets go up. [The failure of one limpet to explode would have alerted Hasler to the probability that some of the devices would fail.]

Evening. Preparing practice limpets. Making out equipment list with Mackinnon.

Monday 23 November

a.m. Navigational training on sectional charts. Troops preparing stores for exercise. p.m. 1415. Embarked on *Jan Van Gelder* with 6 Cockles. Proceeded to Upper Loch Long. 3 p.m.–5.30 p.m. Dummy limpet attacks on *Jan Van Gelder* doing 1.5–2 knots both with and against her.

Evening. 7.30 p.m.–9.30 p.m. Repeat in darkness. Very profitable exercise.

Tuesday 24 November

a.m. Navigation on Sectional charts.

p.m. Speed build and unbuild exercises. Self 5 p.m.–7 p.m. fuzing limpets.

Wednesday 25 November

a.m. 9 a.m.–12.15 p.m. All ranks fuzing limpets.

p.m. 3 p.m.–5 p.m. Went on board HMS *Tuna* and discussed details with No 1 [Johnny Bull].

Evening. Packing cargo bags of *Catfish*.

Thursday 26 November

a.m. Troops packing bags. L'Estrange arrived with all paper work.
Evening: discussions with L'Estrange.
Friday 27 November
Day spent in administration.
Evening. Drinking with Poles. Disastrous results.
Saturday 28 November
a.m. Start painting boats. Discussions with [Dickie] Raikes. Painting Cockle suits. Evening. Sorting out cargo bags. Sewing up bag.

Although he had met HMS *Tuna*'s First Lieutenant (Johnny Bull) on 25 November, it was not until two days later that Hasler was to meet the submarine's captain. Dick Raikes recalled that when he met Blondie for the first time, Hasler was suffering from the worst hangover of his life, the result of the drinking session the previous evening on the *Al Rawdah* with the Polish submariners. The Poles had insisted on offering Hasler and Jock Stewart traditional Polish hospitality, but the particular firewater they were offered – Hasler never found out what it was – knocked them both for six. It was therefore an unusually discombobulated Blondie who shook hands with Raikes the following morning, but despite this the two men hit it off immediately. They were to become lifelong friends. Blondie was a real character, 'a born leader', considered Raikes. 'There was no bullshit about him.' In Hasler's quietness lay singular confidence, determination and strength. Raikes had received a sketchy briefing about the mission, although he alone of his crew had any idea of Frankton's destination:

I was briefed on the operation from the Admiral (Submarines) the week before in London. But just broad details, you know. The job was to take twelve Royal Marines and their six kayaks to the mouth of the Gironde estuary, from where they were to carry out a dangerous raid on the port of Bordeaux. I and HMS *Tuna* had been chosen because I knew the area. I was to meet with the head of this commando unit, Major Herbert Hasler, a highly reputed Royal Marine officer, and over the course of the next few days I planned with him the loading and launching of his commando unit, which was due to depart on the 30th of this month.

When he returned to Gourock Hugh Ionides briefed Raikes in more detail, especially on the methodology he had agreed with Hasler for safely disembarking the canoes from the submarine. Hasler had already briefed Bull on the sling-and-davit approach, and Raikes readily agreed to the device being built on to his 4-inch gun:

> We bolted a piece of rolled steel girder on to the barrel of the gun having first welded an eye to the end of the girder to which we bolted a two part purchase that could be used to hoist the canoes out from the casing into the water. When doing so we used the gun's normal training mechanism to swing the canoes out using the two part hoist to sling them up and lower them into the water.

Lieutenant Geoffrey Rowe, HMS *Tuna*'s pilot, also met Hasler for the first time that morning. Rowe climbed down through the fore-hatch of the submarine into the torpedo stowage compartment (whence the torpedoes were normally loaded, and through which the collapsed Cockles were also loaded into and unloaded from the submarine), turning towards the stern in the direction of the control room. 'As I passed the wardroom the Skipper . . . called to me: "Pilot, I want you to meet Major Hasler. He's coming with us on the next patrol." I shook hands with an outdoor, sandy-haired and moustached Royal Marine commando and, as was customary, exchanged Christian names, although he chose to use his nickname. "We're planning an exercise in a few days" he said. "There'll be a Lieutenant and eight [sic] men with me."'

The last few days before HMS *Tuna* sailed were a flurry of purposeful activity. In the midst of this Hasler observed that HMS *Tuna* was a very happy ship, a testament to the leadership of its commander. Raikes's calm personality, physical stamina and ability seemingly to command his boat without speaking made a strong impression on Hasler.

There were a thousand and one things that needed doing. The compasses were checked to ensure that their deviation was minimised, the men's cargo bags for the raid were carefully packed; and final tests, using the fully laden *Catfish*, were made from the rig Johnny Bull had built for swinging out. Equipment needed to be checked and labelled and canoes, ammunition and limpets packed.

The final meetings were held with L'Estrange, and then a cold Monday 30 November dawned. Geoffrey Rowe recalled that it was still dark when Hasler and his men came on board, trans-shipped from *Al Rawdah* to HMS *Forth* before joining *Tuna*, 'bringing with them, in pairs, long packages which slid down the fore-hatch with the men'. Hasler had said farewell to L'Estrange, Jock Stewart and Hugh Ionides on HMS *Forth*. Ionides had spoken to the men before they climbed down the gangway to the submarine. 'The day that you have all been training for has come,' Bill Sparks remembered him saying. 'I don't know where you're bound or what the job is to be. What I can say is that people of the highest authority are awaiting the results. Good luck to you all.' It wasn't the first indication that the men had had that this was not a drill. The night before they had been told that they were about to embark on a secret operation, and that if they wished they should write a letter to their families. Jock Ewart, like the others convinced that they would soon be en route for a fjord in northern Norway, penned a short letter to his family in Glasgow:

Dear Mum, Dad and brothers,

I'm taking this opportunity to write you these few lines,

> although I hope they won't be necessary. As you know I volunteered for a certain job, which I trust you will learn about at a later period. I've enjoyed every minute of it and hope that what we have done helps to end the mess we are in and make a decent and better world. You will see by recovery [sic] note whether I am a prisoner or otherwise, which at present isn't worrying me in the least. I have a feeling I'll be like a bad penny, so please don't upset yourself over my safety. My heart will be with you always, you are the best parents one could wish to have. Anyway Mum you can always say you had a son in the most senior service, and, though I say it myself, 'one of twelve heroes'.

Jack Mackinnon told his parents that they would not hear from him 'for a number of weeks, so don't on any account worry over the fact that you get no letters'. He assured them that he would 'carry on watching crossing the street'. He finished, as always, with the refrain:

> Well cheerio just now, and above all don't worry about me.
> With lots of love and kisses to you all
> Your loving son
> Jacky

The young Bob Ewart had fallen in love with Heather Powell, the sixteen-year-old daughter of their hosts at the White Heather guesthouse. To her he wrote a letter which she was only to receive if he did not return:

> Dear Heather
> I trust it won't be necessary to have this sent you but since I don't know the outcome of this little adventure, I thought I'd leave this note behind in the care of Norman [Colley] who will forward it to you should anything unexpected happen.

During my stay at South-Sea as you well know made me realise what the good things in life are and I'm glad I have this opportunity to help bring back the pleasant times which I'm sure you always had and what you were made for. I couldn't help but love you Heather although you were so young, I will always love you as I know you do me, that alone should get me through this but no one never knows the turns of fate. One thing I ask of you Heather is not to take this too hard, you have yet your life to live . . . please don't worry and fret yourself about me, with your picture in front of me I feel confident that I shall pull through and get back to you some day . . .

I pray that God will spare me, and save you from this misery, so hoping for a speedy return I'll say cheerio and God be with you. Thanking you and your mother from the bottom of my heart, at present in your care.

God bless and keep you all

Yours for Ever

Bob

Chin Up Sweetheart

The diesel engines chugged purposefully as the crew of HMS *Tuna* went to 'Harbour Stations', and at 10.30 a.m. the vessel slid away smoothly from her mother ship. On HMS *Forth* the crew stood and saluted the black submarine sliding across the quiet waters of Holy Loch. Standing on the narrow deck with his comrades and looking back, Sparks knew then that they were embarking on 'something big'.

TEN

Journey to the Gironde

Within an hour of leaving the safety of Holy Loch, Hasler called his men down to the torpedo stowage room to brief them on the real object of their journey. It was so cramped they sat knee to knee, huddled forward to catch every one of his quiet, carefully thought-out words. Hasler was a man of economy of speech and calmness of approach that accentuated the firmness of his manner and the authority of his delivery. Trusting him implicitly, the men listened in silence, the quiet murmur of the submarine as it was propelled through the water providing an eerie background. The dull yellow light that tried to penetrate the depths of the torpedo stowage compartment from the overhead bulb failed abjectly to illuminate anything other than the men's keen faces, long shadows and darkness comprehensively filling the remaining space.

Carefully Hasler sketched a map of the French Atlantic coast on a blackboard he had propped up at one end of the confined space and, grinning, revealed that it was not the *Tirpitz* they were after, but blockade-runners darting out into the Bay of Biscay from Bordeaux. Their aim was to attempt to sink or seriously damage as many as possible of the twelve freighters they would find lying up at Bassens and Bordeaux. The men listened eagerly. Sparks for one was relieved, considering that a visit to Norway to take on the *Tirpitz*, while undoubtedly glamorous, was tantamount to being given 'a one-way ticket'. Hasler outlined the entire plan to the men for two hours, none of them aware that the submarine had trimmed down to periscope depth for the journey down the Clyde. The trip in the submarine, Hasler told them, would take five days, during which time they would remain surfaced at night, making their way on their diesel engines, and at a much slower speed submerged during the day. In a few hours' time they would reach Inchmarnock, the island off Bute where they would rehearse disembarkation drills repeatedly until Raikes and Hasler were convinced they could leave the submarine quickly and safely when the time came to do it for real. Thereafter they would make their way to a point off the Gironde estuary, where HMS *Tuna* would leave them to carry on alone.

The submarine, Hasler told them, was planned to arrive off the Gironde on 5 December. They would then be hoisted out on the first suitable night, some nine and a half miles off the Point de la Négade, the westernmost point of the peninsula between Montalivet to the south and Soulac to the north. Montalivet, he told them, would be easily recognisable from the sea because of the village's distinctive profusion of red roofs, but it was thought that the Germans had a searchlight battery at the Point de la Négade. The aim would be for the force to then travel up into Bordeaux by stages, helped on the way by the flood tide, lying up during the day and moving only in darkness. On the first good night, at high-water slack, the point at which the flood tide stopped and reversed into the ebb, limpets would be attached to the targets, after which the force would withdraw down the estuary, as far as possible helped by the ebbing tide. At low-water slack the survivors would scuttle their boats and equipment on the east bank.

At this point Hasler stopped, and asked whether there were any questions. The momentary silence was broken by Sergeant Sammy Wallace: 'Sir, how do we get home?' 'We walk,' Hasler replied, explaining that it was not practicable to attempt to make contact with a submarine up to ten days after the attack, not least because the German defences would be fully alert for such an attempt, making it dangerous not just for the escapers but also for the submarine. Instead, it had been decided that the men would attempt to make contact with members of the French Resistance at Ruffec, who would help them escape overland to Spain. Hasler then showed them Ruffec on the map. Escape packs had been prepared for them, containing maps and currency. According to Bill Sparks, someone piped up: 'But we can't speak French!' The five days in the submarine, Hasler replied, would enable them all to learn a few helpful words. Hasler, who had some schoolboy French (and a little German), intended to teach them a few elementary phrases during the voyage.

Before he finished his introductory brief he emphasised that they all needed to understand that the absolute imperative above everything else, including their own safety, was the success of the mission. Nothing else came close. Even if only one boat was left, it was to press on regardless of its condition, and in spite of any other losses, to attack its target.

'Now, what happens if something goes wrong?' Hasler asked, rhetorically. Plenty could. If the submarine was surprised on the surface during the launching process they were on their own, he said. The submarine fore-hatch would close immediately and the vessel would prepare to dive regardless of the state the men were in on deck. Crews left outside were to inflate their lifejackets, load their boats, get in and fasten their spray covers. If the submarine dived, they should endeavour to float clear and proceed independently with the operation. If approached by any other vessel, evasive action should be taken until the vessel got close enough to see the canoes. At this stage boats would stop and remain stationary in the lowest position. If a patrol boat appeared to be coming alongside, the crew would prepare hand grenades and endeavour to capture it by boarding. All the other boats would take evasive action and proceed independently.

'If hailed or fired at from the shore, boats will stop in the lowest position and allow the tide to carry them clear. They will never [underlined] attempt to paddle away or shoot back.' If approached by a person of apparent French nationality while lying up, crews were to remain concealed until sighted, then get hold of him (or her), explain that they are English and instruct them not to tell anybody what they have seen. Children should be told to tell their parents, but nobody else. The men were instructed not to detain such people long, or harm them, unless they were behaving suspiciously. If they were approached by German troops they were to remain concealed until sighted, then kill them as silently as possible, concealing the bodies preferably below high-water mark. They then had to get 'away as soon as it was dark, regardless of the state of tide'.

They would be on their own. 'If a boat gives the SOS signal for any reason,' explained Hasler, 'only the remaining [two] boats of its division will go to its assistance. If the distance was reasonable and the area safe an attempt could be made to get the damaged boat and crew ashore. Otherwise, the boat will be scuttled and the crew left to swim for it with their No. 5 [escape] bag.' If any crew was unable to reach the objective, they needed to make every effort to scuttle or conceal their boat and equipment, go to the nearest safe lying-up place and remain there until four days after leaving the submarine, then escape following their verbal instructions. 'If the alarm is raised during the attack, boats will not withdraw, but will use their own initiative to press home the attack at the earliest opportunity.' Sparks recalled his words: 'I realize that this is a bit more than I originally asked of you, so if any man thinks that he is not quite up to it, let him speak up now. I assure you that no one will think any the less of you for it.' After a pause, he said: 'Does anyone want out?' He was met only with silence, and a determined shaking of heads. Proud, and relieved, he remarked: 'Good. Anyway, it's much less dangerous than a bayonet charge.' Notwithstanding accidents, Norman Colley would not be required.

The first task was to rehearse the disembarkation procedure. Surfacing off the Isle of Bute at 2.30 p.m., the six teams practised throughout the afternoon and well into the evening, until all were exhausted. Geoffrey Rowe was impressed at how this training had dramatically improved the speed at which the entire process could be undertaken:

> To a drill prepared beforehand the marines made ready their canoes in the fore ends and we surfaced. Time and again, getting better at each effort, the men and their canoes were, one at a time, raced up to the upper casing through the fore-hatch which was re-secured after each pair and their boat were up. *Tuna* then dived and resurfaced many times to repeat the drill in simulated operational conditions.

Hasler recorded that by nightfall the time taken to lift out and launch five boats had been reduced to a commendable thirty-one minutes. Unfortunately, during one of the exits the skin of *Coalfish* was ripped on the hatch cover and *Cuttlefish*'s compass was damaged. The process of taking each collapsed canoe up through the narrow hatch 45 degrees on to the foredeck required care, with the chance of snagging the delicate fabric on the fore-hatch latch. The tear could be repaired during the journey, but Hasler and Mackinnon hoped that repeated practice before they set course would remove the chance of error on the real launch.

At 10 p.m., with all the Cockles safely restowed on board, the surfaced HMS *Tuna* got under way, heading south through the darkness, the rhythmic throbbing of her two diesel engines a constant accompaniment. The rounded hulls of submarines make them uncomfortable for surface travelling, their constant rolling in even the slightest swell inducing queasiness in all but the most hardened of mariners. That first night the weather was relatively calm, but on the following morning, 1 December 1942, when *Tuna* was joined by the vessel that would escort her south as far as Land's End, the swell worsened. The presence of the escort vessel HMS *White Bear*, a luxury American steam yacht (previously named SY *Iolanda*, purchased by the Royal Navy for $1 in 1940 and pressed into submarine protection duties), enabled the submarine to travel on the surface until Cornwall disappeared from sight, which preserved the vessel's batteries and allowed for faster passage. However, it induced terrible sickness among the ship's guests, particularly Sergeant Wallace and Corporal Sheard. Johnny Bull observed that the weather 'was foul and there was much seasickness particularly amongst the marines which took the edge off their rigorous training'.

Only Hasler, a hardened sailor, was unaffected. His diary recorded for that first day: '*Tuna* proceeding down the Irish sea with HMS *White Bear* as escort. Rolling slightly. Slept all day between meals. 9.15 p.m.–00.45 a.m. Turned hands to. Restowing bags, paddles etc and boats. Everyone except NCOs pretty useless (because of seasickness). Myself continuing planning till 1.45 a.m.'

The submariners had given the Royal Marines their cramped bunks, while Hasler and Mackinnon were accommodated in Raikes's cabin and the wardroom respectively. Hasler got the Marines up from their beds – feeling quite sorry for themselves – at 3 p.m., and told them that seasickness was nothing more than a question of mind over matter: they should get a grip of themselves. 'From now on, anyone who is sick won't go on the raid,' he insisted sternly. Remarkably, his admonishment worked, and although the lingering smell of diesel fumes poisoned the already fetid air when submerged, the men had all recovered by the second day. From then on Hasler kept them busy with regular briefings and organising kit and equipment, as his diary entries show. At 5.20 p.m. the ship's log indicates that they were 180 degrees west of Wolf Rock, ten miles distant, off Land's End:

Wednesday 2 December

[Dived between 7.20 a.m. and 7.10 p.m.] *Tuna* making south, area of Bristol Channel, Lands End. Slept most of day. 3 p.m. turned out troops and began to go through bags, restowing and sewing up again . . . Lecturing troops, who have all recovered. Parted company with *White Bear*. Proceeded dived. 7.10 p.m. surfaced. Speeding at night on the diesel engines.

Thursday 3 December

Dived all day. Lecturing troops all day. Examining photos of approach. Instructions for escape.

Friday 4 December

Dived all day. Lecturing troops all day. Subjects – the attack, résumé of complete orders, working out detailed timetables for the attack, and the first night's passage.

Hasler later prepared a detailed description of the orders he gave to the men during this phase. Just before hoisting out, Lieutenant Raikes would provide a last-minute estimate of the magnetic bearing and distance to the Point de la Négade, which the men would fix on their compasses. They would then paddle in two arrowhead formations of six Cockles (divided into A and B Divisions, each of three boats) until a mile offshore, when Hasler would determine, on the basis of the high-water mark, whether they would lie up on the east or the west bank. The purpose of this formation was that when the Cockles in A Division stopped, the three boats from B Division would come in behind and pair off, still in arrowhead, with their partner Cockles in A Division. A Division was to comprise *Catfish* (Hasler and Sparks), *Crayfish* (Laver and Mills) and *Conger* (Sheard and Moffatt). B Division comprised *Cuttlefish* (Mackinnon and Conway), *Coalfish* (Wallace and Ewart) and *Cachalot* (Ellery and Fisher).

During the first night's passage Hasler would give final instructions to Jack Mackinnon's B Division, which would then separate from A Division and operate independently for the remainder of the operation. This would give the raiders a greater chance of success if one division were discovered and eliminated. When they reached the target area *Catfish* and *Cuttlefish* were to concentrate on the west bank of Bordeaux docks; *Crayfish* and *Coalfish* the left bank, and *Conger* and *Cachalot* the north and south quays at Bassens.

Passage, of course, would be conducted only at night. Once through the relative shallows of the estuary mouth between the Pointe de Grave and Royan, the Cockles were to keep out of the buoyed channel but not too close to the shore to be a security risk. It was important for the men to remember that the Gironde and the Garonne were sensitive areas to the Germans: a close watch would be kept on the water, and German artillery and anti-aircraft batteries and defensive positions would be found along the riverbanks, well camouflaged and invisible at close range. When lying up during the day it was critical that the men did not move, even in apparently deserted areas. They could only move to stretch their legs after dark. Concealed sentries were required at all times.

Once the advanced base was reached the limpets would be fused, and cargo bags would be restowed to rebalance the Cockles now that the limpets had been moved; the breakwaters would be folded and compasses stowed. The Cockles were given both primary and secondary targets. The primary targets, the four largest merchant ships, were to receive two limpets each, all to be placed five feet under the waterline as follows:

1 A Division Boats – on the upstream end of each ship, one limpet just past amidships and the other midway between there and the upstream of the ship
2 B Division Boats – on the downstream end of each ship, one just short of amidships and the other between there and the downstream end.

In addition, both Hasler's and Mackinnon's boats would carry a specially designed explosive cable-cutter, to cut away the anchor of any vessel lying in midstream so as to beach her, but only on the return journey. Two limpets should be reserved for any such vessels if they were found during the approach to the targets. Secondary targets were allocated in case no primary objectives presented themselves. These included any large tankers in the target area (two limpets each); any smaller vessels (except submarines), and finally any vessels encountered during the withdrawal.

During the withdrawal the boats were to proceed downstream on the ebb with caution, avoiding the ship channel, the middle ground banks, and keeping away from the shore, none of which was an easy task. At low water they were to select a suitable place, land their two bags of escape equipment, destroy reserve buoyancy in the boat and scuttle it with all remaining equipment. They were then to proceed independently in pairs to Ruffec in accordance with the verbal escape instructions.

The journey to the Gironde held numerous hazards for HMS *Tuna*. The seabed was remarkably shallow for vast swathes of the extensive coastline, out to a considerable distance from the shore, forcing Raikes and Hasler to agree that the raiders would disembark some nine and a half miles offshore, a distance that would also reduce but not eliminate the chances of detection by the German radio detection-finding (RDF) station that was known to be at Soulac together with any rudimentary radar the Germans might have scanning the coast. Even at long range, however, the surfaced metal bulk of the submarine would stand out like an aircraft in a clear sky, distinct from the wooden sailing vessels of the French fishing fleet. This was exacerbated by the fact that the shallow waters, out to the 100-fathom line, were very heavily fished by French fishing boats operating the entire length of the Atlantic coast. The war had dramatically increased the demand for fish because productivity on the land had dropped considerably with so many men still in German custody, and any vessel capable of staying afloat was pressed into this service. This, of course, dangerously increased the chance of detection for a submarine. Raikes described the task of avoiding the hundreds of sailing vessels as 'horrible':

> On one occasion I think that there were ten of them within two miles of me. And of course being fishing boats they were facing north one minute, east the next. I think the important thing was that my orders at that stage were that it didn't matter what happened, but I must not be seen, which would obviously affect the secrecy of the operation . . . So I spent at least two nights dodging these bloody tunny fishing boats.

Another worry was the presence off the Gironde of mines scattered by the RAF in an effort to hinder shipping movement. HMS *Tuna* had been demagnetised three times before the operation, in a process called 'degaussing', but the accuracy of records made by RAF aircrews of where mines had been sown was regarded with deep scepticism by their naval colleagues. The task of threading one's way through these hazards was a nerve-racking one. It was known that the Germans sent observers to sea with the fishing fleet, and detection would have roused the air defences along the coastline like a swarm of angry hornets, not to mention the small armada of destroyers protecting the Gironde itself. The result of striking a mine, German or British, was not to be contemplated. Raikes also remembered, from his time in HMS *Talisman* in these waters in 1940, that the currents and water densities behaved strangely. With a periscope depth of 38 feet, Raikes tried repeatedly to trim the vessel so that it remained steady at this level, but sudden changes in the density of the sea water foxed him. On Saturday 5 December he noted in his diary: 'Inexplicable density layers today. Perfect trim at 30 feet became . . . heavy at 35 – entailed blowing ballast and not holding *Tuna* until 150 feet.' An uncontrolled descent of 115 feet was an uncomfortable experience: more than once the seabed intervened to halt the descent in a juddering shock.

*

HMS *Tuna* reached the French coast off the Gironde on the night of Friday 4 December 1942, and surfaced, rolling heavily, amidst a vicious storm. The low grey skies that came down to meet the white-topped waves persuaded Hasler that their disembarkation would have to be delayed at least until the following night, in the hope that the weather might improve. In any case, Raikes could not secure a fix visually with land or with the stars, so was not entirely sure of his exact position. That night, still on the surface and moving uncomfortably from side to side with the deep Atlantic swell – an action that seemed to balance out, for the troops still unused to this type of motion, the welcome fresh air pumped below – HMS *Tuna* patrolled, far enough out to avoid the pestilential curse of the Biscay fishing fleet. Saturday dawned grey and wet, with no let-up as *Tuna* slipped beneath the waves to continue her lonely vigil submerged, away from the prying eyes of any patrolling German aircraft. Hasler used the day profitably, however. His diary records:

> *Saturday 5 December*
> Dived all day.
> a.m. Troops stand off. Self and Mackinnon continue working out detailed timetable and study photographs.
> p.m. Lecture troops on timing of first night and of attack.
> Evening. Mackinnon lectures troops on coastal features around second lying up place. Then spending evening writing up fair copy of orders and studying advanced bases.

The weather remained difficult on Sunday 6 December, and a further delay was agreed between Hasler and Raikes. Identifying his precise location was critical for Raikes, and yet the absence of any clear landmarks, combined with the weather – heavy sea mist had replaced the storms of the previous day – was making it hard for him to be certain enough of where he was to ensure the safe disembarkation of the Royal Marines.

At 1 p.m. landfall was sighted, and an estimated position was recorded to be 'just north of Hourtin lighthouse'. Raikes noted somewhat poetically in his diary: 'Landmarks do not exist or have been removed by the Germans and the charts are as much good as a midwifery course to a rabbit.' In fact the weather by now was perfect, with a heavy sea mist shrouding the area, but ironically it was the same mist that prevented him from taking an accurate astrofix or gaining visual confirmation of their exact location. During the day heavy aerial activity was noted in the ship's log. Raikes did not consider the enemy aircraft were looking for him, however. If they had been, he observed, 'they would have found me in only 30–40 feet of water'.

At 9.27 a.m. an Arado floatplane was spotted. These were small ship-borne reconnaissance aircraft found on German raiders and sometimes used to support coastal defences. The next morning the officer of the watch noted in the ship's log: 'Intense air activity by Arados, JU88, ME109, ME110 and Dorniers.' Raikes's diary likewise commented: 'Many aircraft seen all day. Dornier 18, Arado, 88, ME110 and ME109.' This would have been a mixture of bombers returning to their bases following anti-sea operations, as well as routine aerial security patrols to protect the mouth of the Gironde. The three main aerodromes were at Bordeaux–Mérignac (Focke Wulf 200), Hourtin (Arado 196) and Royan at the mouth of the Gironde (Heinkel 59). Claude de Baissac also reported to London that a considerable amount of flight training took place out of Bordeaux, which would have contributed to this volume of traffic.

HMS *Tuna* spent the whole day submerged, surfacing at 7 p.m. about three miles offshore to spend the night moving from south to north along the coast before submerging to periscope depth again at 7 a.m. on Monday the 7th, which Geoffrey Rowe described as 'a brilliant sunny day'. The surface of the sea had been empty until fishing vessels from the Bordeaux fleet were observed at 4.57 a.m. The submarine had to exercise the utmost diligence to remain undetected – a problem, given the remarkable shallowness of the seabed, the conspicuousness of the periscope and the fact that, as the water was heavy with plankton, the wake of the vessel stirred up telltale luminescence. They had to trust that the minds of the fishermen would be on securing the day's catch.

Raikes finally succeeded in fixing his position about lunchtime. The very conspicuous water tower in Montalivet village, amidst the red roofs, together with the Cordouan lighthouse and the St Nicolas beacon, enabled him to plot his exact position for the first time. It was a relief, accompanied by the onset of much calmer weather. The prospect of disembarking his passengers now appeared possible for the first time. Soon after he had fixed his position he talked it over with Hasler, and both men agreed to prepare for the operation that night. They also agreed a precise location from which to launch the canoes. Preliminary trials at Inchmarnock clearly showed that it was unlikely the whole operation would take less than an hour to complete without damage to the boats (thirty minutes to assemble them, forty-five to disassemble). The original plan was to unload them on to the deck while the submarine was out at sea, before trimming down and travelling to the disembarkation point, close to the entrance to the estuary, on the surface. Raikes described the process:

> It was tentatively decided therefore that I should try to surface in about position 45 degrees 27 minutes North, 1 degree 35 minutes West to assemble boats on fore casing at full buoyancy; then trim down and approach the Gironde, finally disembarking in about 45 degrees North, 1 degree and 23 minutes West. This would only mean being stopped for about 45 minutes. This position was considered to be the closest possible from my point of view, and the furthest possible from the point of view of the Military Force, to the Gironde.

Hasler had carefully written out the disembarkation procedure in note form for the men to rehearse while in the submarine. The entire process was to begin four hours before disembarkation, when the crews would build up each of the canoes, one by one. Buoyancy bags were to be inflated, then: 'Paint patches. Put on modified operational clothing. Load boats with B. Bags; paddles, 4 and 5 bags [containing dry clothes and escape kit]; compasses. Grease hatches (breakwaters down). Stow boats in ready use position. Eat and drink. Complete operational clothing.'

At 3 p.m. the canoes were removed from the torpedo tubes, and then opened up. The fore and aft buoyancy bags were inflated and the no. 4 and 5 bags stowed away. Hasler's diary noted calmly that he had a sleep in the afternoon, before talking to the men at five, and they ate a final hot meal from the galley in the submarine at 5.45 p.m. They were all set to disembark. By this time the sea had settled to the consistency of a millpond. The mist had cleared and the evening threatened to be cold but clear and still. In fact, Hasler worried that the 'visibility was too good for comfort'. He would have preferred the sea mist to hide the Cockles as they entered the estuary.

But a further difficulty had presented itself. Sitting off the Gironde during the late afternoon Lieutenant Johnny Bull, who was officer of the watch, spotted through the periscope at 6.10 p.m. a German patrol vessel exiting the estuary entrance some five thousand yards distant and loiter conspicuously between Soulac and the Cordouan lighthouse, precisely where Raikes had intended to disembark his camouflaged saboteurs. Bull handed the periscope to Raikes.

Raikes knew from his intelligence briefing that there were six minesweepers in the Gironde, together with a number of small destroyers and about twelve torpedo boats. All could be expected to contribute to surface patrols off the estuary. After watching the stationary vessel for some time he concluded that they needed to change plan. The disembarkation would need to be carried out further from the estuary mouth, so he reluctantly turned the vessel south to halt three miles off Montalivet-les-Bains. This was in the midst of the supposed RAF minefield, so taking the risk that the degaussed submarine would not offer any magnetic attraction to any unswept mines still lurking in the water. 'I don't think those mines could have been laid in a more embarrassing position as they seemed to interfere with every possible plan of action from the very start,' wrote Raikes. 'This plan quite evidently required extreme accuracy in navigation even allowing for the rather touching faith of the authorities in the accuracy of the positions given by the RAF – a faith which I did not share.'

The Royal Marines would need to canoe along the coast rather than directly into the mouth of the Gironde from Cordouan, although the much reduced distance they would need to paddle pleased Hasler considerably. This closer position to land meant an extra hour of flood tide to help the canoeists through the estuary and into the river, but it also entailed them having to travel parallel to the coast, with the waves breaking on the beach to their right. At least the submarine would not be seen by the watching Germans, as in its trimmed-down state the darkened boat would only show its conning tower and main deck which, at a distance, would be invisible to the enemy vessel against the darkness of the sea. The only added danger was that, because the submarine was now much closer to shore, and away from the main channel that entered the estuary, it would show up like a bonfire in the night on the German radar at nearby Soulac.

At 7.13 p.m., sitting at periscope depth, Raikes asked Hasler, who was dressed in his combat smock and with blackened face liberally daubed from a tub of new camouflage cream that the RMBPD had trialled at Southsea only six weeks earlier: 'Are you willing to go?' The firm reply: 'Yes.' 'OK,' replied Raikes, ordering Bull to surface.

Gradually releasing ballast, HMS *Tuna*'s conning tower broke surface and the submarine trimmed so that the deck was a matter of a foot or two above the water. It was now 7.17 p.m. Two minutes later both engines were stopped. In the conning tower, Hasler turned to Raikes and shook his hand. 'Book a table at the Savoy on April 1st,' he told him. 'Not on your life,' Raikes replied. 'I'll book a table on March 31st or April 2nd.' Raikes was struck by Hasler's calm confidence. 'Blondie never ever showed emotion,' he remarked. 'He was a consummate professional. For him it was just the next job.' Geoffrey Rowe, HMS *Tuna*'s pilot, provided a detailed account of the disembarkation:

> Darkness had only just arrived when we surfaced. The Skipper, the First Lieutenant and myself went to the bridge, with three look outs. 'Pilot, get up the periscope standards and keep your eyes skinned' said the Skipper. I climbed the rung ladder aft to the rear standard and sat on top – this brought me about 15 feet higher than the other eyes with consequently a further horizon. From that position I could see the Boom Defence vessel showing faint signal lights, but otherwise my binoculars found nothing to report. The sub was not blown up to full buoyancy. The fore hatch opened and up came the canoe and two men, fleet of foot but silent. They brought their small craft beneath the muzzle of our 4-inch gun which, like the jib of a crane, protruded beyond the bridge structure. To the muzzle of the gun the First Lieutenant and Coxswain hurriedly affixed a sling which the former had made, of such a length that with the barrel of the gun depressed the cradle rested on the casing and the Marines could lay their canoe in it, and get in. Slowly the gun was elevated as *Tuna* was flooded a little deeper; the gun was traversed to starboard carrying the manned canoe and, when it was at right angles to the sub the gun was again depressed enabling the Marines to paddle away, and lay off waiting. Using low pressure air blowers to keep down noise, the Skipper brought *Tuna* partially up again and the routine was repeated four times further.

Despite the hours of preparation at Inchmarnock, the canvas side of *Cachalot* was ripped badly by the same catch that had snapped *Coalfish* during training the week before as it was passed up by members of the submarine crew. The boats were passed up part-loaded, with the no. 4 and 5 bags already on board, the crew and remaining three bags then being loaded on the wet and shifting deck. By this time *Catfish* with Hasler and Sparks had been launched, and was waiting off *Tuna* to be joined by the remainder of the boats. It was immediately clear to

Raikes's orders were unequivocal: responsibility for the Cockles during disembarkation lay with the him. 'The two Marines were devastated,' he recalled. 'They were almost in tears, but I was quite adamant I was not going to let them go. It was my decision at that stage because it would have given away the whole operation if they'd been picked up swimming.' Hasler, bobbing on the sea alongside *Tuna*, agreed. Hasler told the two men: 'You can't come in this. Bad luck. Take the boat below again. You will have to go back with the submarine.' Eric Fisher broke down and cried. Bill Ellery pleaded with Hasler: 'It's a calm night. We won't hold you up – I can mend the tear while Fisher bales. Between us we'll catch up.'

Reluctantly but firmly Hasler refused, the wounded *Cachalot* was reshipped and the men could only watch helplessly from the deck as their comrades were lifted out, one by one, and placed gently on the calm sea. Then, at 8.22 p.m., after the matelots whispered farewell to the Royal Marines (who, much to Hasler's annoyance when he subsequently discovered it, had saved up their rum ration and secretly given it to their comrades in medicine bottles), the ten camouflaged men vanished into the night. Rowe:

> 'Clear the bridge' ordered the skipper. Lookouts disappeared below. I came down from twenty minutes of numbing periscope standard and we turned south to retrace our passage. As I landed on the bridge deck I saw the searchlights probing the surface at the river's mouth.

By 8.30 p.m. the sea had washed over the place where, minutes before, HMS *Tuna* had sat atop the waves. The only evidence remaining of her presence, as she sought the sanctuary of the deep, was a swirling patch of phosphorescence. Moved, Raikes wrote in his diary that night: 'The keenness shown by the Marines was an inspiration, and I hope very much to have a reunion with them by and by.' He continued:

> Operation completed in a time that reflects very great credit on Lieutenant Bull and his upper deck hands. Waved 'au revoir' to a magnificent bunch of black-faced villains with whom it has been a real pleasure to work.
>
> I should like to place on record the outstanding cooperation and spirit of the whole Marine contingent carried for this operation and in particular of Major HG Hasler OBE GM [sic] Royal Marines whose example and courage were of the highest order.

Within a few hours of disembarkation two of those courageous Marines would be dead, and a further two washed up on shore and taken prisoner a few short days before meeting their deaths at the hands of a German firing squad.

Once under way, Raikes dictated a simple message to be sent to the Admiralty. It arrived on Admiral Sir Max Horton's desk the following afternoon: 'Operation Frankton completed at 9 p.m. 7 December.' German radio detection units on the coast picked up a signal at 6.49 p.m. (5.49 p.m. GMT), which they identified as coming from 'naval grid square NF 9440'. The presence of HMS *Tuna* had been spotted, although it was to be some time before the Germans were to recognise the significance of this information.

ELEVEN

The First Night

Hasler's post-operational report described in his precise, detailed manner the story of the first few hours after pulling away from HMS *Tuna*:

> The five cockles MKII moved off . . . led by *Catfish* steering 035 degrees magnetic to pass two miles to the west of La Pointe de Grave. Weather oily calm with low ground swell. No cloud. Visibility good with slight haze over the land. At about 11.50 p.m. the boats passed over the Banc des Olives, whose presence was evident from sounding the way in which the ground swell began to build up into steep rollers over the shallows.

The night was too clear for his liking, but the sea was calm and the fifteen-mile journey north, skirting the coast, meant a problem-free start to the operation, to make up for the disappointment of leaving without Bill Ellery and Eric Fisher. Hasler noted that these rollers over the relative shallows of the Banc des Olives would have been dangerous if the boats had been a little further inshore. Far to the right he could hear in the distance a low rumble where the south-western swell, barely perceptible offshore where the canoes were travelling, built up into steep rollers when the water shallowed to about three fathoms, and broke heavily on the western side of the Le Verdon peninsula.

The heavily laden craft, riding low in the water, were

exhausting for even the fittest men to propel for long distances, which had led Blondie during training to institute a formal five-minute rest for every hour of paddling. After the first fifty-five minutes, therefore, he gave the signal – the palm of one hand flat on his head – to raft up. Sergeant Sammy Wallace had suffered a bout of seasickness, but otherwise everyone was in good spirits. Setting off again, the canoeists could now feel the force of the flood tide pulling their boats irresistibly towards the mouth of the estuary, and noticeably hastening the pace of travel. Hasler changed course to take the party further eastwards so that they followed the line of the coast, now clearly visible about one and a half miles away on the right-hand side. They had now been paddling for three and a half hours. After a while Sparks, sitting in the rear crew seat, realised that *Catfish* was leaking. The leak was not large, but nevertheless necessitated bailing out during each of the hourly breaks.

At about midnight Hasler suddenly heard a disquieting booming sound breaking the rhythmic slap of the bow wave on the sides of the canoe, and the regular if muffled splash of the paddles as they dipped and strained through the water. This was not the sound of the breakers off the beach, but something much, much closer. A spasm of anxiety surged through him. Immediately stopping, he and Sparks strained to identify the sound, the other canoes in formation around them quickly doing the same. The flood tide was pulling them on, even without their help, and as they drew nearer the sound grew rapidly louder.

Hasler was shocked. It was a roaring of *breakers*, coming not from their right, where they might have expected them as the sea broke over shallows near the shore, but *directly ahead*. He tried to tell himself he was mistaken, but he knew at once what it was. Astride their track, where the swollen waters collided and clashed in their frantic haste to pass over the shallows, they were confronted by a foaming cataract known to sailors as a tide race. He had experienced this before, at Start Point, Portland Bill and St Albans

Head on the south coast of England, though not in a canoe. It was frightening enough in an ordinary boat. A naturally occurring phenomenon, races occur when fast-moving tides, such as the one that was even now forcing their canoes in the direction of the Gironde estuary, pass over a constriction such as a shallow sandbank, forcing the waters together and creating potentially dangerous eddies, waves and even whirlpools.

Hasler knew that none of his novice canoeists would ever have encountered anything like it. Even worse, because no such threat had been envisaged during planning (there was no mention of tide races to warn him, either on the charts or on the Admiralty's Bay of Biscay pilot), no instructions had been given to the men as to how to deal with this type of threat. The darkness would add to the terror. The group was suddenly in serious danger. It looked as though the mission faced catastrophe before it had even begun.

The five canoes were by now all bunched up together, the men holding on to the gunwales of the craft next to them, open-mouthed at the increasing cacophony in front of them. *Catfish* was at their head, facing the oncoming storm. Somehow Hasler had to warn them, without starting a panic, of the perils ahead. The tide was carrying them swiftly forwards, and the roar in their ears was swelling to such a crescendo that it was plain they hadn't much time. Hasler estimated later that he had had about two minutes to warn his men of the danger they faced and to explain as best he could how to deal with this unexpected threat.

'What you hear is a tide race,' he shouted back over his shoulder, above the now deafening roar of the waves. He was not even able to turn his craft around, to face them. He shouted, hoping that they would hear, understand, and act. 'The waves will rush at you from all directions and they may be four or five feet high. Somehow we must keep head-on to the worst of them. I'll go first, the rest of you follow one by one. We'll meet up on the far side.'

They had barely braced themselves when the tide race was upon them. Against the flimsy, heavily laden canoes the turbulence burst like a deluge. Hasler and Sparks hit the frothing cauldron bows-on but were instantly tossed about in the warring currents. Yet, as suddenly as they were drawn into the maelstrom they were through it. Hasler observed with relief that the Cockle proved quite able to weather the storm provided it was kept head into the waves and the cockpit cover was securely fastened.

Restraining their canoes as best they could on the far side with their double paddles, the two men waited to rendezvous with the others. Three boats quickly followed them through. They waited for the fourth, but there was no sign of *Coalfish*. The crew, Sergeant Sammy Wallace and Bob Ewart, had vanished. They waited silently, the Cockles bobbing on the seething surface, watching anxiously for sight of their comrades. But there was no sight or sound of them. Their disappearance was inexplicable. Even had they capsized, they would have been swept through the tide race with their flooded canoe. They all carried special signalling whistles that imitated the mournful cry of a seagull. Sparks sounded the call repeatedly, but no answer came. Hasler concluded that Wallace must have turned landwards to avoid the vortex of the tide race and been washed ashore.

In his post-operation report written in April 1943 he remained unsure of what had become of the crew. 'Since both men and the boat had buoyancy equipment, it seems possible that they had not capsized, but had turned further inshore on finding themselves separated from the remainder. Nothing further was heard of this boat.' Hasler, who was taking sextant readings regularly because his compass was proving unreliable, possibly due to the presence in the canoe of the eight limpet mines, later estimated the position of the first tide race to be 45 degrees 31 minutes north, 1 degree 10 minutes west, almost 1.875 miles (3 kilometres) due west of Soulac-sur-Mer and four hours before high-water mark. 'This entailed heavy overfalls with waves four feet high and with breaking crests,' Hasler recorded. All the crews had been briefed to carry on independently if they lost formation, and Wallace and Ewart would do that if they could. Above all Hasler hoped that they could avoid capture, as at least three days lay ahead for the remaining canoeists, and any hint to the Germans that their ships in Bordeaux were at risk of commando attack would compromise the entire operation.

'We'll have to go on,' Hasler ordered grimly, when he realised that Wallace and Ewart would not be rejoining them. Of the six Cockles that were to participate in the raid, only four remained. One can only imagine what was going through Hasler's mind – within four hours of HMS *Tuna* surfacing he had lost one third of his force.

But the night's problems were far from over. The remaining canoes – *Catfish*, *Conger*, *Cuttlefish* and *Crayfish* – continued their steady approach to the estuary, reluctantly leaving their friends to their fate, in part because of the inexorable pull of the flood tide. They were nearing the mouth of the river, and ahead they could see the tall outline of the lighthouse at the Pointe de Grave, their turning point, mercifully unlit. The island of Cordouan, too, was in darkness. However, just as they began to think that the worst was over they heard the unmistakable sound of a second tide race, again, directly ahead. Barely an hour had passed since the last one, Hasler's meticulous sextant work recording that they were now at 45 degrees 33 minutes and 30 seconds north, 1 degree 6 minutes and 30 seconds west.

Again they scarcely had time to brace themselves before they were swept into it like flotsam. This time the overfalls were similar but the waves were more severe, at five feet high. Hurled into the rapids broadside on, Hasler and Sparks were saved only by frantic paddling and by the secure fastenings of the cockpit covers, which kept out the water. Once through the tide race they stopped paddling, breathing exhausted sighs of relief. They watched as two boats were seen to hurtle through the foaming surf, drawing up alongside *Catfish*. Then the third arrived, bursting free from the corrugated whirlpool of eddies as though fired from a gun. Hasler thought that he had heard a shout: he was right. It was the flooded and capsized *Conger*. Clinging to it were the crew, Corporal 'Jan' Sheard and Marine David Moffatt. These two men, with Sergeant Wallace, were the comedians of the party and, even as they gasped with the bitter chill of the December sea, they managed a grin. 'We're OK,' they said. 'Hold onto the other canoes, then,' Hasler told them, his heart sinking at the capsizing and possible loss of yet another crew.

The cruel sea was doing huge damage to his force, before they even had a chance to come to grips with the enemy. 'We'll tow your canoe,' he said. 'If we can get you inshore you can empty and refloat it.'

But turning inshore proved impossible as the flow accelerated through the estuary mouth, and they crabbed through it in confusion. It was impossible to bail out the flooded *Conger* as they raced along, but Hasler hoped to beach it when they got into the Gironde. Meanwhile, towing one canoe and with two men in the water, they were rapidly approaching their biggest hazard so far, the patrols and sentries at the mouth of the river. The tide carried the party round the Pointe de Grave, no more than a quarter-mile offshore, then through a third, but less violent tide race, where the waves reached three feet. 'Hold on!' Hasler shouted to the men in the water. Somehow they negotiated it, with Sheard and Moffatt, half paralysed now by cold but supported by their lifejackets, still gripping on desperately. Then, as the flood tide swept them round the point and into the river, the revolving beam of the lighthouse, with its 25,000 candlepower, lit up the darkness with startling intensity, blinding the canoeists and lighting the estuary like day. It was now 2 a.m. on the morning of 8 December.

With the whole operation now under serious threat of discovery, Hasler redoubled his efforts to tow the waterlogged *Conger* and its shivering crew to the shore. But the encumbrance was just too great. Try as he might, he could make no headway against the current with the capsized canoe behind acting as a sea anchor, preventing any forward motion against the current. Regardless of how hard they paddled, the current was still sweeping them parallel with, rather than towards, the shore. The only thing to do was to cut the enfeebled canoe adrift, and allow the crew to swim to the shore. They would have to take their chances of capture. All the while the Pointe de Grave lighthouse illuminated the surface of the estuary, but as yet no hue and cry had erupted. Hasler knew that the lighthouse was designed to provide guidance to vessels in the far distance, not act as a searchlight to spot local intruders, and from the silence he deduced that the lighthouse keeper was not, for the moment at least, looking in their direction. The minute he did so, however, or if patrolling sentries looked in their direction, the game would be up.

Hasler made up his mind – there was only one thing to do. 'Sink the canoe!' he ordered sharply. Sparks slashed at the canvas sides with his knife but the built-in buoyancy defeated him, the boat refusing to disappear under the water. They were forced to cut it adrift, Sheard grabbing the back of Laver's boat and Moffatt clinging to the back of *Catfish*. But the two men were now effectively themselves acting as sea anchors, and neither canoe could make headway towards the shore against the grip of the current.

At the Gironde estuary between Le Verdon on the south bank and Royan on the north, the Germans had garrisoned anti-ship and anti-aircraft artillery and naval patrol vessels, as well as setting up airfields and radar. The records of the German 708 Infantry Division, responsible for the defence of the coast, make it clear that HMS *Tuna* was spotted between 7.17 and 8.30 p.m. when she had surfaced off Montalivet. At 9.50 that evening (8.50 p.m. GMT)* Major Beyer of the Luftwaffe, based at the Pointe de Grave,† reported

* From 2 November 1942 to 29 March 1943 the Germans used the standard Mitteleuropäische Zeit (Middle-European Time, MEZ), which equated to GMT plus one hour. Thus the German clocks in Bordeaux were an hour ahead of HMS *Tuna*'s. This difference makes sense of the otherwise conflicting times between German accounts and those of HMS *Tuna*.

† Nine 20-mm guns and four searchlights.

to the Divisional Operations Officer the following message: 'Radar station W.310 has detected a ship 2.48 miles south-east of La Pointe de Grave. No further information.' As this was twenty minutes *after* HMS *Tuna* had dived, the delay must have been in the length of time it took to report the alarm.

In any event, it served to place the German defenders on the alert. The headquarters of 708 Division across the water at Royan sent a message to its battalion garrisoned at Soulac to exercise 'increased vigilance'. At 10 p.m. the HQ ordered Captain Panzel, duty officer of the Navy Artillery Division 284, responsible for the anti-ship artillery positioned along the peninsula, to turn on his searchlights. Twenty minutes later Panzel reported to the Duty Officer at Divisional HQ: 'Nothing to be seen, searchlight seen about 8 k.m. away, sighting likely to have been a fishing boat that has lost its way.'

The naval commander at Royan at the time was Korvettenkapitän Max Gebauer, ordinarily the commandant of the Naval Anti-Aircraft School in south-west France, who was standing in for Korvettenkapitän Lipinski, who had returned to Germany for three weeks' leave. In the early hours of the morning he was awakened by the news that the radar station at Soulac had detected a target out to sea. Gebauer promptly ordered that the lighthouse be switched on, and that other searchlights (including those normally used for anti-aircraft purposes) sweep the area of the coastline. 'This was done,' Gebauer reported, 'but without result.'

Hasler's tiny party, struggling to make headway in the heavy currents between La Pointe de Grave and the little fishing and ferry port of Le Verdon, remained undiscovered, despite a now alert enemy. Ahead of them on the near side of the river was Le Verdon, a mile or so distant, with the pier stretching out into the Gironde and blocking their path. If they went on trying to tow the men inshore they would all end up tangled in the pier, for that was where the current was sweeping them. Once again, Hasler gave the sign to raft up. Then he leaned over to talk to the two men in the water. 'I'm sorry but we'll have to leave you. Try to get to the shore and hide up. Then make your escape over land.' Even as he spoke he realised the hopelessness of it: the men were literally dying of cold. 'I'm terribly sorry,' he heard himself say. The effects of hypothermia would not be long delayed. 'That's alright sir,' stammered a near-frozen Sheard. 'Thanks for all you've done. And good luck.'

This time Hasler's voice failed him. Sparks caught a glimpse of his contorted expression in the sweep of the beam; he had never seen Blondie show emotion before. Grasping the gloved but frozen hands of the men in the water, Hasler knew that he, as their leader, was probably abandoning them to their death.

He then saw Corporal Bert Laver, No. 1 in the third boat, pull out what looked like a flask and thrust it inside Sheard's lifejacket. Somewhere in the rapids Sheard had lost his medicine bottle of rum. It was the first Hasler knew of the gift. At any other time he would have been furious at this defiance of orders, but now he blessed the submariners for it.

With sinking hearts the six remaining canoeists bade farewell to their comrades, wishing them Godspeed and promising to meet up at the end of the war. Drawing quickly away with the flood tide, Sheard and Moffatt were left in the water about one and a half miles south-east of the Pointe de Grave. With any luck, Hasler thought, they would be carried by the flood tide and washed ashore around Le Verdon pier. Some days later David Moffatt's body, together with *Conger*, was found far to the north, near La Rochelle. On the official German *Totenlist* (Death List) No. 128, part of the Third Reich's careful attention to the bureaucracy of death, is recorded the following: 'Body of Moffatt, David Marine PLY/X.108881 washed ashore 17.12.42, Le Bois Plage en Re, and buried on the Ridge of Dunes'. This date was later decided upon as that of Moffat's death. There is a story among the harbour personnel at Le Verdon that Sheard's body was found on the beach at La Pointe de Grave on 8 December, and taken to a German infirmary from where it subsequently disappeared. As the Germans were scrupulous note-takers, and as no written confirmation has been found, it is likely that this story will remain speculation.*

With time now against them Hasler realised that they had to keep moving. The lives of his men were important, but he was no longer in a position to help Sheard and Moffatt, and the delays so far were threatening to prejudice the entire mission. But by now the remaining six men were exhausted. It would simply not be possible, in the state they were in, to make their way across the currents sweeping the estuary to the planned lying-up place on the east bank of the Gironde, about twelve miles from the estuary mouth near Saint-Georges-de-Didonne, in the time available. With only three or four hours of darkness left, Hasler needed to think fast about reaching landfall and a safe lying-up place. They would need to find somewhere to hide on the more barren, exposed west bank, which Hasler had initially ruled out in his planning because of its lack of cover. The only option available, given the strength of the flood tide, was to pass by the pier at Le Verdon.

But therein lay a further threat. Half a mile off the pier-head were three patrol boats, which the men could see silhouetted in the distance against the night sky, yellow lamps blinking from the top of their superstructures. Hasler recognised them to be French Chasseurs – small destroyers – and they were anchored in line ahead as though ready for an inspection. There was no alternative to braving the channel between the ships and the pier.

There would be armed sentries on these ships, which they would have to pass one by one, as well as on the pier. They had reached the shadows of the lighthouse beam, but a blue light marked the extremity of the jetty, and they would be flooded with light from the Chasseurs if they were seen. Ahead lay the supreme test of their training and camouflage. In order to get through this defile

* I am grateful to M. Eric Poineau for this information. The Germans recorded a body being washed up at Les Sables d'Olonne at the same time, but they did not think it belonged to a saboteur.

unobserved, it was necessary to change to single paddles and proceed with caution, and the three boats separated to a distance of several hundred yards to lessen the chances of being seen. 'We shall go through individually in low position,' Hasler told the other two crews, 'using single paddles, three or four hundred yards apart. I'll go first, Corporal Laver in *Crayfish* second, and Lieutenant Mackinnon in *Cuttlefish* will bring up the rear. We'll meet up again 100 yards on the far side. But make sure first that I get through. If I'm caught, you must try something else. Remember, if only one cockle gets through, it may be enough.'

Separating the paddles, which fitted together in the middle, he and Sparks each stowed one half-paddle, fastened the canvas covers, leaned forward hard to flatten their silhouette, and single-paddled as stealthily as they could for the gap, letting the tide do most of the work, blades scarcely rippling the water. Sparks, peering under his eyebrows, caught sight of a sentry on the end of the pier and ducked down. They were immediately opposite the jetty when a signalling lamp on one of the destroyers, shattering their night vision, began winking messages to the man on the pier. Alerting him, surely? What else could it be? In any case he must have seen them. Hasler tried to tell himself that unless the defences were specifically looking for a canoe they might still get away with it. But in his imagination he could feel the bullets hitting his back.

When they felt they were safe Hasler and Sparks stopped to wait for the others. Laver and Mills came next as arranged, and they too got through. They rafted up with Hasler, and the four men waited for Mackinnon and Conway.

The twenty-one-year-old Glaswegian was taking his time – wisely, no doubt. Was he, perhaps, leaving it just a little too long? He should have been through by now. But as *Catfish* and *Crayfish* drifted gently upriver there was no sign of the third canoe. Then they heard a shout. They listened intently, but there was no further sound. It must have come from one of the destroyers. The signalling lamp would have alerted the sentry, too late perhaps to apprehend the first two canoes but delaying Mackinnon. There was absolutely no reason to think he had met with any mishap. He and twenty-year-old Jim Conway, his No. 2, were in excellent shape. The night was so still that any alarm or disturbance would have been audible. There had been just that single staccato shout, and then silence. Sparks tried his gull's whistle, and they strained their ears for an echo. None came. A second and third whistle were succeeded by the same empty silence. Could the shout have come from Sheard or Moffatt? Drifting with the tide, they could have overtaken Mackinnon. All Hasler knew was that Mackinnon and Conway could be trusted to follow them upriver, when their immediate problem was solved, and if necessary carry out an independent attack.

Once again Hasler put their recent experiences behind him. The time was 6 a.m., nine and a half hours since they had left the submarine, with dawn approaching and their planned lying-up place, four miles across the river, inaccessible. Time was now his enemy, not only because first light was beginning to seep through in the east but also because the tide would turn soon. If they didn't get ashore quickly they would be carried back to the river mouth, on the ebb, in daylight. Furthermore, the four men were now wet and exhausted, the near-freezing water soaking through their mittens and chilling them to the bone.

Turning to starboard to pick up the nearside bank, he steered the two canoes on a course of 196 degrees magnetic for a stretch of uninhabited shore that he recalled from the charts, and picked up the west bank of the estuary near the navigation channel known as the Chenal de Talais. The shore was shallow on this side, but it was almost high water and the canoe could make it all the way in. Hasler noticed there was a swell breaking with which they would have to contend. Then, as they headed in thirty minutes later, they encountered a row of half-submerged stakes on a shingle bank. Put there to reduce erosion, they offered an insurmountable obstruction as the groundswell breaking over them made them impossible to negotiate in safety, the stakes threatening to rip through the canvas side of an unwary canoe.*

Continuing upriver, obliged to paddle more vigorously now, they could detect no feasible landing place. Daylight was almost upon them when they spotted a narrow sandy promontory, pointing across the river like a finger, where above the high-water mark lay a rash of low scrub marked on the map as the Pointe aux Oiseaux.† The mudbanks extended for several miles along the west bank of the Gironde, and were separated from the farmland beyond by a tall dyke some twenty feet high, along which ran a path used extensively by local farmers and fishermen. It looked far from ideal, but it would just have to do. Stepping ashore, leaving the others sitting in the canoes ready for a quick getaway, Hasler did a rapid reconnaissance of the area. The bushes were too sparse for perfect concealment, but the camouflage nets they carried would help considerably. He could see no signs of habitation – 'Come on!' he called to the others.

Unlike conventional canoes, the Cockles, with their longitudinal stiffening and flat hulls, could be manhandled ashore, and after dragging them into the bushes they arranged the camouflage nets. Then, using their combat rations, they prepared a meal – their first, apart from the occasional biscuit, for more than twelve hours. Each pack, containing bully beef, tinned cheese, an oatmeal block with tea, powdered milk and sugar, together with chocolates and boiled sweets, was high in calories but unappetising, and needed to be heated through to provide nourishment. For this, miniature metal stoves containing solid fuel called 'Tommy cookers' were used, although clearly cooking could only take place when it was safe to do so.

Hasler relaxed with his men to the extent of taking a sip of the submariners' rum. Then, while the others slept, he took the first

* They remain there to this day, clearly visible at low water.

† This name was unknown to the locals. It is known locally and shown on maps as the Saint-Vivien Plage.

watch. It was 7.30 a.m. They had travelled twenty-three miles but it had been, unexpectedly, the toughest and most dangerous canoe journey of his life; and now only one-third of his tiny force – four men in two canoes – remained. At least three nights' travel and innumerable obstacles lay ahead. If any of these held as much danger as the night that had just passed, Hasler mused, there was no possibility of success. But one of Blondie's most striking personal attributes was his inability to be depressed or overwhelmed by failure, and he entertained no thought of doing anything other than persevering with his mission. If it meant travelling into Bordeaux with four men, or alone, so be it.

Scrutinising the surroundings, he was now able to take a better look at the wooden groynes, the stakes planted in rows across the mud that protected the upriver side of the promontory. Beyond the promontory a small creek, or canal, curved inland out of sight. From his map he could see that it led to the tiny hamlet of Saint-Vivien, three miles along the canal to the south. What Hasler did not know, however, was that Saint-Vivien was a fishing hamlet, the local fishermen travelling out every day down the canal at the start of the ebb tide and returning at the start of the flood. The life of the fishermen was governed by these twice-daily periods of high water. Only then was the creek navigable. Hasler's arrival on the promontory at high water had coincided with the departure from Saint-Vivien of around thirty small fishing boats. When Hasler first saw them some distance inland they gave the bizarre impression of travelling across land. The creek flowed into the river at a point away from their hide-out, and he was satisfied they would not be seen from the boats.

Suddenly, however, the situation changed. The boats, emerging from the creek, turned and approached the hide; and simultaneously a party of peasant women, burdened with baskets and children, emerged from a path beside the canal bank and advanced down the promontory in their direction. It was now 8.30 a.m.

Soon, adjacent to the promontory, the boats disgorged their fishing crews. In order to catch the tide the men had left early.

'Blondie' Hasler as a newly commissioned Royal Marine Second Lieutenant in 1932. (Mrs Bridget Hasler)

The photograph taken of Hasler in Barcelona in late March 1943 for his identity documents, which presented him as a travelling salesman. His luxuriant moustache, hacked off in Lyon in January on the orders of Mary Lindell, had already grown back to its former glory. (Mrs Bridget Hasler)

A photograph of Bill Sparks taken later in 1943 after he received the Distinguished Service Medal. (Getty)

Men of the RMBPD photographed off Southsea on 10 September 1942. (RMMC)

One of the collapsible Folbots used by the Army commandos, and rejected by Hasler for use by the RMBPD in preference to Fred Goatley's Cockle. (RMMC)

Two Royal Marines of the RMBPD in a Cockle MkII off Lumps Fort, Southsea. (RMMC)

Hasler and Stewart demonstrate 'walking' the flat-bottomed Cockle MkII off the beach. (RMMC)

Manhandling a Cockle through the torpedo hatch of a T Class submarine. (IWM)

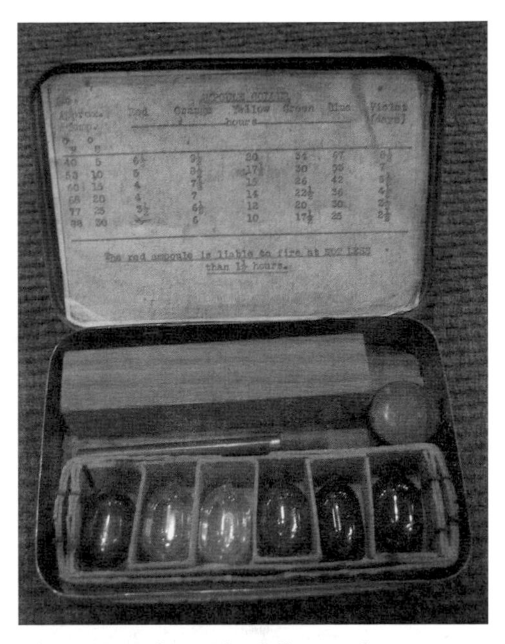

Glass Limpet fuses. The different colours represented varying delay timings. (Combined Military Services Museum)

A limpet mine. (Combined Military Services Museum).

A Cockle MkII preserved at the Combined Military Services Museum, Maldon, Essex (Combined Military Services Museum).

Lieutenant Richard Raikes RN, Officer Commanding Her Majesty's Submarine *Tuna*. (IWM)

HMS *Tuna*. (IWM)

The crew of HMS *Tuna* at firing practise with the vessel's 4-inch quick firing gun. (IWM)

The results of the raid. One of the ships in Bordeaux resting on the river bed after the attack. (Francois Boisnier)

Yves Ardouin (right), one of the oyster fisherman who met Hasler's party at the Pointe aux Oiseaux, with his wife and daughter after the war. The presence of the RM party remained a secret. (RMMC)

The elf carved by Hasler in hiding. (Mrs Bridget Hasler)

Irène Pasqueraud. (Mrs Bridget Hasler)

Clodomir Pasqueraud. (Mrs Bridget Hasler)

Hasler with Mr and Mrs Alibert Decombe of La Présidente Farm.

Hasler and Sparks in London in 1956.
(Mrs Bridget Hasler)

Mary Lindell, Comtesse de Milleville, in 1961.
(RMMC)

Blondie Hasler, Mary Lindell and Bill Sparks at a reunion in London, 15 June 1961.

At the unveiling of a memorial to the raiders in Bordeaux on 3 April 1966, Mary Lindell (third from left, front), Hasler and Sparks, met up with many of the French men and women who had helped them during their escape in 1942 and 1943.

Reunion at Windsor Castle, 15 June 1961, arranged by the Royal Marines to bring together the French helpers of the two survivors of Operation Frankton. Left to right: Mary Lindell, Clodomir Pasqueraud, Yvonne Mandinaud, Yve Rullier (with her daughter behind her), René Flaud, Jean Mariaud, Armand Dubreuille and Maurice de Milleville. (Getty)

Clear of the creek, which would dry out as the tide ebbed, they were ready for breakfast, which their women had come to cook, no more than fifteen yards from the hide. *Catfish* and *Crayfish* had been hidden in the middle of the spot of beach used every morning by the villagers for their breakfast. Such proximity made camouflage useless. Furtive looks, whispers, averted gazes spoke eloquently of the locals' embarrassment. It was a timely reminder to Hasler that he was in a defeated, occupied and partially hostile country, where the native population lived in fear. Meanwhile they would be taken for what they were – four highly suspicious characters, faces streaked with dark camouflage cream, with two odd-looking craft, and trying to hide, ineffectually, under a net in the bushes. The penalties for helping them, even for ignoring them, would be severe.

The only hope was that these simple fisherfolk had no love for the Germans and would not betray their presence to the occupying power. Realising that their cover was blown, it was now up to Hasler to make the first move. He stood up, calmly approaching the fishermen and their families who had unwittingly discovered them. 'Bonjour,' he began in his halting schoolboy French. 'We are British soldiers. We are your friends. Our presence here must not be revealed.'

Hasler had only one thought in mind: to persuade them to keep silent. Silence would be taken by the German occupation forces, if discovered, as traitorous, incurring penalties that included the death sentence. The suspicions of the normally conservative country folk were already aroused. The twenty-eight-year-old Hasler, with his bald head and fair, bristling handlebar moustache, looked too much like a stage Englishman. The whole set-up smelt like a trap. In addition, he was aware that he spoke French with a distinctive guttural accent. 'You are Germans!' one of the Frenchmen replied. The trick was too transparent. What would a tiny group of English soldiers be doing here on the Gironde? Where could they have come from? Where could they be going?

These were questions Hasler could not answer without giving the game away. 'All I can tell you is that we are British soldiers. We simply ask you to tell no one you've seen us. Wouldn't it be better anyway just to say nothing?'

Although this is nowhere recorded in Hasler's otherwise meticulous notes, the French historians François Boisnier and Raymond Muelle discovered evidence that the local fishermen persuaded him to move a short distance to a more secure location. One of them, Yves Ardouin, a local oysterman from Saint-Vivien-de-Médoc, told Hasler: 'If you want to hide, carry on upstream a further 220 yards and get into the next mouth of a small river. It doesn't lead anywhere. The canal where we are now is the Gua Canal which leads to the port of St-Vivien. It's used by other French fishermen and the Germans have a building site near here. As for your safety,' he added, 'I'll tell the other fishermen and it's obvious we won't say anything to others, but I can promise nothing.'

Hasler thanked them, and did as they suggested. The French were true to their word. The news of the hideaways quickly spread through the tiny village, but went no further. Presently the women and children strolled back home, while the men returned to their boats. 'We can promise nothing, M'sieur,' they repeated to Hasler as they left. The Royal Marines could do nothing but await their fate, and make themselves as comfortable, and inconspicuous, as possible.

TWELVE

The Garonne

Whatever their suspicions or their allegiance, the most sensible course for these fisherfolk to take, Hasler recognised, was to report what they had seen to the police. But since the French police were controlled by Vichy, and the Vichy government was collaborating with the Nazis, discovery and capture would then be almost certain. There was nothing further he could do. All day they waited and watched for a German patrol to appear, fingering their Colt 45s and the silenced Sten guns. When a light aircraft with Luftwaffe markings began circling their position, Hasler's worst fears seemed to be confirmed, but nothing came of it. His insistence during training on the highest standards of camouflage was bearing dividends.

At four that afternoon two figures approached their hide-out from inland. As they came into focus they proved to be two of the women who had come down that morning. Evidently they had decided to find out a bit more before their menfolk came home. To Hasler it seemed a remarkably brave act. He crept out of the hide to talk to them, and they chatted as freely as Hasler's limited grasp of the language would allow. The husband of one of them had been deported to Germany. Suddenly she said something in German and Hasler, caught off guard, replied, 'Ja.' 'So you are German!' the woman exclaimed. Hasler hastily explained that he had learnt German, too, at school. Afterwards Bill Sparks asked: 'Did they believe you?' 'One can hardly tell with women,' he replied, 'whether they believe you or not.' The two bachelors laughed. The women did tell him, to his disquiet, that German soldiers were working on the far side of the creek.*

The situation looked bad. They had been away from HMS *Tuna* for less than twenty-four hours, but in that time Hasler's effective force had been reduced to two canoes and sixteen limpets between them. Even worse, their presence had been revealed to the entire adult population of a French fishing village. They had no knowledge of what had happened to Sergeant Wallace, Corporal Sheard, Marine Ewart and Marine Moffatt, but had to assume that at least some were in German captivity. If that were the case, Hasler had no choice but to accept that the enemy were now aware of the threat to the blockade-runners in Bordeaux.

On the positive side, however, at least two fully equipped canoes had managed to survive the tempests of the first night. They had not, so far, been discovered by the enemy, and if the villagers of Saint-Vivien could be trusted there was every chance that the canoes could slip away into darkness on the new flood tide, leaving behind only memories. Assuming that nothing else untoward were to happen, Hasler considered that sixteen limpets were sufficient to deliver enough damage to the blockade-runners to judge the operation a success: after all, his original plan, before Mountbatten had ordered the number of canoes to be doubled, envisaged only three craft embarking on the enterprise. Hasler's relentlessly positive temperament allowed no space for doubt or pessimism: if Operation Frankton were to fail, he considered, it would only be at the hands of the enemy. There was absolutely no other reason for not pressing home his attack, even if he were the only man left alive to do so. This is precisely the instruction he had given his men while on HMS *Tuna*: to deliver their attack with resolution, even if they found themselves the last man standing.

* François Boisnier suggests that M. Ardouin also revisited the men during the afternoon, carrying bread and wine, although this is not mentioned in Hasler's detailed account.

They spent the rest of the afternoon in a state of nervous anticipation. As it grew dark the tired men's worst fears seemed to be realised. Out of the dim stillness ahead of them appeared a long line of men, advancing slowly towards them. Clutching their weapons they waited for the inevitable. Watching the grey-clad figures approach, Sparks thought they were going at last to meet their enemy: 'We waited and waited, then eventually as it got darker, the Major was watching through his glasses, then he began to chuckle. They were a load of invasion stakes that we had been watching, and in the dusk they looked like Germans.'

They now needed to get moving again. The next flood stream began at 11.30 p.m., which meant wasting some of the hours of darkness. After repacking, and removing or burying all traces of their stay, they began tugging their canoes across the slimy, glutinous mud that separated them from the river at low tide. Fully laden, their canoes were a hard pull for two men, and despite the bitter December cold they were sweating heavily when they got to the water's edge three-quarters of a mile from their camp, just as the flood tide began to flow. The Cockle's flat plywood bottom was ideally designed for this type of task, entirely vindicating the changes Hasler had insisted upon for the Mark II.

'Getting the boats clear of the shore was difficult owing to the large areas of outlying sand banks on which the ground swell was running in the form of small breaking rollers which had to be met head on,' Hasler recorded, 'but eventually we got clear and out into the shipping channel.' His plan was to cross to the east side of the river during the night and look for a hide-out before dawn on the far shore, which he knew was sparsely populated. The buoys marking the navigation channel were flashing a faint blue light, making navigation easy, and with the aid of his compass he kept them in view at about a cable length to the north-east. The weather was flat calm, no cloud, with good visibility although there was a haze over both shores. Hasler decided it was time to cross the channel. Halfway across, they spotted a ship heading upriver for Bordeaux, which forced them to hurry their stroke. When it overtook them they were so close they could see the reflection of the vessel's port light dancing on the ruffled surface of the water. In case there was someone on deck they froze into the well practised low profile, heads right forward, paddles still, until the danger was past.

At first they rested for five minutes in every hour, but as the night wore on and the temperature slumped, the salt spray from their bow wave froze on the cockpit covers, and they were glad to keep going. With the aid of the flood tide they were averaging four or five knots. Continuing on the same course, they eventually picked up the east bank just north of Portes de Calonges, and followed it about one mile off shore until the approach of daylight made it necessary to lie up. As they paddled along parallel with the shore, Hasler was able to make out the vague shapes of scattered farm dwellings through the darkness, and a wealth of hedgerows for cover.

With the last of the flood tide he took advantage of high water to step lightly ashore for a reconnaissance, and saw facing him the perfect hide-out – a deep trench with bushes on either side. They got the boats in against a thick hedge inside the ditch and placed the nets over them. They had covered twenty-two miles in seven and a half hours. They were on the east bank of the Gironde about one mile north of the Frèneau canal at Le Montalipan. Having dragged their canoes into the hide, they brewed tea on their tiny solid-fuel cooker and ate some of their primitive combat rations, before settling down for the day as dawn rose. It was 9 December. One man kept watch while the others slept. In the light they could see, according to Hasler's notes, a 'steam cargo ship in the floating dock on the west bank of the Gironde, opposite'. By standing up the sentry could just see a farmhouse through the hedges about four hundred yards away, and as on the previous day light planes with German markings disturbed their slumbers. But otherwise they were uninterrupted during daylight, in spite of the arrival of a herd of cows in the field.

They had thirty miles to go to Bordeaux. The next night's passage would be a difficult one, complicated by the many islands in the river. But the main problem was once again the tides. When darkness fell that evening there would be only three hours of flood tide remaining. After that they would have six hours of ebb, during which they would have to find an intermediate lying-up place, then make use of the three hours of flood tide they would get before daybreak. To lighten their loads they dispensed with everything they could spare, burying it in the ditch.

At twilight the weather was still flat calm, with no cloud. Visibility was excellent. Anxious to make the best possible use of the tide, they began manhandling their canoes over the riverbank while it was barely dusk. With one man at the top and one at the bottom they managed it without damaging the boats, but they got caked in mud and slime.

The four men at the top were still silhouetted against the sunset when an urgent shout froze them. The tenant farmer from the nearby Présidente Farm, Alibert Decombe, had come down towards the river to look after his cattle and had spotted them. Before leaving the hide they had blacked their faces, so they could hardly have presented a more sinister picture. Perhaps this was why the farmer believed Hasler's story when Blondie climbed back up the bank to greet him. From the outset Decombe exhibited genuine friendliness, seeming to understand immediately that he had stumbled upon a covert British operation. He never doubted the nationality of the black-faced, camouflaged men in front of him. 'It's cold!' he commented to Hasler. 'Why don't you and the men come up to the house for a drink?' Hasler politely declined, and after further polite if stilted conversation Decombe ambled back to the farmhouse and the Royal Marines, grateful that they had not been rumbled by a collaborator, got on with the business in hand. Hasler recorded: 'We repeated our story of the day before, and he seemed quite convinced by it, and was rather upset when we declined to go up to his house for a drink. "I'm sorry, M'sieur, but we have to get on. Will you be sure to tell no one you've seen us?" "I shall say nothing. You can depend on that."'

Once again they had encountered a patriot. Decombe didn't even tell his wife until after the war.

The course now lay between two islands, and as the waters grew more restricted they became uncomfortably conscious of the amount of noise the boats made when they paddled at cruising speed, the whoosh of their paddles and the slap of the bow wave echoing back at them from the darkened shore. Above them the river opened out to accommodate a sprinkling of islands as they approached the town of Blaye, ten miles upriver to their left. Hasler's plan was to cross the shipping channel again to the right-hand side of the river and run between the islands, using them as cover for their intermediate stop somewhere opposite Blaye. At about 8 p.m. they were bisecting the first two islands when the nocturnal silence was shattered by the roar of marine engines not a hundred yards ahead off the Ile de Patiras. A clump of reeds to their right offered the only hope of concealment, and they paddled vigorously towards it, any noise they might make drowned by the revving of engines.

Crashing into the reeds, they then moored in an almost impenetrable thicket, through which they could barely discern what was happening. But as the chug of the oncoming motor settled into a regular beat, they glimpsed a dark shadow passing their hide-out and heading downriver. Its furtive probing convinced them the search was still on. An island to their left seemed invitingly untenanted, but a smaller one to their right – Bouchaud, opposite St-Julien – looked even more desolate. Waterfowl scurried in all directions as they forced their way ashore and they were appalled at the commotion they made, but there was no one to hear. Hasler:

> 'Desert Island' proved to be covered in thick reeds six or seven feet high with occasional trees, but the landing was difficult owing to the vertical mud banks on which the reeds, for the most part,

> were almost impenetrable. After many attempts, at 8.45 p.m., we found a place where we could get ashore and where the boats could safely be left to dry out as the tide fell.

Determined to catch the first of the flood tide Hasler tried to get them launched again five hours later, just before 2 a.m. on 10 December, but the ebb tide had stranded them on a mudbank and it was a long and messy business getting the canoes to the water in the dark. At last they got going, and an hour later they were running down the seven-mile channel that separated the land to their right from Ile de Cazeau on their left. Somewhere on that island they would have to find a hide for the two remaining hours of darkness. The channel was so narrow that anyone standing on the bank would easily spot them, and they adopted their usual low position, using single paddles and leaning forward to reduce their silhouette, at the same time hugging the reeds fringing the island. They then proceeded across the ship channel and entered the shallow passage to the west of Ile Verte. Hasler:

> We saw no sign of life in this area, but as the passage was narrow we made ourselves as inconspicuous as possible by using single paddles and keeping right in close to the shores of the island, which are covered with tall reeds. By 6.30 a.m. we were approaching the southern end of the Ile de Cazeau, which lies just beyond the point where the Garonne and Dordogne rivers meet to form the Gironde (Bordeaux lies on the Garonne), and began to look for a lying up place on the island.

At length they spotted a small plank which seemed to give access to the shore. Hasler, fearful of where it might lead, traversed it gingerly. Then he followed an overgrown path through the trees until it came to a sand-bagged emplacement. It was a German anti-aircraft battery. Creeping back down the path he rejoined the others, but dawn was upon them, the riverbank was becoming more populous, and like it or not they would have to get ashore before they ran out of island. At 7.30 a.m. they finally landed on the extreme upriver tip, where cover was scarce. They would have done much better to stop earlier, but there was no time to turn back.

They found themselves on the edge of a marshy field grazed by cows. The very long grass lay in the middle, and they dragged their canoes to what proved to be scant and inadequate cover, doing the best they could with the camouflage nets. Sleep was impossible, and for all their craving for a smoke that too was unthinkable. It was going to be a nerve-racking few hours. All day Hasler and his men sat uncomfortably in the canoes, not daring to brew up and hard-pressed even to relieve themselves. It was bitterly cold, and a penetrating drizzle fell continuously.

During the afternoon they found themselves being slowly and ponderously encircled by a ring of cattle. Any attempt to drive the cows off could have been fatal, so the four men stayed dumb and immobile under their nets. To the light aircraft that passed overhead the cows must have stood like target indicators, but mercifully none of the pilots came down to investigate. A man walking at the edge of the field with his dog also failed to draw any inference, and perhaps because of the cows the dog did not pick up their scent. Sparks's account suggested also that two German soldiers wandered to the edge of the wood looking out into the field in which they were hiding, but after some heart-stopping moments they wandered away.

That very day, on the opposite side of the island, Jack Mackinnon and Jim Conway also lay hidden, having successfully negotiated their way past the waiting destroyers at Le Verdon and made their own independent journey up the Gironde.

Thus the men's third day in hiding faded into dusk. As they prepared for an early start, dark clouds gathered over the river, a breeze sprang up and it began to rain again. These were the conditions they wanted – pitch-blackness and the noise of the elements to deaden the sound of their progress. The attack on the ships was originally scheduled to take place that night, 10 December. But Hasler's tide calculations forced him to conclude that it was not possible to get high enough upriver to have any chance of withdrawing in darkness on the ebb tide after a successful attack. Another night of travel was required.

He planned to move that night to an advanced base nearer the target and thus make the attack on the night of the 11th. There was a risk, he thought, that one of the other crews might still be at large on the water somewhere and might be attempting an independent attack, as they had all been instructed, and that this attack might be mounted on the original date.

Catfish and *Crayfish* were duly launched at 6.45 p.m. on 10 December – with considerable difficulty, owing to the slippery near-vertical banks. The weather was good, Hasler recalled, cloudy with occasional rain and a moderate southerly breeze. For the first two miles they proceeded up the centre of the river, then changed to single paddles and followed close along the western bank which was lined with thick reeds. Both boats, swinging round a bend in the river at 10 p.m., caught their first glimpse of the docks at Bassens South, a mile away on the left-hand side of the river. This was the smaller of the dock areas, but under the arc lights they could see two sizeable ships – admirable targets, if there was nothing more attractive in Bordeaux. Suddenly ahead of him Hasler saw a pontoon pier, with what looked like a coaling lighter moored at the tip. Ducking their heads, they glided under the pier and somehow got by unseen, finding a small gap in the reeds into which they were able to force the boats. The reeds were between six and eight feet high, and provided the perfect camouflage. It was about 11 p.m. They had travelled eleven miles. 'As soon as the tide began to ebb, the boats dried out and we made ourselves comfortable for the night,' Hasler recalled.

Next morning, completely concealed and inaccessible from the bank, they were able, by standing up in the canoes, to monitor the river traffic and study the two vessels opposite. A cargo ship and a cargo liner (later identified as the *Alabama* and the *Portland*) anchored some way from the shore, they were scarcely more than half a mile distant. Hasler incorporated them into his revised plan. This was that *Catfish* would proceed along the western bank to the main dock on the west side of the river two miles further upstream in the heart of Bordeaux. Laver and Mills in *Crayfish* would cross to the east bank and so travel into Bordeaux on the other side of the river. If they found no suitable targets there they were to return downriver and attack the two ships at Bassens. There was no plan to rendezvous afterwards. Two men travelling across country might merge into the background. Four would arouse suspicion.

During daylight there were a good many small craft under way, chiefly tugs and harbour launches carrying workmen. Sparks recalled that the day was relatively comfortable, despite intermittent drizzle: they were able to brew hot tea on their Tommy cookers, smoke, and talk in low whispers. They rearranged the stowage of the boats so as to have all the escape equipment in two bags, and in the evening they completed the fusing of the sixteen limpets, two fuses on each – a time fuse at one end and a 'sympathetic fuse' at the other, designed to explode in the event that another limpet on the same hull went off prematurely. They readied the orange ampoules (giving a nine-hour delay) in the mines without activating them as yet, and removed the safety-pins from the water-soluble sympathetic fuses.

The miserable, drizzly weather unfortunately cleared up in the evening, and by twilight it was once again flat calm with a clear sky and good visibility. Owing to the fact that the moon would disappear after 9.32 p.m. Hasler considered it essential to delay leaving their lying-up place until 9.10 p.m., which was about thirty minutes later than would have been desirable from the perspective of the tides. High water was at midnight: they needed to have completed their attack before the start of the ebb tide, which would carry them quickly back towards Blaye. Accordingly, the time fuses were activated at 9 p.m.

They were committed to the attack. Shaking hands, Hasler and Laver wished each other good luck, promised to meet up one day in the Granada pub in Southsea, and at 9.15 p.m. pushed out from the reeds on the final leg of their journey.

THIRTEEN

Murder by Telephone

On the night of 7 December Max Gebauer welcomed Vice-Admiral Julius Bachmann to Royan. The Flag Officer in Command (FOIC) of HQ Naval Command Western France, based at Nantes on the Loire, Bachmann was to undertake an inspection of the land, sea and air garrisons, and watch the test-firing of batteries on the Gironde estuary due to take place on 8 and 9 December. Bachmann was not well liked by his subordinates. Nearing his retirement, it seemed to his staff that his primary concern extended merely to the enthusiastic obedience of orders.

In preparation for Bachmann's visit the three small French destroyers of the estuary defence flotilla had been drawn up in inspection array off Le Verdon pier. Bachmann, together with his Chief of Staff (Captain Franz Bauer), adjutant (Lieutenant Frass) and aide-de-camp (Lieutenant Heinz-Günther Lell), plus staff officers from both headquarters, would cross to Le Verdon by civilian ferry the following morning. Breakfast provided Gebauer with the opportunity to brief Bachmann on the radar reports that had come through during the night. The Navy was always interested in the effects of radar, and the apparatus at Soulac, which provided a detection range of between fifteen and twenty miles out to sea, was considered an important element of the Atlantic coast defences.

Then, at 8 a.m., the telephone rang. It was Oberleutnant Wild, the commander of the harbour defence flotilla across the estuary mouth at Le Verdon. Wild reported that two Englishmen had been seized by a Luftwaffe anti-aircraft unit at 5.30 a.m. in Le Verdon itself. Gebauer considered the news, and discussed it with Bachmann. The admiral was immediately interested. Nothing warlike ever happened in his area, so here was something that added a certain frisson to his visit. Perhaps it had something to do with the radar report from Soulac the previous night? As he and Gebauer would be crossing over shortly from Royan on the ferry, he instructed that he wanted to meet the two prisoners after the inspection of the three destroyers. The men were then to be escorted to Royan, and there interrogated by officials from the Abwehr's Section M (naval counter-intelligence), who would travel up from Bordeaux to undertake a proper questioning of the captives.

What had happened to *Coalfish* and her crew? Sergeant Sammy Wallace and Marine Bob Ewart had capsized in the first tide race, and been swept ashore on to the beach at Soulac some 330 yards short of the Pointe de Grave and directly in front of an unoccupied German artillery battery site. Freezing cold and separated from their canoe, they were without any of their escape kit or maps. In fact, they had nothing but what they stood up in. Disoriented too, and unwilling to surrender, they decided to try their luck by knocking on the door of one of the houses scattered across the sandy promontory. The only other likely option, in their state, was a rapid descent into hypothermia. They walked some distance through the dark, struggling in their weakened state through the pine forests that covered the peninsula, towards the outskirts of the port at Le Verdon. They were not to know that many of the houses on the promontory were empty at this time of year, being holiday homes; nor that they had stumbled unwittingly into one of the most heavily defended areas of the Atlantic coast.

The responsibility of the 708 Infantry Division, the coastal area was heavily garrisoned with a miscellany of units including an anti-aircraft battery (Flak Unit 595), an infantry battalion at Soulac, naval units guarding the estuary mouth and naval artillery units manning the shore defences. These last included anti-ship artillery in newly built concrete gun emplacements, together with searchlights. The 708 Division had been formed in May 1941 specifically for the defence of the area between Royan and Bordeaux, and comprised 728 and 748 Infantry Regiments (with six battalions between them), 658 Artillery Unit, 708 Pioneer Company, 708 Intelligence Company and 708 Supply Troop.

Ever since the Combined Operations raid on St Nazaire on 27/28 March, the Dieppe raid on 19 August and now the Anglo-American invasion of North Africa the previous month, the German High Command had been distinctly jittery about the security of its ports. If Wallace and Ewart had moved south, they might have stood a chance of remaining undetected. Unfortunately, they moved north to the tip of the peninsula and straight into the heart of the German defensive zone, whence there was no chance of escape.

The house whose light drew them in, which they had believed to be French and therefore offering the prospect of help, proved to be accommodating members of Flak Unit 595, next door to the first-aid post of the Fahren Flotilla (ferry boat) service at Le Verdon, manned around the clock and guarded by a sentry. The Germans recorded that the two men were exhausted when they were captured, 'wet through and trembling with cold'. They were immediately taken before the Kriegsmarine medical officer, reported their mishap and asked to be taken prisoner. They were treated well, received clothes, blankets and an opportunity to sleep. They were plainly recognisable by their uniforms as members of the enemy forces and declared repeatedly (in English) that they were both 'fighting soldiers'. The medical officer was intrigued by the fact that both men's faces were 'painted green'.

The day that followed was busy, if chaotic. Wallace and Ewart's initial claim that they were shipwrecked sailors, survivors of a torpedoing at sea, was quickly recognised by their captors as an ill-disguised fiction, the truth revealed by the obviously combatant nature of their uniforms. Mere sailors would not have worn camouflaged, waterproof clothing or streaks of camouflage paint on their faces. On their combat jackets were emblazoned their Royal Marine and Combined Operations shoulder flashes and badges of rank. Likewise, the Germans, alerted to the possible presence of an enemy vessel the previous night, assumed that this was likely to have been the men's mother ship.

Later in the day, when what was believed to be a 'rubberised dinghy' was spotted offshore (heavy surf prevented its recovery at that time), and maps of the Gironde estuary with colour-marking of military positions, two aerial photographs of the submarine pens at Bacalan and other small but telltale pieces of equipment – containers of drinking water, tins of food, a magnetic mine, a Sten gun with silencer and several clips of ammunition – were washed up on Soulac beach, it was realised that the men were commando raiders of the kind that had plagued the German-defended coast for the previous eighteen months. As fighting personnel, they were given the full protection afforded to prisoners of war under the international laws of war. However, in a subtle though perhaps unintentional demonstration of the new German attitude to British military sabotage missions, the naval authorities in France issued a communiqué on 8 December, the day of the capture, asserting that 'a small British sabotage squad was engaged at the mouth of the Gironde and had been exterminated in combat'. Wallace and Ewart were of course still alive at this juncture, the hyperbole of the German announcement hinting perhaps at the fate that awaited them.

At midday on 8 December the Luftwaffe anti-aircraft detachment at Le Verdon (Flak Unit 595), having transferred their surprise guests to the Kriegsmarine, only then decided to report the incident up their own chain of command, through the infantry battalion at Soulac, to the HQ 708 Division. Their report described Wallace and Ewart as 'Anglo-American marines'. Only weeks before,

Operation Torch had landed tens of thousands of Anglo-Americans on Vichy French territory in Morocco and Algeria. Were these dishevelled commandos harbingers of a similar attack on metropolitan France? The part of the Atlantic coast that stretches in a wide, inviting arc from Biarritz in the south to La Rochelle in the north had always seemed, to German assessments at least, an obvious location for an Allied landing. Its vast beaches opened up into swathes of weakly defended territory.

They were right to be worried. Combined Operations had come within a whisker of launching at least one significant military action against this region – Operation Myrmidon – in early April 1942, in what was designed to be a copy of the St Nazaire raid. Three thousand troops (comprising No. 1 and No. 6 Commandos, one and a half battalions of Royal Marines together with an armoured regiment and a motorised infantry battalion) were directed against the harbours of St Jean de Luz and Bayonne, inside the Adour estuary. The plan was to disrupt road and rail transport between France and Spain before re-embarking for home. The force, embarked on HMS *Queen Emma* and HMS *Princess Beatrix* disguised as Spanish merchant ships, spent a month sailing off the French coast. On 5 April the ships approached the mouth of the estuary in order to carry out the landing, but in the midst of bad weather encountered an unexpected sandbar and, lacking local navigational expertise that would enable them to proceed, were forced to return to Britain.

Clearly a monumental cock-up, the abortive raid had nevertheless demonstrated Combined Operations' interest in raids against the region. Generalleutnant Hermann Wilck, the commander of 708 Division, recognised the vulnerability of his seaboard flank only too clearly; and given what was happening in North Africa as well as the extensive raiding activity against the French coast that year, was understandably nervous.

So on receipt of the message from the anti-aircraft gunners at Le Verdon, over seven hours after their arrest, Divisional HQ responded with surprise and concern at the news: why had it taken so long to report such a serious incident? The hapless commander of Flak Unit 595 said that he had believed they were shipwrecked sailors, and had informed Naval Command Gascony accordingly, as they were responsible for the interrogation of shipwrecked prisoners. He did not think it necessary to inform his own chain of command. Exasperated, HQ 708 Division ordered an immediate search of the coastline and the extensive forest belts that lay to the rear of the beaches and sand dunes, and demanded full details of the captured soldiers.

At 3.40 p.m. Unit 595 explained that the men had been taken for interrogation and that a search of the coastal forest area was taking place. At four o'clock, when the staff of HQ 708 Division telephoned the Inshore Squadron Gascony at Royan to confirm the details of the emerging story, they were told that it was suspected the men were part of an 'explosives commando' and that Oberleutnant Helmut Harstick of the Abwehr's counter-intelligence unit in Bordeaux was on his way to carry out a detailed interrogation. At 6 p.m. Hauptmann Rosenberger, 708 Division's intelligence officer, passed on the information to Generalleutnant Wilck, who ordered that OBWest (Field Marshal Rundstedt's HQ in Paris) also be informed. This was done at 6.30, and OBWest passed on the report to the WFSt (the operations department of the Oberkommando der Wehrmacht (OKW), Hitler's Supreme High Command), then at 7.50 to the HQ of Admiral Wilhelm Marschall, C-in-C Navy Group West.

On meeting the two bedraggled prisoners late that morning, following his inspection of the coastal defences, Bachmann's suspicions were immediately aroused. Were these men not commandos of the type for which the Führer had recently ordered 'special' treatment? If so, interrogation was the business not of the naval staff at Royan, but rather of the specialist interrogators of the Astleitstelle (the naval counter-intelligence branch), the Abwehr or the SD. Perhaps even the Gestapo. In the first instance, however, it was a naval matter, so he instructed his staff to order the Astleitstelle accordingly. The Abwehr's Section IIIM was based in Paris under the command of Fregattenkapitän Dr Erich Pheiffer, but had in Bordeaux a subsection reporting to Oberleutnant Harstick.* In the meantime Pheiffer ordered a professional interrogator from the naval POW transit camp at Dulag Nord† near Wilhelmshaven to make his way with all speed to Bordeaux to interview the two men. Hauptmann Heinz Corssen was duly instructed to pack his overnight bag and make his way to Bordeaux by train, via Paris.

In Bordeaux, Oberleutnant Harstick needed some persuading that he was really required, he too suspecting that the men were merely shipwrecked sailors who needed to be sent directly to the naval POW camp at Fallingbostel, but Bachmann insisted and Harstick complied. Climbing into a staff car with Hauptmann Glatzel, the two men made their way by road out of Bordeaux on the A10, along the eastern bank of the Garonne and Gironde towards Royan, to where Wallace and Ewart had been escorted by Oberleutnant Wild to await interrogation. Harstick and Glatzel arrived at 6 p.m. and met first with Bachmann, who briefed them on what course of interrogation to pursue. *Were* these men commando raiders? What was their target? If the answer to the first question was affirmative, Bachmann told Harstick, he would give orders for the two prisoners to be shot.

According to his war diary, Admiral Bachmann telephoned Admiral Marschall in Paris at 5.30 p.m. and told him of the situation and of his plans to execute the men, should interrogation confirm his suspicions that they fell under the Führer's *Kommandobefehl*.

* Abteilung III was the Abwehr's counter-espionage and security section, responsible for the security of the Abwehr and the armed forces. For the latter purpose it worked in close connection with the Geheime Feldpolizei (GFP), the security police of the Wehrmacht. The Abwehr's principal departments were IIIA (administration), IIIH (Wehrmacht), IIIM (Kriegsmarine) and IIILuft (Luftwaffe)

† 'Dulag' is an abbreviation of *Durchgangslager*. The Dulags were transit camps through which all POWs passed for processing and distribution to more permanent abodes. Wilhelmshaven closed in June 1943.

Bachmann was energised by his responsibility, and determined to be seen as an exemplar of military obedience: as soon as the formalities of questioning were completed, the two men would be shot. He had absolutely no qualms about this course of action: the law decreed summary execution for sabotage, and he was nothing if not obedient. His telephone call to Marschall was followed up by a signal that Bachmann dispatched at 8.15 that night. The fifth paragraph of this message stated: 'I have ordered immediate execution at conclusion of interrogation (if present facts confirmed) on account of attempted sabotage.'

The arrest of Wallace and Ewart that morning, the flurry of signals along the naval and Army chains of command, together with Bachmann's insistence on the 'immediate execution' of the men at the end of the interrogation process, created a whirl of activity in Paris. On the evening of 8 December a conference was held at HQ Navy Group West (based at the Ministère de la Marine on Paris's Place de la Concorde) to discuss the matter. The principal question related to the appropriateness of Bachmann's execution order rather than to its legality, despite the fact that to professional military officers the irregularity of the order was startling. But there was no attempt in HQ Navy Group West to challenge the basis of Bachmann's decision. They knew that it emanated in the first instance from the Führer, and totalitarianism brooked no dissent, even from senior military staff officers. Rank, status, family connections, even previous exemplary service and battlefield success, provided no protection from the fury of a Führer scorned, as countless Germans with otherwise spotless reputations, such as Erwin Rommel, were to find.

Fregattenkapitän Lange, head of the enemy intelligence section at HQ, a reservist officer and lover of opera (a foible which earned him the undying scorn of Marschall), meekly asked whether it would be more prudent to postpone the execution at least until a full and comprehensive interrogation had taken place. He was concerned to ensure that the men talked. In this regard he asked

Pheiffer whether there were such things as drugs available to force the men to tell the truth under interrogation. Pheiffer demurred at such a naive request, no doubt aware that the Gestapo and SD had long perfected the art of making men and women talk against their will. They certainly did not need drugs for the purpose. Nevertheless, the HQ staff agreed that permission to delay the execution, in the context of Hitler's explicit instructions in the *Kommandobefehl*, would need to come directly from the WFSt itself. Marschall, who like Bachmann had the reputation of a toady, refused to call Hitler's HQ because he was too precious of his reputation among the officers that surrounded his leader. His deputy, Admiral Wilhelm Meisel, agreed to do so.

Meisel had served with distinction in the raider *Möwe* in 1914–18 and had commanded the cruiser *Hipper* during a raiding journey in the Atlantic in 1941. He had joined Marschall's staff only three weeks before Operation Frankton, and there is some evidence that he was horrified at the peremptoriness, if not illegality, of Bachmann's proposal. When his telephone call went through to the duty officer, however, Meisel was told that both Colonel General Alfred Jodl and General Walter Warlimont were at the cinema with the Führer. The duty officer, Oberst Werner von Tippelskirch, was surprised that the HQ Navy Group West had bothered to ring the WFSt on such a trivial matter, von Tippelskirch haughtily insisting that there should be no delay in implementing the Führer's orders, which had to be carried out to the letter. He added, according to the record of Navy Group West, that no methods were to be spared in order to extract the truth from the captured men.

This is, on reflection, unsurprising. The German military conscience had long been blunted. A full year before, on 10 October 1941, Field Marshal Walther von Reichenau, Commander-in-Chief of the German Sixth Army, operating in the Soviet Union, published an infamous order – entitled 'Conduct of Troops in the Eastern Territories' – instructing his soldiers to take 'drastic measures' against guerrillas. This was meant to be, and was, interpreted as meaning that they were to be shot without mercy. Hitler ordered that a similar instruction be disseminated across the German armies in the East. The notion that enemy *francs-tireurs* were to be executed out of hand was therefore old hat to the staff officers of the WFSt. Major Bill Barkworth, the British war crimes investigator and wartime SAS intelligence officer, commented in his report in 1948 that Wilhelm Meisel, 'with the possible exception of Lange, seems to have been the only member of Marschall's Staff with sufficient moral courage to voice his protests, and although his main motive may have been the understandable wish to have the prisoners interrogated his spirited attempts on the telephone to the WFSt must be booked to his credit'.

Nevertheless, and despite Meisel's concerns, obedience to the Führer took priority over either his conscience or his commitment to upholding the international laws of war. At 0040 on 9 December Marschall's HQ sent Bachmann this instruction: 'With no methods barred, also using the subterfuge of sparing their lives and assurance of good treatment[,] try to obtain before execution the following information of operational importance . . .' In a signal sent at precisely the same time Marschall informed the Seekriegsleitung (SKL, the Admiralty) in Berlin that 'if previous findings [of interrogation] are confirmed, I have ordered immediate shooting on account of attempted sabotage'.

Meanwhile, in Royan, Harstick and Glatzel began their own interrogation of the two Royal Marines, assisted by an English-speaking naval officer, Oberleutnant Weidemann. By now the evidence that the pair were British 'commandos' on a sabotage mission was clear. Sergeant Wallace did not attempt to deny it, instead trying to persuade his questioners, neither of whom used force against the men, that he and Ewart were the only survivors of a mission that had gone badly wrong. The interrogation lasted about four hours. At 10.30 p.m. Harstick phoned Admiral Bachmann's office to explain the outcome, after which, at 11, Bachmann made his own calls. The two Abwehr men then worked through into the early hours to prepare their full report.

At 3.52 a.m. on 9 December, Hauptmann Glatzel called Lieutenant Wild to give him a preliminary report of the interrogation, before ringing through a similar report to Hauptmann Rosenberger at HQ 708 Division. Rosenberger was told that the two men insisted they were one part of a pair of canoes, dropped off by submarine, tasked with travelling up the Gironde, paddling at night *to fix explosives to German ships using the limpet mines they were carrying to cause explosions and sink the ships* (my italics). The first canoe of the pair had been damaged on launch, and they had capsized in the surf.

The secret was out! Hasler's greatest fear, that captured men would reveal under duress the nature of the mission before the others had the chance to complete it, had been realised. The interim report made by Glatzel ran as follows:

> The two captured Englishmen left Portsmouth about two weeks ago. Due to the bad weather the submarine cruised until yesterday evening [7 December], setting down the two early in the night, in a canoe, in the Bay of Biscay probably just outside the Gironde estuary. They were given a course, which they followed. After some time they saw a fire and made towards it. In the morning at around 4 a.m. their boat capsized in the surf at La Pointe de Grave. They say that they only just managed to save themselves. They went ashore, allegedly to give themselves up. They are wearing British uniforms, without headwear, consisting of a type of twill trousers and blouson, similar to a camouflage shirt. On their sleeves are rank and insignia, and the wording 'Royal Navy', plus badges for Combined Operations . . . The prisoners allege their orders were to paddle at night and to hide during the day. They were to travel up the Gironde and fix explosives to German ships using the limpet mines they were carrying to cause explosions and sink the ships. They had maps of the Gironde up to Bordeaux

> as well as two aerial photographs dated November 1942. The maps are marked to show occupied and enemy-free territory. Magnets, and some ammunition, camouflage netting, and other items of equipment have been found. The capsised boat has not yet been recovered . . .
>
> The commander of submarine P49 only gave the attack orders to the two men once they were on board the vessel, and after it had been at sea for about a week.* They belong to a troop of about fourteen men gathered together by the Navy at Portsmouth. This troop was put together about nine months ago. Apart from the two captured, the submarine was to deploy another two men, but this was aborted because the second canoe was damaged during the launch.
>
> After carrying out their orders the two prisoners were somehow to make their way to unoccupied territory. They claim that they were not given any French papers nor addresses nor any money.
>
> The leader of the enterprise [Sergeant Wallace] is quite willing to give information, but the second man [Marine Ewart] is reluctant to tell the truth, and claims not to have been informed about the purpose of the mission.

Would the Germans believe the story that the entire operation had now been aborted because the other pair never left the submarine, and that they, the only ones to leave on the mission, had capsized in the surf off Soulac? By telling their interrogators their objective Wallace was clearly jeopardising the safety of the other members of the operation who were still at large. Perhaps he assumed that his interrogator would believe the story that they were, to all intents and purposes, alone, and that the operation was now over. Perhaps he thought that enough time had elapsed for the remainder of the raiding party to have made it into the Garonne, and to be close enough to completing their task for it

* This may have been an attempt at subterfuge by Sergeant Wallace. P49 was HMS *Unruly*. HMS *Tuna* was in fact N94.

not now to matter what information the Germans were given. The account that Wallace provided was so replete with obvious misinformation that it seems clear that this was his intention.

But it was a considerable risk to take. Bachmann for one did not believe the story. On hearing the news from Harstick on the night of 8 December he warned Fregattenkapitän Ernst Kühnemann, commander of the Port of Bordeaux, of the threat of commando raiders against the ships nestling in the supposed sanctuary of the docks at Bassens and Bordeaux, as well as the submarine pens at Bacalan. Kühnemann was told to place his men on their guard against canoeist saboteurs who might have escaped the net.

On the evening of 9 December Bachmann returned to Nantes. When he reached his office he noted in his war diary that Marschall's HQ had ordered a delay to the execution in order to ensure that the men were properly cross-examined by an expert naval interrogator, Heinz Corssen, but that otherwise the execution of the men was not in doubt:

> About 8.33 p.m. the two prisoners are handed over to SD Bordeaux.* Accomplishment [of the execution] to be reported to Navy Group West and to Admiralty [SKL] by 11 a.m. 10 December.

The war diary of the naval operations staff of the German Admiralty in Berlin on the same day read:

> Group West communicates C-in-C West's report to Supreme Command of the [WFSt] concerning the capture of two English naval ratings off La Pointe de Grave . . .

* The SS's Sicherheitsdienst (SD) in Bordeaux were based at the Hafenüberwachungsstelle (Hüst), alongside the Gestapo, located at 13 and 16 Allée de Chartres, Bordeaux.

> FOIC Western France reports that, in the course of the day, explosive charges with adhesive magnets, chart material of the Gironde Estuary, aerial photographs of Bordeaux harbour installations, camouflage material, provisions and drinking water for several days were found. Salvaging of collapsible boat did not succeed.
>
> FOIC Western France has ordered that if the interrogation of the two men . . . confirms previous findings, they should be shot immediately; but has postponed this in order to obtain further information. According to Armed Forces report, both men have meanwhile been shot. This measure would be in accordance with the Führer's special order; it represents, however, an innovation in international law, as the men were in uniform.

It was not just the Navy who wanted to delay. On the morning of 10 December the SD asked Bachmann's Flag Lieutenant (Heinz-Günther Lell) to request a further postponement of the shooting. After his uncomfortable experience at the hands of von Tippelskirch, Meisel told the SD to obtain permission themselves. They did so, asking Hitler's HQ (the WFSt) for three days' grace. The SD received the same negative response as Navy Group West. As there would be no time now to get Heinz Corssen to Bordeaux to effect this interrogation, his journey was cancelled. His train had made only the short distance to Oldenburg before he was turned back to Wilhelmshaven by the Railway Police.

The Naval High Command in both Paris and Bordeaux fell over themselves in their haste to accomplish the Führer's bidding. Late on 10 December a teleprinter in Nantes clattered out the final unequivocal orders in the process leading to the judicial murder of Sergeant Wallace and Marine Ewart. Making specific reference to the telephone call from the Chief of Staff Navy Group West to the FOIC Flag Captain, the message directed as follows:

> The two prisoners are to be handed over from the FOIC to the SD with explicit reference to paragraph 4 of the Führer order No. 003830.42 Top Secret dated 18 October 42. SD will interrogate the men concerning questions still open. Measures pursuant to the Führer order are to be carried out by 11 p.m. on the 10th of December at the latest. The SD is requested to report accomplishment to FOIC C-in-C West, C-in-C West, Navy Group West and OKW/WFSt.

During the afternoon of 9 December both men had been moved from Gebauer's HQ in Royan to the town's fort. They were then transferred from the authority of the Kriegsmarine to the SD on the morning of 10 December, and taken to the Naval HQ in Bordeaux located at the Château Dehez at Blanquefort (today known as Château Magnol), there to await the arrival of Heinz Corssen. But even the bureaucracy of murder could not be rushed. Proper procedures had to be complied with and the veneer of legality observed, in part to absolve any of those involved, in their own minds at least, of personal responsibility for carrying out what was, under all accepted conventions of war, murder.

At 10.35 a.m. on 10 December the teleprinter at FOIC West clattered out its baneful orders once more: this time it was the head of the Bordeaux SD, SS Sturmbannführer Dr Hans Luther, a pre-war Frankfurt lawyer,* demanding a Navy detail consisting of a petty officer, sixteen ratings and an officer from FOIC Bordeaux 'for special task on orders of the Führer which was to be carried out by 11 p.m. Report at 9.45 p.m.' The acting duty officer that night in the Naval HQ, Bordeaux, was Lieutenant Theodor Prahm, the Adjutant of the FOIC, a man described by his post-war British interrogator as 'a colourless bank clerk'.

* His defence at his trial in Bordeaux after the war, that he was 'only obeying orders', succeeded. Three members of the Bordeaux SD were tried in the city between 28 April and 6 May 1953 for their crimes. Hans Luther was sentenced to five years' imprisonment.

At about 7.30 p.m. his telephone rang. On the other end of the line was Chief Petty Officer Otto Reckstadt, stating that the execution detail had been assembled by the HQ Company Defence Platoon at the Admiral Lütjens Barracks. Prahm knew all about Bachmann's order to execute the two British marines, had seen the instructions that morning to provide a firing squad, and had thought nothing more of it. That was, until the telephone rang again, at 10 p.m.

This time it was Luther on the line, demanding to speak to the officer responsible for the port of Bordeaux, Korvettenkapitän Ernst Kühnemann. Kühnemann, however, had stepped out earlier and had told Prahm that he would not be contactable for the remainder of the evening. Luther demanded that Prahm, in Kühnemann's absence, come 'at once' to the Gestapo HQ in the Place de Tourny on 'a matter of urgency'. Prahm was irritated by Luther's bossiness, and asked why Luther could not instead come to see him. Luther replied that 'he was in the town with a convoy, which he could not possibly leave', and arranged to send a car to collect Prahm. At the Place de Tourny Luther told Prahm that he was required at the execution, in accordance with orders, of the two English prisoners. On his arrival at the Place de Tourny he noticed that the firing squad from Chief Petty Officer Reckstadt's HQ Company Defence Platoon were sitting there in the dark in the back of an open-topped truck, while Sergeant Wallace and Marine Ewart were sitting, under an SD guard, in a large car. The stuttering yellow street lights provided a mournful illumination of the scene.

According to Prahm's testimony to war crimes investigators in 1945 he refused to be associated with the execution, arguing that it was the responsibility of the SD. This claim does not ring true. Prahm knew of, and did not contest, Bachmann's execution order; he knew also of the orders that morning to assemble the firing squad and, following his conversation at 7.30 p.m. with Chief Petty Officer Reckstadt, that it had been assembled. What is more likely is that Prahm objected to his *personal* involvement in the affair, perhaps with an eye to the future. According to him, Luther then pulled out his trump card: a warrant giving authority over all units of the armed forces, effectively ordering him to comply. In any case, Luther asserted, it was he who was ultimately responsible, not Prahm. His conscience salved, Prahm duly fell in line.

Luther insisted on haste, as he had to report completion to one of the higher headquarters by 11 or 12 p.m. Prahm's recollections of the events that followed were provided to the war crimes investigators less than three years later:

> I joined the head of the SD [Luther] in his car and the column moved off (a truck with the execution squad consisting of one Petty Officer and 16 Ratings, a big car with the two prisoners and 3 or 4 members of the SD as guard, a further car with the head of the SD, his driver and me. We drove first to the submarine base [at Bacalan] where we fetched a naval surgeon, as the harbour surgeon had not been available. When I asked whether a priest was coming with us, the head of the SD replied that a priest had been with the two prisoners for the whole of the afternoon. He also said that the death sentence had been read out to the prisoners before their departure.
>
> The column then drove into a wood which lay as far as I recollect to the north-west of the town, approximately 5–10 km away. Thc SD alrcady had two coffins put ready on the edge of the wood.* These coffins were taken along by the lorry to the place of execution. The place of execution itself was a sandpit, the far side of which served to stop the bullets. The SD men dug in two posts, which were lying there. The prisoners were tied to the posts; this was the first time that I saw the prisoners. The two cars were then placed in such a position that the beams of the lamps fell on the prisoners.

* The precise location remains a mystery. There has been supposition that the execution took place at Château Magnol, but this is not borne out by Prahm's testimony.

> I placed the 16 men into two rows, the front row kneeling, gave each group its target and gave the order to fire. Immediately after I ordered the squad to turn about and march off. The surgeon went to the men who had been shot, while at the same time two SD men, who had already drawn their pistols, fired several shots into the backs of the necks of the victims. The surgeon then established that death had taken place.
>
> The SD men placed the dead bodies in the coffins and loaded these on the truck. As it appeared to me and to my men too irreverent to get into the lorry with the coffins, we therefore went on foot up to the road to the edge of the wood. The truck also came up there, after the two coffins had been placed in a building, which was also at the edge of the wood.

The official German death notice stated that the bodies were buried in the POW cemetery in Bordeaux. However, as no such cemetery existed, it is possible that they were buried either in unmarked graves in the wood where they were executed, in the German military cemetery in the town, or even in a public graveyard. The Germans, however, left no records of the final resting place of the two men; or if they did, such records have long since disappeared, destroyed perhaps in the German evacuation of the city in 1944. In a German attempt the next year to cover up the truth of their actions it was falsely stated that the men had died (presumably by drowning) in the harbour in Bordeaux on 8 December 1942. The veracity of the official German account with respect to the final resting place of the two men therefore remains suspect. The only good thing that can be said is that, as coffins were provided, the bodies were afforded the semblance of a burial and not merely dumped in an unmarked, hastily dug pit where they had been shot.

The complex procedures undertaken to provide the events of that night with pseudo-legitimacy still irritated the German Navy, hypocritically unwilling to have its hands sullied by murder when it had, after all, initiated the process that led to the two men's executions. On 22 December Marschall noted: 'According to the report, to which reference is made, the shooting of the two saboteurs has been carried out by a detail from the NOIC Bordeaux at 12.30 a.m. on 11.12.42. Since the execution of saboteurs is a matter for the SD it is ordered that in future cases the culprits should be handed over to the SD for shooting.' The complaint rang hollow. It was Admiral Julius Bachmann, and therefore the Navy, who ordered the execution in the first instance, not the SD. Both were complicit in the illegal execution of the two Royal Marines, the Navy for ordering their deaths, and the SD for arranging the killing and the disposal of the bodies. The Navy could not wash its hands of the consequences of its own orders.

What did the SD discover from the two men? Although they admitted, when faced with the limpet mines, maps and other paraphernalia from the stricken *Coalfish*, that their target was the blockade-running ships in Bordeaux harbour, the Germans appeared to believe Sergeant Sammy Wallace's claim that only two teams of canoeists were involved, and that only one of these teams managed to exit the submarine. Extraordinarily, although on 10 December the military authorities across the region were warned that an attempt against Bordeaux shipping had taken place, the assumption was that the threat had been nipped in the bud. Under interrogation the two men did not reveal that other canoeists were, even as they spoke, making their way surreptitiously into the heart of Bordeaux. The SD had not been given much time for the interrogation. Had Bachmann not been in such a hurry to shoot the two men the SD might have resorted to more persuasive measures, and extracted this information. But the SD were denied their chance, and Wallace and Ewart died silent, the full extent of their secrets going with them to the grave.

Major Bill Barkworth, the British war crimes investigator, felt moved to conclude his otherwise clinical investigations into the murder of Sergeant Wallace and Marine Ewart in 1948 with the following observation:

> This case at Bordeaux is a classic case of the working of the Commando Order, and gives the full picture from the Führer, surrounded by his staff of cynical toadies down through the various formations to the simple and obedient members of the execution squad. The contemplation of a crime of violence is often less sickening than the dissection of the moral attitude that inspired it. Here, then, we are faced with the spectacle of Senior Staff Officers, some of them men gently born and bred as Christians, without the moral courage to stand up to the Führer's vicious and sadistic bombast, or even taking the way out, so easy in the German army, of requesting a posting to a combatant unit, bullying lower formations to a servile imitation of their master's manner, refusing to listen to the protests of humanity, conscience or reason and exerting all the weight of their authority and position to extort the immediate execution of the prisoners, captured in war . . .
>
> Nothing can excuse the keenness with which certain officers expended time and energy . . . in pestering lower formations, until they were able to present themselves before their Führer for a pat on the back, with the satisfactory sensation of a job well done; for after all, if killing there had to be, it was done by others, less well-connected, probably less religious and not upon the Staff. They themselves had no share in the dirty work. They only used the Staff Officer's weapon: they only murdered by telephone.

FOURTEEN

Attack

Hasler and Sparks left their hide in the reeds opposite Bassens at 9.15 p.m. on the night of 11 December, about the same time that Wallace and Ewart were told that they had been sentenced to death. Excited, though nervous at the same time, the four remaining Royal Marines paddled with the slowing flood tide towards their targets, Hasler and Sparks on the southern bank in Bordeaux itself just two miles ahead, Laver and Mills on the northern bank targeting ships in the Bassens area some way short of the city.

They had come so far, and were close to carrying out one of the most audacious attacks of the war. Yet many impediments remained in their way. The orange ampoules had been set in each of the limpets, four of which now sat between each of the Royal Marines' legs as they paddled strongly towards their targets. Each would explode at about 7 the following morning. One thought that plagued Sparks's mind as they travelled to their target was the need to keep the soluble simultaneous fuses dry. He admitted to feeling very lonely, but *Catfish* didn't have far to travel.

Moving along the riverbank, the constant drizzle of the day now mercifully ceased, Hasler and Sparks rounded the final bend into Bordeaux some ninety minutes later, and were horrified by the wall of light that confronted them. Bordeaux had no blackout, and the docks that stretched from the Quai Carnot to the Quai des Chartrons (just short of the Pont de Pierre) alongside the river were fully illuminated. They had not expected this final challenge. As they crept along the dock wall, keeping in its shadow, presented ahead was the well lit entrance to the submarine pens at Bacalan. The only way to avoid this was to risk the other lights along the river, and to head out into mid-stream to avoid the lock gates (with their inevitable sentries), before heading back into the sanctuary of the deep shadows alongside the dock wall. Although they were exposing themselves to anyone watching the river from the northern bank, Hasler knew he had no option. To the relief of the two men no shouts emanated from either bank, and *Catfish*, like a cockroach startled by the light, scurried back to the shelter of the darkness on the southern bank, the brightly lit lock gates falling behind them.

Almost as soon as they returned to the quayside they encountered their first ship, a tanker, which they ignored. Hasler had warned the men when on HMS *Tuna* not to bother with attacking fuel tankers: their hulls were subdivided into too many watertight compartments to allow limpet mines to have much effect. Likewise, they passed silently by a second ship, a cargo liner. By now they could feel the flood tide diminishing in strength, the effort required to continue paddling increasing with every stroke. The third ship was clearly a blockade-runner – of about 7,000 tons, the MS *Dresden* – but what looked like a small tanker was moored alongside, preventing them from laying any limpets amidships, so for the moment they ignored this one too.*

They hadn't much time left before the tide began to ebb, and pull them back down the river. The next vessel, MS *Tannenfels*, proved to be the first available target. Hasler estimated it too to be in the region of 7,000 tons; precisely the sort of target for which

* It has been suggested that this was the *Cap Hadid*, a 1,680-ton fruit-carrier built in 1938 belonging to the Saga Company of Paris. The *Cap Hadid*, however, had been sunk by an RAF attack on 8 December 1940. The vessel attacked by the RMBPD was in all likelihood one of the anonymous ones used in the Garonne and Gironde to supply fuel oil to vessels in Le Verdon, to the submarine pens at Bacalan, as well as to the quays at Bassens and Bordeaux.

Lord Selborne had long advocated an attack. Near the bow Hasler attached the first limpet on to the placing rod and lowered it carefully below the waterline, while Sparks steadied the canoe from behind with the magnetic holdfast. They repeated the process three times, during which time the high-water slack turned into the ebb tide. They needed a few strokes with the paddles to reach the ship's stern, and with the change in the flow they had to swap roles, Hasler grabbing the holdfast to stop them drifting back while Sparks took the placing rod and attached the third limpet. Paddling now against the force of the ebb tide, they moved to the next target. Unfortunately, a tanker was moored against a nice fat cargo ship alongside the quay. So they moved on.

Another cargo vessel quickly presented itself, which Hasler decided to attack on their return. Reserving three limpets therefore for this target, both men pushed hard against the flow of the river. The bright dock lights showed two further vessels ahead, moored together. The outside one appeared to be an armed minesweeper, a *Sperrbrecher*. It was not what they had come for, but they could get no further up river, and there was only one suitable target behind them – the cargo ship flanked by the tanker. Hasler decided to put a couple of limpets on the engine room of this vessel and then go for the cargo-carrier downstream. Again he held on while Sparks placed the limpets. Then, with their last three limpets saved for the cargo ship behind them, they slunk down into their canoe to begin the tricky manoeuvre of turning it downstream. For this they had to venture beyond the shadow of the *Sperrbrecher*'s hull. Using single paddles, they moved smoothly and silently. Then potential disaster struck. Hasler:

> Whilst *Catfish* was a little distance from the side of the *Sperrbrecher* in the act of turning to go down stream, we were seen by a sentry on deck, who shone a torch on us. Fortunately we were able to get back close to the ship's side and drift along with the tide without making any movement. The sentry followed us

> along the deck, shining his torch down on us at intervals, but was evidently unable to make up his mind as to what we actually were, owing to the efficiency of the camouflage scheme.

The sentry's hobnailed boots twenty feet above them and the light of his torch playing on *Catfish* seemed inevitably to spell the doom of their mission. But the sentry was confused about what he could see only vaguely in the light of his torch, amidst the swirling brown waters of the Garonne. Lying absolutely still and leaning forward, they managed to drift under the relative sanctuary of the overhanging bow, out of the direct sight of the sentry. There they waited, in some trepidation, using the holdfast to keep hold of the boat and to prevent being swung out into the river with the ebb tide and again into the sentry's view. They could hear the heavy boots above them, as the puzzled sentry wondered what he had seen. After about ten minutes Sparks gently released the holdfast and *Catfish* drifted out from under the bows.

Unbelievably, no shout or shot followed the men as the canoe floated off with the ebb tide. The sentry had clearly convinced himself that he had seen nothing unusual and had wandered off. Shaking from their lucky escape, Hasler and Sparks now needed to plant their last three limpets on the SS *Dresden* and the fuel tanker anchored alongside. Within thirty seconds they had borne down on the two vessels. Hasler quickly saw that the ideal approach would be to go between the two ships, allowing them to place two limpets on one vessel and one on the other. As they were about to attach the first limpet, however, the tide began to push the two ships together, threatening to crush *Catfish* in the middle. Instantly aware of the danger, Hasler and Sparks desperately pushed back out of harm's way. They made it with seconds to spare. They still had three limpets to place, so edging down the side of the tanker they put two on the stern of the *Dresden* and one on the stern of the tanker, aiming to blow a hole in its engine room. Then they turned and rejoined what had become a flowing ebb tide.

The mission was complete! Without a word they exchanged a handshake, and then pushed quickly out into mid-stream, far away from the glaring lights of the quayside and of the now doomed blockade-runners, the two Royal Marines paddling furiously, sweeping along with the ebb tide. 'We pulled out to the middle of the river,' recalled Sparks, 'and then bashed away as fast as we could away from the target area.'

The two men made their way downstream with a mixture of jubilation and pride. All the weeks of planning had reached their climax, and despite the devastating losses to No. 1 Section the RMBPD had repaid, with interest, the trust that had been placed in it. *Catfish* now bounded along with the rushing tide, freed from the dead weight of eight limpet mines, almost seeming to exult in the men's quiet satisfaction. They had nearly thirteen miles of paddling in front of them before they reached Blaye, which they needed to get to before dawn and the return of the flood tide. They were then going to scuttle their boats before heading across country in the direction of Ruffec. 'In order to reach the Blaye area by low water slack,' Hasler wrote in his report, 'it was necessary to abandon much of our former caution and proceed in mid-stream using double paddles, and although we must have been clearly visible and audible at least 200 yards away, we did not see any further signs of life.'

After a short while, however, a rhythmic splashing sound could be heard behind them. Stopping *Catfish*, Sparks blew on his seagull whistle. A moment later an answer came across the water and out of the darkness appeared *Crayfish*. By an extraordinary chance, in the middle of the Garonne and in the blackest night, they had been unwittingly but joyously reunited with their fellows. Pulling the canoes together they chatted for a while, both crews exuberant with success. Laver told Hasler that they had proceeded some distance along the east bank at Bordeaux without encountering any targets, and that as the ebb tide had then turned against him they returned and attacked the two ships previously seen at Bassens South, placing five limpets on the large cargo ship (the SS *Alabama*) and three on the smaller cargo liner (the SS *Portland*). It was easy, Laver reported, 'just like in training'. There was no sign of the enemy.

Hasler was pleased: all his men had displayed courage and initiative. They had done all, and more, of what he had asked of them. Later he was to record that Laver had handled his boat skilfully and had displayed initiative and coolness in making his independent attack. Likewise, Marine Mills and Sparks did their work in a cool and efficient manner, showing considerable eagerness to engage the enemy. But at precisely the same time that he and the surviving three Royal Marines had been placing the limpet mines on the targets, Sergeant Sammy Wallace and Marine Ewart were facing their murderers in a forest only a few miles away.

Hasler's plan was to carry on beyond the southern point of the Ile de Cazeau before stopping for a rest, leaving the heavily lit port area well behind them. Anxious to make the most of the ebb tide, they said their farewells. It was a poignant moment for them all. They were to split up: two men on foot stood a better chance of blending into the countryside than four. They would then meet up, somehow, in Ruffec. If not, they would do so in Blighty. 'See you in the Granada,' they said as they shook each other's hands. 'Don't forget you owe me a pint,' Sparks said to Mills. 'Hardly,' Mills replied. 'You owe *me* one. It's my 21st birthday in two days.'

Staying in mid-stream, the two canoes now proceeded rapidly downriver, clearing the northern end of Ile Verte before crossing the shipping channel and passing between Ile du Petit Fagnard and the Ile du Paté, then on past Blaye before they felt the flood tide begin to run against them. Crossing to the right bank, Hasler and Sparks found a landing spot at 5 a.m., Laver and Mills continuing for another 440 yards.

Exactly an hour later, on the Bassens quayside, the first of the limpets exploded, sending a sheet of water high into the air on the river side of the *Alabama*. Three minutes after that, a second limpet exploded, sending water rushing into the hull at two points. Consternation reigned. The alarm was sounded, the vessel evacuated and guards began rushing about to secure the docks. On the *Portland* two of the mines had detached themselves and exploded when hitting the river bottom, but no geysers had been reported. The sentries, when interrogated later, admitted only to feeling a 'slight vibration of the ship' at these times: they had not felt it important to raise the alarm.

Then, at precisely 8.30 a.m. the first limpet further up the river in Bordeaux detonated on the *Tannenfels*, moored at the Quai Carnot. A short while later a second mine exploded, causing the vessel to begin gradually to list, threatening to capsize. Thereafter mines exploded with unpredictable regularity throughout the morning. The *Dresden*, against which Hasler and Sparks had placed two mines after nearly being crushed against its hull, sank stern first on to the riverbed after suffering explosions at 8.45 and 8.55 a.m., and the fuel tanker moored alongside suffered a fire in her engine room, together with flooding, after a limpet went off at the same time. In all, six vessels had been attacked, mines exploding with various effects on five of them. According to the German records, of the sixteen mines placed, eleven detonated against their targets' hulls and five either fell off or failed to explode:

1 Five exploded on the SS *Alabama* at Bassens, and although the hull was twisted the vessel remained afloat.
2 One exploded on the SS *Portland*, while two had earlier dropped off and exploded harmlessly on the riverbed. Only a small amount of water entered the ship.
3 Two exploded on the stern of SS *Dresden*. The leaks were sealed by 9.30 p.m. but work was necessary till the evening of 13 December. By the morning of the 14th the holds were emptied.
4 One exploded on the stern of the fuel tanker moored alongside the SS *Dresden*.
5 Two exploded on the SS *Tannenfels*, while one either dropped

off or was a dud. The ship remained afloat but listed about 24 degrees, although measures were undertaken successfully to prevent the ship from capsizing.

6 None exploded on the *Sperrbrecher*, the three placed on the vessel having dropped off and exploded on the riverbed at 10.30 a.m.

The port authorities under Korvettenkapitän Kühnemann rapidly recovered from their embarrassment and, with the help of Italian divers from the submarine base and civilian *pompiers* based also at Bacalan, the holes in the ships were rapidly closed and within two days the water had been pumped from all the vessels.

Kühnemann's initial premise was that the damage had been caused by floating mines, somehow released upstream, either by aircraft or by saboteurs. The discovery later that day of two camouflaged canoes off Blaye made the Germans suddenly wake up: the mines had been left by commando raiders. The two Royal Marines shot in the forest the night before the attacks must have been part of a group, some of whom had made it successfully to their targets. Clearly, Bachmann's warning late on the night of 8 December that the blockade-runners in Bordeaux had been the target of the two captured Royal Marines had not led to extra vigilance. And there is no evidence that the alert sentry on the *Sperrbrecher* ever came forward to admit to having very nearly caught the Royal Marines red-handed.

The *gendarmerie* and the German forces across the region were placed on full alert to watch out for strangers making their way through the area. Kühnemann instituted the following countermeasures:

1 Patrols and pickets guarding shore installations were to be strengthened, and patrols in the harbour area increased.

2 A boat was to patrol the whole of the harbour, including Bassens, at night.

3 The crew of the guard vessel at the harbour entrance was to be increased. Its searchlight was to sweep the shore at irregular intervals.
4 Ships in the harbour were to be illuminated from shore as from 12 December.
5 The peacetime quay lighting, which was out of order, was to be restored.
6 Shore installations which could not be included in the rounds were to be protected by barbed-wire entanglements.
7 The Pauillac floating dock, the gate of the Gironde wharf and the large stone bridge at Bordeaux were to be protected by river booms.

Extra sentries were posted on vessels in the harbour, searchlights would be used more extensively off the coast, and coastal artillery would fire on the area of any questionable radar contact at sea. Claude de Baissac wrote in his report, dated 24 March 1943:

> There were no [security] controls in Bordeaux [before Operation Frankton] . . . but since our raid on the ships in the harbour, there has been very strict control on the river. Double sentries are stationed all along the bank equipped with hand grenades; they shoot anything moving, even floating logs. Searchlights are also in operation guarding against any intruders. Everyone is searched when he enters the harbour, and searched again when he leaves.

FIFTEEN

Escape

On 12 December at about 5 a.m., Hasler and Sparks drew ashore some 1,640 yards north of the old river port of St Genès-de-Blaye, site of an imposing fort built between 1685 and 1689 by Louis XIV's chief engineer, Sébastien le Prestre de Vauban. The imposing brickwork of the Sun King's fortifications genius could not be seen by the men riding the receding current as they made their way to a position where they could strike their boats. The angled walls of the grey fortress would have passed by them in the quiet darkness on their starboard bow, the small unoccupied Ile de Paté passing to their right, in the centre of the Garonne. They could see, however, the dark, imposing bulk of the two-funnelled Cammell Laird liner SS *De Grasse* on the eastern bank, lying quiet and forlorn, laid up for the duration of the war.

Operation Frankton had, until this point, been thoroughly planned and rehearsed, most of it in the minutest detail. Hasler himself had ensured this. The entire focus of his and the RMBPD's efforts had been to execute a successful attack on the blockade-runners at Bassens and in Bordeaux; and in truth, thoughts of how the escape to Spain would be undertaken had never been at the forefront of Hasler's mind. Lieutenant Commander L'Estrange had coordinated the details with Langley and Neave, and Hasler was left to trust that, somehow, members of the Resistance would show up to manage the process of their safe return to Britain.

From the point at which they were to scuttle their canoes,

however, only the sketchiest details were known; nothing had been planned or rehearsed, save for the escape kits that had been packed with the advice of MI9. These included a quantity of French francs, a good-quality 1:250,000-scale road map for the region with the demarcation line drawn carefully by hand in thick pencil, and a number of disposable compasses together with emergency rations (including tablets to enable them to digest raw vegetables) and items such as balaclavas and gloves, essential in the cold of the Aquitaine winter. The extent of the information available to all four evaders was that their rendezvous was to be the town of Ruffec, ninety miles north-east of Bordeaux. Walking, the journey would take five days, of which they had emergency rations for two. They would need to scavenge food on their way, either from fields, hedgerows and orchards or directly from the populace.

There was no time to ponder on the problems they faced, however – only for action. They had to get to Ruffec, through country that was occupied by the Germans and inhabited by people who had no reason to risk their necks to provide support and succour to four fleeing Britons. Hasler knew that they would just have to trust themselves to luck. He wrote to the French writer Robert Chaussois on 3 January 1968:

> The escape plan placed a heavy load both on the French population, and on us. For us, it was alarming to have to throw ourselves on the mercy of complete strangers, when we had no way of knowing whether they were for or against us. For the first time, we felt that we had lost the initiative, and were depending too much on good luck. For the French, the load was much greater: every man or woman who helped us risked not only himself but his whole family: until we reached Mary Lindell's organisation, nobody whom we approached had any reason for believing our story, or had even heard of the Bordeaux raid . . . I marvelled that we received so much help and so few refusals . . . we were merely soldiers trying to save our own lives; they were civilians, risking

> their lives in a cause which they did not understand, but which they hoped was a blow [struck] for France and her allies.

Throwing oneself on the mercy of the local population was indeed a matter of chance. In the early days of 1940 the speed with which Britain had deserted France in her hour of need was much pondered. Churchill had refused to send the entire RAF fleet to support the Battle of France, and the evacuation from Dunkirk was despised by some as the fullest extent of British military incompetence. When the Royal Navy opened fire on the French Fleet anchored at Mers-el-Kébir on 3 July 1940 to prevent it falling into German hands, but killing 1,297 French sailors in the process, anti-British sentiment built quickly on a much older hatred of perfidious Albion.

There was no guarantee, therefore, that 'ordinary' French people would be willing to offer sanctuary to escapers or evaders. Moreover, when escape circuits and resistance groups began to grow, the Germans worked assiduously to infiltrate and turn them, often exploiting the deep social and political divisions in French society to persuade activists on the political right, whose natural inclination was to fight the Germans, that the real enemy was the left. The argument the Germans deployed was that intolerable though the occupation of France might be, the greater evil was rampant communism, against which a strong Germany provided the only bulwark.

When *Catfish* drew into the lee of a muddy bank, the only light to illuminate the scene was the dying moon reflected on the water, the ubiquitous dry reeds in the shallows crackling loudly as the canoes came to a halt. Hasler and Sparks clambered out into the shallow water, enjoying the opportunity to stretch themselves for the first time in ten hours. Having struggled through the thick mud that lined the river bank, they removed their camouflaged waterproofs and life vests, stuffing them into the boat, at the same time recovering their escape kits. Throwing the remaining Sten gun into the river, then slashing the sides of the faithful *Catfish* and pushing the hulk into the river, they climbed awkwardly up the bank and began to make their way on foot on a north-east bearing, still in darkness, carrying their No. 5 bags slung over their shoulders. They were so deep in hostile territory now that they would hardly be able to shoot their way out of a confrontation with the enemy, but they kept their Colt automatics.

Hasler was soaked to the waist and Sparks's feet were wet. Hasler wanted to put as much ground as they could between them and the river as quickly as possible, but they could not take the risk of moving during daylight. The curfew made travelling at night dangerous, but for two evaders it was the lesser of two evils. At least at night, if they were careful and avoided towns or roads, they could easily remain hidden. They were still in uniform and would remain so until they could scavenge some civilian clothes. But first they needed a warming cup of tea and some shelter to prepare themselves for the next stage of the journey. After struggling for a short while against the nuisance of strange rows of low-standing wire fences, they realised they were in a vineyard attempting to cross against the grain of the vines. Changing course, they made much faster progress, and found a wood in which they could hide, between St Genès-de-Blaye and Fours. Warming themselves with the tea, the exhausted men then attempted to clean off the mud clinging to their clothes before curling up on the damp ground to snatch a few hours of fitful sleep.

They remained under cover for the whole day, sleeping when they could. The skies were damp and grey, the cold piercing, and they spent their waking hours shivering. Sparks recalled that Hasler remained determinedly positive about the outcome of their journey, the two talking together about what they needed to do to survive.

It was a relief when darkness descended that first night at about 7 p.m., and they could generate some warmth by walking. The rain fell steadily now. It pattered on to the treetops above, and a steady fall of drips made their way through the dense foliage on to the two men as they struggled out of the heap of sacks and leaves with which they had made their bed, stretched, and prepared to move off. It was now colder than ever. Frosts are rare in the region, but the mercury in December can drop as low as 2 degrees Celsius. Hasler balanced one of his small compasses in the palm of his hand, watching the tiny needle dancing in its capsule, before it halted, hesitantly, pointing north. Without a word he shouldered his pack and both men began to make their way steadily through the trees, alert to the possibility of encountering a woodsman or a peasant making his way home from the fields at the end of the day. The sound of their crunching footsteps over the forest floor was drowned out by the steady drone of rain on the canopy above, which also helped shelter the men from the worst of the wet. But the rain contrived to keep people indoors in the comfort of their small cottages, wispy smoke drifting slowly up from chimneys before scattering in the drizzle.

They walked all night. As dawn threatened on the morning of 13 December they found themselves about a mile south of Reignac, having made slow progress. The river was about thirteen miles behind them, and they had crossed the busy main road running north-west to Royan. Finding a convenient copse through which ran a clear stream, they had at least some water to make tea and to help with tidying up their beards. Hasler had now decided to take the risk of approaching a farmhouse, and they needed to look as presentable as they could. They needed food if they could get it, and some civilian clothes. The plan was that Hasler would approach the house while Sparks remained hidden. If he did not come out, Sparks was to make his way independently. At about 7.30 a.m. near the village of Brignac they walked cautiously up to an isolated farmhouse. Already the elderly farmer was in the garden. Using his simple French Hasler asked for help, but received a cold response. The owners were clearly scared and suspicious, although Hasler managed to secure a dirty beret for himself and a cap for Sparks before being hustled off the premises.

The peasants had nothing spare to eat, the first sign to both men that there was in fact little food available in the French countryside in this sparse, wartime winter. But they did manage to get a sack in which to carry their food, water and spare clothes. Dressed now a little less conspicuously although still wearing their military hobnailed boots, they now took the risk, for the first time, of walking in daylight, although as soon as they could do so they disposed of their remaining weapons (the two Colt 45s and a grenade) in a wood. They kept their identity discs: it was crucial to be able to prove their military identity if they were caught, but concealing weapons while wearing civilian clothes would have elicited a swift and fatal response from their captors.

It is clear that Hasler's expectation was that the worst that could happen to them was to be taken prisoner and presumed to be spies – not that, if captured, they would be tied to a stake in a forest and shot because they were Royal Marines on a commando mission. The thought never entered his head. Not one of the Royal Marines on Operation Frankton, nor in all likelihood those in Combined Operations who had sent them, had an inkling of the real consequences of their arrest now that the Kommandobefehl. They believed, until told otherwise by their German captors, that if they could prove they were bona-fide servicemen they would be protected by the full force of the Hague and Geneva Conventions in respect of prisoners of war. They never realised that nothing would now save them from the Führer's wrath, and one of his firing squads, if they were captured.

A mile or so further on Hasler again tried his luck with a farmhouse, but to no avail. They were, however, waved on to a third house in a small village four miles distant, where the middle-aged occupants gave Sparks a very old jacket and trousers and Hasler some trousers. More importantly, they received a smile from the woman who donated these rags – the first positive response from the civilian population so far. That night, having made only limited progress during the day, they bedded down on their sacks on the cold ground in a wood just south of Donnezac. About an hour before daylight the next morning, 14 December, keen to get their blood circulating and warm up, they began the day's walking, heading for Donnezac, which they passed through before the lights were fully on in the town. There was no one about. Before starting out, they had eaten virtually the last of their emergency rations, the oatmeal biscuits, which they chewed, having insufficient water to boil them into porridge.

It was at 4 p.m. that day that Sheard and Moffatt's *Conger* was discovered, washed up on a beach on the Ile de Ré sixty miles to the north, where the contrary Biscay tides and currents had swept it. It startled the German troops responsible for the defence of the area, 80 Corps, but they drew from its discovery the wrong conclusions: 'Oberleutnant Willemer reported to his HQ at around 4 p.m. a 4.5 metre long canoe with green and black camouflage paint drifted ashore south of the Ile de Ré. There is no sign of the occupants. They were without doubt British sabotage troops who are now at large on the Ile de Ré or near La Rochelle.' The defences were put on increased alert, fearing that the coastal artillery batteries were the target.

Meanwhile, far to the south, Hasler and Sparks had been eking out their rations, and were now feeling famished and weak. Hasler's report stated that they began the day by turning 'north east to the main road and north east up another road which brought us approximately to the T in Montendre (Sheet 29, France, 1:250,000).'

> We then went north west on a side road to a village under the figure 6 on their map. On the main road we walked south east for a short distance, and then turned left to Ruffignac (the light railway shown on the map does not exist). From Ruffignac we followed a cart track to Villexavier (Sheet 24), and thence to Ozillac and St Germain-de-Vibrac, near which we spent the night of 14 December in a wood . . .

They had travelled eighteen miles but were now hungry and tired. They were insufficiently clad to keep out the cold, and without any food the threat was that their bodies would soon succumb to exposure. To make things worse, it rained intermittently during the night, the men shuddering in the cold and wet under their inadequate clothing. They would need to get help soon, Hasler mused. They simply could not go on like this for much longer, and would be forced again to put their lives in acute danger by approaching members of the civil population.

Up early the next day, they trudged determinedly on. Hasler remained nothing but positive. Bill Sparks recalled that when things got tough he (Sparks) would often let off steam by bemoaning their fate, shaking his fist at the sky and 'shouting at the gods'. Hasler never did, quietly continuing with the business in hand, carefully planning the next stage of the journey or solving the particular difficulty in which they found themselves at the time. He wanted to survive, and to get back home to demonstrate that the RMBPD concept of harbour attack could be successful. What was more, he knew he could survive, with careful attention to detail, thorough planning, determination and just a little bit of luck. Looking back over the last few days he knew that they had been lucky, and prayed that luck would not desert them.

It was now the morning of 15 December, three days after the attack in the Garonne, and there had been no sign of a hue and cry breaking out. Hasler did not doubt, however, that the authorities, both German and French, would be on full alert for them, so any further approach to the civilian population would need to be made circumspectly. They walked on in the damp morning air to the village of St-Ciers-Champagne, and then east along a main road from which they turned left for the village of Barret, continuing along the St Médard road and eventually turning left for Touzac. At a village six hundred yards south of Touzac they tried to get food at a garage, but were turned away brusquely by the fat proprietor and his wife. 'Certainly not,' she replied to Hasler's halting request. 'We don't have enough for ourselves.'

About half a mile north-west of Touzac, however, they had better luck. Approaching a young woman working in her garden, Hasler slowly explained that they were escaping British soldiers, that they were hungry and needed food. It was clear to her that the two men were in poor shape and she was immediately moved to compassion. 'Stay here,' she instructed Hasler. Going into her house she returned with a piece of bread and cold chicken. She had no idea just how important this morsel of food was to them. While they ate gratefully, she warned them that the nearby town of Lignières contained Germans, and should be avoided. Proffering their thanks, the two men went on their way, and avoided the place.

Luck remained on their side that night. The rain was now incessant, and they were weakening, despite the food they had secured. Hasler knew that they had to find warmth and shelter that night, or they soon would be too weak to continue. The first door on which they knocked, a farmhouse belonging to a Madame Malichier, did not appear promising. Nervous about sheltering the men herself she knew, though, where they would be safe. A local man, Clodomir Pasqueraud, who lived with his wife Irène and his children at a remote farmhouse nearby, had well known anti-German sympathies, and would, she believed, be prepared to help. Guided by the teenage son of one of her vineyard workers, the two exhausted Royal Marines duly made their way through the dark along paths between vineyards set amidst the low and undulating hills of the Charente, to the door of what they were later to know as Nâpres Farm, a few miles south of Saint Preuil. They had travelled nineteen miles that day, and were now utterly exhausted.

In the original account of the 'Cockleshell Heroes', written by Brigadier C.E. Lucas Phillips in 1956, the name that Hasler and Sparks gave to M. Pasqueraud, not knowing until many years later his real name, was the 'fiery woodman'. This was because the nervous young man who escorted them (M. Cadillon, the son of a farmworker from the farm at La Pitardie, a mile or two to the south-west) received a barrage of angry hostility from Pasqueraud when the farmer opened the door of his cottage. It was well into the curfew, and any stranger knocking on his door after dark would probably have something to do with the law (he was well known to the local *gendarmerie* both as a smuggler and communist agitator). Nervous and angry, M. Pasqueraud wanted to know who the men were, and why they had been guided to his farm. According to François Boisnier, who interviewed one of Pasqueraud's sons (Robert, who was eleven at the time), Cadillon replied: 'The boss's wife, Madame Malichier, told me that they're escaped Englishmen. She said the Trouillets didn't want to know them at La Pitardie and she couldn't keep them at Maine-Laurier, so I should take them to Clodomir Pasqueraud at Nâpres . . .'

Fearing a trap by provocateurs, Pasqueraud continued loudly to deny that his home was a suitable place for supposed Englishmen. While this discussion was going on, Hasler picked up an English voice in the background. It was the unmistakable sound of the BBC. Hasler now spoke directly to Clodomir, explaining that they were escaping British soldiers and needed food and shelter. Softening, the 'fiery woodman' ushered the men into the house, and the frightened Cadillon was sent back home.

Thereafter, fear and suspicion were banished, and Clodomir and Irène were hospitality itself. Desperately poor, they nevertheless unhesitatingly shared the family's evening meal, a steaming pot of broth followed by roast chicken, garlanded with potatoes and onions, with the starving Royal Marines. Despite the fear and hostility the pair had encountered so far, the selfless kindness of the Pasquerauds was a pattern that repeated itself hundreds of times during the war. In Mary Lindell's recollection, the poorest and those with least to give were invariably the most generous.*

* For decades after the war, as the Paris representative of the RAF Escaping Society, Mary Lindell regularly visited these retired wartime *passeurs*, many of whom were still the poorest of the poor, with gifts of food and money.

'Le poulet est bon!' exclaimed Hasler gratefully, to a beaming Irène.

It was the first hot meal the men had had for eight days. Hasler and Sparks had had the good fortune to fall into the welcoming arms of true patriots. The Pasqueraud household was pitifully poor, but Hasler always believed that these simple French peasants, by their unrequited generosity, saved the lives of both fugitives that night. The tiny cottage comprised two storeys, a single room with a rough earthen floor downstairs, heated by an open fire, together with a single room above, accessed by stairs running up against the far wall. Downstairs, the three boys all slept on a single bed, Clodomir and his wife upstairs. That night Hasler and Sparks slept like babies, in the downstairs bed. The next morning, anxious to keep on the move and unwilling to allow the Pasquerauds to suffer any danger, the men, now warm, dry and well fed, prepared to move off. 'When you get back to England,' Clodomir said, 'send us a message on the BBC that you are safe. Say, "Le poulet est bon."' Laughing, Hasler agreed, and in due course the message was sent.

During the first part of their journey that day, 16 December 1942, in which they had to cross the Charente River and the busy road that ran to its north (the Route Nationale 141) between Cognac in the west and Angoulême in the east, they were escorted by the two eldest Pasqueraud boys, Marc and Yves, on their bicycles. Before the river was reached they travelled through St-Même-les-Carrières, the first place they saw German soldiers. 'We got the impression there were only a few, and were told they had moved in a few days before,' recalled Hasler. Much to Sparks's consternation a group of them burst out of a house they were passing in the town, elbowing past the startled evaders. Sparks was relieved that on this occasion he suppressed an urge to complain about their rudeness.

The presence of the two French boys did much to enable the Englishmen to relax, and blend into the surroundings. They looked no different from the many other vineyard labourers and farm-workers they passed on their way. Hasler's report recorded: 'That day we continued to Triac, Lantin, Fleurac and Vaux-Rouillac, and spent the night in a disused hut south of the light railway near Le Temple, Rouillac.' It had rained all day, and both men were soaked to the skin. They had made another eighteen miles, the two unstintingly courageous Pasqueraud boys leaving them at the bridge over the Charente at Vinade, seven miles along the way. During the day, Sparks recalled, they had found a small pile of potatoes and turnips by the side of a freshly ploughed field. They would have been left over from the harvest two months before, so would not have been in good shape. Without the means to cook them, they devoured them nevertheless, with the help of the digestion tablets in their escape packs.

The hut that provided shelter that night was verminous, recalled Sparks, and had a leaky roof, but it was better than lying out in the wood. All the same, they remained wet and cold. They had run out of food, having eaten the remains of the chicken that Irène Pasqueraud had pressed into their hands when they left Nâpres Farm that morning. They did not really sleep that night, dozing off instead for short spells before the cold shook them awake once more, clutching them in its icy embrace. Before dawn broke they had started on their journey, desperate once again to get warm. It was now Thursday 17 December. They made good progress during the day, walking to Montigne, Bonneville and Mons. Avoiding Aigre, they turned left at its outskirts on the road for Oradour, from which they turned right along a cart track to St Fraigne. It was now approaching early evening, and dusk was beginning to fall. They then continued into a small hamlet called Beaunac, which Hasler noted in his post-operational report was not marked on the map, just east of St Fraigne.

'After trying several houses,' he recalled, 'we found one where we got some food, and were allowed to sleep in an outhouse.' It was here that the men came very close to being caught, escaping only by their wits and the courage of a villager.

Knocking on a succession of doors was in retrospect a serious mistake, because Hasler and Sparks inadvertently brought their presence to the attention of the whole village, a hamlet of less than a dozen houses. It would have been better to make themselves known to no more than two households before moving on, but they were tired and hungry and the evidence of the past few days was that some kind soul would eventually take pity on the two vagrants.

In the fading light one villager, André Latouche, had watched the men enter Beaunac, and when they reached his door he ushered them quickly inside. He fed them and allowed them to sleep in his barn. No sooner were their heads laid on the warm straw than both were fast asleep. They planned to be up and away well before dawn. Small rural communities like this were notoriously suspicious of strangers, and there was every chance that even now news of their presence would be on its way to the local *gendarmerie.* Latouche decided that he needed to warn the mayor of the neighbouring town, Ebréon, perhaps so that when the authorities inevitably learned of their presence the villagers would not be accused of giving sustenance to the escapers, although hopefully by the time the Germans found out the two Britons would be long gone. It was a naive gesture that was to have ultimately disastrous consequences for some of his neighbours.

While the two Royal Marines slept soundly in their barn, the village was awash with gossip. One of Latouche's neighbours, Lucien Gody, unhappy that the authorities had been called and fearful of what might happen to the men who had innocently sought sanctuary in the village if the Germans caught them, quietly made his way into the barn at about 11 p.m. Shining a torch into the sleepy faces, he urged the two men to make haste out of the village, as the whole district would soon be roused and the *gendarmerie* had been called. 'We heard in Ruffec two days later,' recalled Hasler, 'that the police had actually been enquiring in the area for two people answering to our description. We got out at once, and went by cart tracks to a road south east of Souvigné, where we spent the night' (in an old, rotting haystack). They had travelled a total of nineteen miles that day, and had survived capture in Beaunac by the skin of their teeth.

But the implications for the village of the two men's short sojourn were disastrous. François Boisnier tells the story:

> Meanwhile the mayor of Ebréon detailed his local policeman, Monsieur Picot, to go and investigate. He was also obliged to advise the local gendarmerie. For safety he chose to contact the gendarmerie at Aigre, since he knew they would not come until the next day and hence would find nothing. However, the gendarmerie did write up a report on the incident, as was their duty and this document was forwarded to the Préfecture in Angoulême. From there it was passed on to the German authorities. The Germans duly arrived in Beaunac on 22 December and immediately arrested Messieurs Bineau, Picot and Latouche, followed the next day by Messieurs Gody, Souchaud and Maurice Rousseau. On 26 December the Germans returned and arrested René Rousseau . . .
>
> Messieurs Bineau, Picot and Latouche were freed on 31 December and two others were liberated the day after. They had been interrogated separately and no violence was used on them. But Lucien Gody (43 years old), Maurice Rousseau (28) and René Rousseau (16) were deported. They were never seen again.

When they awoke the following morning – Friday 18 December – Hasler consulted the map, telling Sparks that their flight was nearly at an end. It had been a miserable night, the rain teeming down, and they were, as ever, hungry and cold. Ruffec, a small provincial town situated on the Route Nationale 10 and straddling the Paris to Bordeaux railway line, was a mere nine miles distant to the northeast. There, they confidently expected, the Resistance would have its spies out along the main roads and would quickly sweep them both into its embrace. Hasler had been – naively – directed to no more than the town of Ruffec where, he assumed, a *réseau* contact would make himself known and all would then be well. Perhaps there they would also meet up with Laver and Mills, who were unlikely to have made better time to the rendezvous than he and Sparks. Looking at the map, he decided to enter the town later that day from the west along the road that led from La Faye through the village of Veillemorte.

Hearts considerably lightened by the prospect of nearing the end of their exhausting journey, the two men set off, taking the paths that skirted the winter fields. As an added bonus the endless drizzle had ceased, for the time being. They were unaware that Ruffec was teeming with the enemy, with two regiments of German troops garrisoned in the town.

Hasler would have been far less sanguine about the future had he known that absolutely no one knew of their arrival. The first flaw in the arrangements for their escape had been Mary Lindell's refusal to take a radio operator with her when the RAF Lysander dropped her into Limoges two months before. MI9 had no means of warning her, therefore, of the possible arrival of up to a dozen fleeing Royal Marines. We can only assume that Langley and Neave made every effort to get a message to her, perhaps via the British consul and MI9 agent in Geneva (Victor Farrel) or through one of the couriers of the Pat Line, but even this remains uncertain.

The second flaw in the plan for the escape was that there now existed no formal demarcation line between the German occupied zone and the *Zone Libre*. In response to the Allied invasion of North Africa the Germans had moved into what had previously been Vichy-controlled territory. For the evading Royal Marines, what had been the free zone had suddenly become much more dangerous than it had been under direct Vichy control.

Entering Ruffec in daylight was perilous. The German garrison was substantial, and the *gendarmerie* were alert. Reports of the two men were circulating widely across the region. It was only a matter of time before they would be picked up and interrogated by the police, so it was essential that they find sanctuary as quickly as possible. Without a detailed map of the town, however, when they entered late in the day Hasler and Sparks were forced to walk around trying to look inconspicuous, while searching for the *résistants* who, they still believed, were somewhere waiting for them. It was nerve-racking, but fortunately no one gave them a second glance.

Before long they came across the Hôtel de France, a prominent edifice sitting on the western side of the main road that led into the town from the south.* However, Hasler immediately concluded that in their condition they could not possibly enter the building, displaying as it did both French and German flags. They would be like two vagrants attempting to gain access to the Ritz, he thought. They needed somewhere much less conspicuous. Walking two hundred yards further on they spotted a scruffy restaurant on the other side of the road, at the junction with Rue de l'Hôpital. The two men crossed the road, and carefully peered inside while pretending to peruse the menu placed in the window. It was quiet, with a few patrons engaged in conversation. Making a snap decision, and trusting that their luck would hold, Hasler nodded to Sparks and pushed open the door.

They had now been on the run for six days. They were completely cut off from any information about the success or otherwise of their attack, about the German response or indeed about their colleagues. Had they been captured? Were they still at large, and if so, where might they be?

London, likewise, had heard nothing as yet from the saboteurs. The only information about the raid came from decrypts of enemy communications. From mid-1940 every morning, a locked buff-coloured box – to which only Churchill and Sir Stewart Menzies, the Chief of MI6, had keys – was placed on the Prime Minister's

* It remains there still, empty and somewhat forlorn, on the Rue de General Leclerc.

bed. Inside was a daily batch of files, each of which was marked 'MOST SECRET' and enclosed in a folder entitled 'Special Messages'. Churchill could then read the heavily paraphrased intelligence summaries that had been decoded at Bletchley Park (near today's Milton Keynes) during the previous twenty-four hours.

On the morning of 12 December, only hours after the first of the explosions, a teleprinter at Bletchley Park reproduced a message sent from Bordeaux to Marseille:

> Following landing of the English sabotage party on southern bank of the Gironde on December 8 four [sic] ships in Bordeaux harbour were sabotaged on December 12.

Then, on the morning of the 14th, Churchill was able to read a decrypt of a German naval intelligence bulletin (No. 528) that reported:

> German SS *Tannenfels*, SS *Portland*, SS *Dresden* and French SS *Alabama* were damaged by underwater explosions in Bordeaux on the morning of December 12th, and it was therefore appreciated that members of the sabotage party landed on the south bank of the Gironde on 8/12 had succeeded in reaching Bordeaux. All these ships were reported empty at the time of the damage.

This was not the first information London had received about the fate of Operation Frankton. As has been seen, four days earlier, on 10 December, a German High Command communiqué had announced the destruction on 8 December of 'a small British sabotage squad', and in the local Bordeaux newspaper *La Petite Gironde* on the 11th the same essential message was published: a party of British saboteurs had been eliminated on the coast. Despite the hyperbole regarding the nature of the 'combat', this communiqué related only to the capture of Sergeant Wallace and Marine Ewart, but at face value it seemed to indicate the failure of the operation. Commenting on the communiqué, Mountbatten wrote to the Prime Minister on 16 December with an update of the situation as he saw it. He had received no confirmation that Hasler had pulled off the raid (nor indeed that Churchill already knew one way or the other). But he was hopeful, as the German report seemed to understate the size of the raiding party.

'It seems possible,' Mountbatten noted, 'that the Germans may have only intercepted one section of the raiding party. The commander of the party was Major H.G. Hasler R.M. who would probably have been with the leading section.' Did the reference in the communiqué to a 'small British sabotage squad' indicate that not all the raiders had been intercepted? That certainly was Mountbatten's hope. 'The capture by the Germans of one section,' he noted, 'would not necessarily have compromised the other section since no papers were carried other than charts.'

He was right, but the Prime Minister already knew the outcome of the raid. The news from Bletchley on 12 December, therefore, provided the first evidence that Hasler had succeeded, Churchill being informed on 13 December and receiving confirmation on the morning of the 14th. For some reason, however, Mountbatten did not know the outcome until the 16th.

Something had clearly gone wrong with communications within Whitehall. It was only when Churchill received Mountbatten's note dated 16 December, in which the CCO commented on the German communiqué of the 10th, that the Prime Minister realised that his Chief of Combined Operations had not heard the good news. The following day Mountbatten informed the Chiefs of Staff Committee that 'apparently successful results had been achieved by part of the Frankton force'. The Prime Minister immediately placed on record 'his appreciation of what seemed to have been an extremely gallant and enterprising operation'. Also on this day a German newspaper picked up the story, and ran a virtually verbatim report that 'a British sabotage group was intercepted and annihilated in the mouth of the River Gironde', a story that was then picked up by the international news services and published in British newspapers during the days that followed.

Further confirmation that the raid had achieved at least partial success was not long in coming. Bletchley Park decoded a secret German message on 19 December that had been sent at 11 a.m. the previous day: 'The steamships in Bordeaux, which were the object of an attack by a British sabotage party on the 12th, are now known to have been heavily damaged.'

Keen to avoid the embarrassment of not keeping Mountbatten informed, in neat sloping handwriting at the side of the typewritten sheet was the message (probably by General Pug Ismay): 'I am informing C.C.O.' Two days later, on 21 December, further confirmation was received at Bletchley Park in a secret German naval report that the 'merchant ships DRESDEN and ALABAMA and three others were damaged by mysterious explosions on 12th December. Two of the ships were at BASSENS and three at BACALAN. The damage can be repaired.'

For their part, the Germans were quickly on the trail of the men. Unfortunately, *Catfish* did not disappear under the swirling brown waters of the Garonne as Hasler had hoped, but had drifted out into mid-water off Blaye early on the 12th with her stern peeking above the surface. That afternoon it was discovered by a river patrol and, along with *Cuttlefish*, recovered. In a message to NOIC Gascony the following day Bachmann's HQ reported: 'In the afternoon of 12/12/42 two canoes with sketches, limpet mines, air sacks, hand grenades, iron rations and some pieces of equipment were found near Blaye outside of Bordeaux and were secured.'

The hunt was on. The enemy escapers were clearly on the north side of the Gironde. German posts and the French authorities were told to be on the lookout for four dangerous commandos at liberty in the region.

SIXTEEN

Execution

In the darkness and confusion of the first night *Cuttlefish* had separated from both *Catfish* and *Crayfish* at Le Verdon pier. Hasler and Laver had waited in the dark beyond the three small enemy destroyers, Sparks repeatedly blowing the seagull distress whistle. There was no response. But Mackinnon and Conway had not fallen victim to an alert sentry or an obstacle in the water: it was merely the vastness of the water and the darkness that combined to separate them from the others. Once he realised that they were alone, Mackinnon used his initiative and pressed on in search of a hiding place for the night.

For the next three nights they proceeded safely upstream, on the night of 10 December hiding on the Ile de Cazeau in a location that can only have been a few hundred yards from that chosen by Hasler, Sparks, Laver and Mills. Many years later it transpired that *Cuttlefish* had in fact been spotted by two Frenchmen fishing under cover of darkness in spite of the curfew. At about 10 p.m. on their second night on the Gironde, M. Raymond and his son Jean were sitting in their punt with their net fully extended when they heard a strange beating-like noise approaching. It was bitterly cold, and fearing a German patrol, the two men ducked down under the gunwale, hoping that the darkness would hide them. It did. They watched silently as a solitary canoe swept by, only a few yards away, the two occupants talking quietly to each other in a language that they recognised not to be French. In a moment or two the canoe had disappeared into the night, but the two men, frightened by this encounter, quickly hauled in their net and made for the shore. The story of the sighting remained a secret until revealed to François Boisnier in 2001.

On the night of 10 December when they left Ile de Cazeau, after three days of good progress, disaster struck *Cuttlefish*. What happened is described briefly by Hauptmann Heinz Corssen on 29 December, following his interrogation of both men. He noted that the information came from Conway, Mackinnon remaining stubbornly silent:

> His first Lieutenant and he himself had an accident at the Bec d'Ambès near the confluence of the Garonne and Dordogne rivers during the last night before carrying out the mission. They ran into an obstacle in the water which they could not see in the darkness. The boat was holed, and sank. They were forced to abandon their boat together with explosives and the rest of its contents, except for the sack with the money, iron rations and maps. They were no longer in a position to continue with the mission. They had spent the night on the Ile de Cazeau, so swam back there. A fisherman rowed them in a small boat to the western bank of the Garonne, where they found help in Margaux. The name of the village was given to everyone on the submarine as a place where they would find help. The prisoner claims that from here he and his Lieutenant walked to La Réole. They walked for three days; during one night they slept in the open and during the second in a barn.

According to subsequent evidence provided to his interrogators by Conway, he and Mackinnon lost contact with each other in the water. They had swum independently to the western bank of the Garonne and met up the next day in a village entirely by chance. There they had received help from civilians, including food and clothing to replace their sodden uniforms. That night –

12 December, when a few miles downstream *Catfish* and *Crayfish* were making their final approach to their targets in Bassens and Bordeaux – a fisherman from the village where they had sought refuge had ferried them across to the other bank of the river to the Bec d'Ambès. They began to walk south and, after crossing the main Bordeaux to Paris road (the A10), began to head south-east for the demarcation line where they believed they would be safe.

Corssen questioned whether Conway was telling the whole truth about the 'village with the helpful Frenchmen', assuming that it must have been Margaux. Chillingly, he observed: 'SD Bordeaux will find out about this village, but there are signs that the marine is trying to obscure the real name of the village to spare the Frenchmen.' There is no doubt that the two men had received considerable help from the local population, although we have no information of their activities between the night of their sinking – 11 December – and five days later when they were seen in the small village of Baigneaux, on the road from Bordeaux to Sauveterre-de-Guyenne, some forty-three miles from Margaux and thirty-one south-east of Bordeaux.

It is clear that Mackinnon and Conway had decided they would not travel north to Ruffec – perhaps the daunting prospect of crossing the Garonne and Dordogne rivers put them off this route – and that they would instead seek either to make their own way to Spain or attempt to cross the demarcation line – vividly marked on their map – and meet up with members of the Resistance who could help them on their way. When questioned, Mackinnon insisted that they were heading for Spain. On 20 April 1956 Hasler wrote to C.E. Lucas Phillips:

> I don't think that Mac was breaching security by saying he was heading for Bilbao – this would be the opposite direction from Ruffec, and could be a case of drawing any pursuit in the wrong direction. He might easily have actually intended to get to Bilbao, as a result of some info[rmation], collected while he was at large.

> I think it is almost impossible to guess what happened before he got to Cessac. The only known facts are that he was last seen off Le Verdon, and that he did not place any limpets in Bordeaux. There is really nothing to show where he came ashore, or when. I think it is quite possible that, feeling a sense of guilt at not having achieved the objective, he could have deliberately kept right off the Ruffec route, in order to give us a better chance of escape.

The dates correspond with the two men walking during the hours of darkness from the point at which they received help and civilian clothes on the western bank of the Garonne at or near Margaux. Assuming that they left their initial place of sanctuary on foot on the night of the 11th, after being ferried to the eastern side of the Garonne, they would have found themselves in Baigneaux, exhausted and hungry, on the evening of the 14th. Using the 1:250,000 maps found on them when arrested, the two men had walked the forty miles to Baigneaux over three nights.

What happened next was related to François Boisnier in an interview in 1999 with M. Edouard Pariente, the man who encountered the exhausted Jim Conway in the centre of Baigneaux at about 6 p.m. on the evening of 14 December.* Pariente worked in a nearby quarry, and was returning home after a long day. It was growing dark:

> Near the church he saw a young man, good-looking and wearing neat civilian clothing, but looking a little bothered. Probably a traveller, just off the bus which had passed a few moments before. The young man came up to him, speaking in a language Edouard did not understand. However, he did catch the word 'English', repeated several times as the man pointed to himself.

* Pariente remembered this as 16 December, but Jaubert's evidence was that they arrived in Cessac on the 14th. It must have been the 14th, as this would have allowed the three days and nights to be spent in Cessac, followed by their arrest in La Réole on the 18th.

Pariente quickly realised that this was an escaped English soldier, looking for shelter for the night. He was immediately sympathetic and thought quickly as to how he could help. As he pondered, Conway gestured to Mackinnon, who had been hiding nearby. Pariente noticed that he walked with a limp. The men clearly needed shelter and food. His own house was far too small, so he wondered whether any of his acquaintances might be able to help. One of his workmates, M. Pouget, agreed instantly to look after the two men; and on the following day another workmate, M. Cheyraud, escorted them along a disused railway track to the small isolated farm of M. Louis and Mme Louise Jaubert near the village of Cessac.

In 1967 Louise Jaubert described being asked by Cheyraud to look after the pair, which she and her husband did without a second's thought. Like Clodomir and Irène Pasqueraud, they were true patriots, although not members of any resistance organisation. Their son Roland had been in the Army, and evacuated in 1940 by the British from Dunkirk. He had been looked after well by a family in Dover, but as soon as he was repatriated he was taken prisoner and mistreated by the Germans:

> Two days before Christmas 1942* we looked out of the window of our small house and saw our neighbour, Monsieur Cheyraud, coming along the railway tracks. Behind him were two strangers who – he told us – were Englishmen who had come from Bordeaux. I felt very sympathetic towards the young men, but we made sure they were not German secret-police agents. During the night I washed their clothes. Mackinnon had a blue sateen suit, and while washing the underclothes I was relieved to see that they bore English trade-marks.

Somewhere during their journey Mackinnon had suffered a wound on his knee, which was by now infected and inflamed, and

* This, of course, was not correct. Mme Jaubert's memory was a week out.

causing him difficulties in walking. Louise Jaubert treated it as best she could. In spite of his injury Mackinnon was eager to get away – 'mainly perhaps because they both knew in what terrible danger their presence put us'. Mme Jaubert recalled that he said they wanted to travel on in the direction of Bilbao in northern Spain. Meanwhile, her husband tried, without success, to contact members of the Resistance across the demarcation line in La Réole, a small town on the railway route between Bordeaux and Toulouse. If the men could be taken over the demarcation line, they would have a much better chance of escape. But he was able to negotiate with a local man to drive them over the line at Langon and deposit them in La Réole, where they could catch the train to Toulouse.

After three days with the Jauberts the men said their farewells. 'We said goodbye to them with tears in our eyes,' recalled Mme Jaubert. 'We embraced them like our own sons – they were such nice boys. Sometime later we heard to our horror that the two had fallen into the hands of the Germans after all.' They had no idea of the fate that awaited their British visitors.

It was obvious to Corssen when he interrogated them some weeks later that the men had received considerable help in getting to La Réole: 'It can be assumed that the two Englishmen very soon received civilian clothes and help, and that they reached the place where they crossed the demarcation line either by train or car, especially as the marine is wearing very light canvas shoes which show no signs of wear. The place where the demarcation line was crossed is allegedly near Langon.' Louis Jaubert in 1945 suggested that the night after leaving them (17 December) Mackinnon and Conway stayed in the village of Sauveterre, before crossing the demarcation line.

It was the morning of 18 December when the ever observant wife of La Réole's police chief, an equally officious German-pleaser by the name of Captain Olivier, spotted two strangers walking through the town. She thought that they looked lost. In any event, she had never seen them before. So it was that Adjudant-chef Jean Barbance and Gendarme Pierre Hennequin were sent to obtain the identity of the two men, and reluctantly took Mackinnon and Conway into custody. On approaching them, it was immediately obvious that they were British. Hennequin, who spoke English well and was already a member of a resistance group, talked to them both.

Mackinnon, he observed, was clearly the leader. In a deposition made on the day of their arrest Hennequin said the former had explained that they were evading south towards Spain, following their involvement in the Dieppe raid in September that year. He talked openly, admitting that they did not have papers, and was clearly under the impression that as they were in the *Zone Libre* they were safe from the Germans. He described himself as a volunteer in command of thirty men who had landed from an unnamed ship at Dieppe, and had been cut off by fighting in the town and thus prevented from being evacuated. 'Realising this,' Mackinnon explained, 'we set off for the countryside, and since that time, with one of my men, we have been living from farm to farm in the country with the intention of getting to Spain.'

They had left their uniform at Dieppe, he insisted, and had been provided with civilian clothing by friendly farmers. Mackinnon was at pains to explain that they had never been captured by the Germans and were therefore entitled to be considered *evaders* by the Vichy French, which entailed internment or imprisonment at the very worst. If they had been *escapers*, it would have entitled the German authorities in the occupied zone to claim them back as prisoners. But somewhat confusingly Mackinnon then proceeded to explain that their task was the destruction of some factories, and that when they had failed to achieve this they had dumped the explosives they had been carrying.

The destruction of factories at Dieppe? Surely not. The clear purpose of the raid was to wrest physical control of the channel port from the German defenders, if only for a time. The fact that explosives were involved, with factories as their targets, might suggest that Mackinnon and Conway were in fact saboteurs rather than the simple soldiers they claimed to be. On being searched, Mackinnon was found to be in possession of an army pocket knife, a small metal saw, a Michelin 1:250,000 map and 600 francs. The police report stated that he had 'a knapsack containing one pair of shoes, a rectangular box containing some vitaminised iron ration tablets, a box containing some tablets for sterilising water, a sweater and a pair of stockings'. These were hardly the contents of the pack of a soldier on a day excursion to France, and suggested a more covert explanation.

As experienced police officers Barbance and Hennequin were undoubtedly suspicious of these two well equipped English vagrants. Their report was a model of thoroughness. Mackinnon was described as being five feet five inches tall, with light-brown hair and eyebrows, a straight forehead, straight nose, small moustache and 'normal' mouth. He had blue eyes, an oval face and a fresh complexion. He was wearing a grey overcoat over a blue jumper, with beret, shoes and yellow socks. The police officers noticed that he was limping slightly, having been hurt on the left knee.

After they had been taken to the police station, Hennequin acted as interpreter for the men. He actively sought to protect them from his chief, whom he knew to be pro-German, by mistranslating; Olivier, however, tumbled to this and furiously threatened Hennequin with punishment if he continued. 'On telephoning his colonel at Montauban, Colonel Olivier received the order to "fix" the matter for the Englishmen,' by which he meant to keep the information away from the Germans and to enable the pair to continue their journey to Spain. 'The procurator, on being informed,' said Hennequin, 'was also party to hushing up the affair.'

So it was that on the morning of 24 December the telephone rang in the office of a local lawyer, Marcel Galibert, who lived and practised at 89 rue Marcel-Badue, La Réole. The call came from the office of La Réole's *juge d'instruction*, the public prosecutor, with the request that Galibert represent the two men in civil court. By being in France without appropriate papers the men had offended against Article 2 of the 1938 Criminal Code. The prosecutor was at pains to explain that he wanted the law complied with to its minimum degree, so that the two men could be issued with papers and escorted quickly the 150 miles or so to the Spanish frontier. He had chosen Galibert because of his known anti-German sympathies.

Mackinnon was at this stage in the local hospital, Conway in the local prison. Accordingly Galibert visited both. Conway was dressed in rather worn working clothes. Galibert recalled, when asked to recount the incident in 1945, that Conway did not speak French and in any case was unwilling to talk about why he was in La Réole. It was Mackinnon's situation in the hospital that most alarmed M. Galibert. Suspecting that both men were involved in underground activities, he was worried when he saw Mackinnon in an open ward, freely conversing with the other patients and surrounded by ten or so young people offering him books, cigarettes and fruit.

'He told me that his name was Mackinnon and that he was an officer, but did not want to tell me from what branch of the service, neither how he had landed in France nor how he had arrived at La Réole. I gave him to understand that the Juge d'Instruction had put them under close arrest to prevent their being handed over to the Germans, and that in due course they would probably be freed. I said that I would endeavour to accompany them to the Spanish frontier.' It was clearly wrong, in his opinion, to allow Mackinnon to be surrounded by all those young people. 'They talked to their families about it, and it is perhaps because of this that the Germans became aware of the Englishmen's presence.' Hennequin agreed, noting that two of Captain Olivier's sons were part of the group that went to see Mackinnon in hospital, with the result that 'the whole town got to know about it, and the arrest of the Englishmen was the result'.

Mackinnon asked Galibert if he could find a way of getting a message to his mother at 22 Clarendon Street, Glasgow. On 29 December the lawyer penned a note addressed to the Red Cross in Switzerland, which Mrs Mackinnon received in April 1943. The message, poorly translated, read:

> Dear Mrs Mackinnon
>
> I expect that you and the family are rather well. Seen John who is healthy and well.
>
> Sincerely yours
>
> Marcel Galibert

After leaving the banks of the Gironde at Blaye, Corporal Laver and Marine Mills initially made good progress in their effort to get as far away from the river as they could. They were both wet and covered in mud, though, after their scuttling of *Crayfish* and the struggle up the bank.

Carrying their escape kit, they managed to find a wood in which to hide during the first day as they made their way north-west on the first stage of the journey to Ruffec. On Saturday 12 December they walked through the night, the town of Reignac on their left and Saint-Savan on the right. Like Hasler and Sparks, they successfully crossed the busy Route Nationale 10. During the next day they hid, presumably in a wood, moving on again as dusk fell on Monday 14 December. During the early hours of Tuesday the two men, having used up their emergency rations, came across a godsend: a small but remote and unlocked hut with a stash of food in a cupboard including bread, milk, wine and some cold meat. Although the food was old, it was still a feast, given the fact that they had not eaten properly for a week, and they devoured it all greedily. The owner of the hut, Raymond Furet, then a boy of only fourteen, was interviewed by François Boisnier in 2000:

> The farm is situated in the commune of Orignolles and is called Chez Ouvrard. It used to belong to my parents who lived in the neighbouring hamlet of Clérac . . . I used to go there every morning at eight until nightfall. The house was left unoccupied at night, with the door unlocked. On that morning I was surprised to find that the larder cupboard was empty and that whoever had been there had eaten and drunk the contents. There was seldom anyone around that isolated spot. But whoever they were [they] had left on the table a note on a piece of paper, written in English. My father hurried to burn it, for fear of having problems with the Germans.

It was at this stage that Laver and Mills became complacent. Having seen not a soul so far and having studiously avoided built-up areas, they now let their guard down and decided to continue their journey in daylight – they were still in uniform – and find a less conspicuous hideout where they could sleep. They had, of course, no reason to believe that if captured they would not be treated simply as prisoners of war and, following perhaps a rough interrogation, be transported to a prison camp in Germany. Like Hasler and Sparks, they had no idea of the end planned for them, were they to be captured, nor indeed that Wallace and Ewart were already in their graves.

During the morning they were spotted by two farmworkers who, recognising strangers in their midst, hurried off to the village of Montlieu-la-Garde where there was a small German garrison, to tell the *gendarmerie*. So it was that the hunt began for Laver and Mills. On being told by the farmworkers that two scruffy men in what looked like uniform were making their way through the area, the police reluctantly began to follow up the lead. The two locals were not British sympathisers, and were insistent that it was their patriotic duty to help in the capture of the fugitives.

Adjutant-chef Dupeyrou duly mounted his bicycle and began

the hunt. It ended later in the day when the two exhausted men were found sleeping in a barn not more than a mile from the site of their breakfast. They remained in the custody of the *gendarmerie* for several days, then on Saturday 19 December were handed over to the SD in Bordeaux and put in the municipal jail. Interrogation by the SD began immediately. Laver asked one of his interrogators – Kapitänleutnant Franz Drey of the SD – whether, in his opinion, they would be treated as soldiers or as spies. Drey replied (or so he told the war crimes investigators several years later) that he 'regarded them as soldiers by reason of their special uniform with rank insignia on their arms'.

On hearing of the arrest of Laver and Mills on 17 December, and realising that the commando raid on the port was a significant affair, Oberst von Auer, Chief of Staff of 708 Infantry Division, tried to close the stable door in a proclamation to the entire division:

> On 17/12/42 two members of a British sabotage unit were taken prisoner in the district of Jonzac north of Bordeaux. From interrogation there is no doubt that there is a connection between these men and the acts of sabotage carried out on 12/12 against ships in Bordeaux harbour, and that the men taken prisoner in the area of the Gironde estuary on 8/12 also belonged to this sabotage unit. The British sabotage unit had a strength of approximately 13 men. They came by submarine with collapsible boats and then reached Bordeaux harbour with five boats by taking advantage of the flood tide. When the tide turned against them, the boats would find secret harbour. By attaching limpet magnetic explosives on ships some damage was caused.
>
> Some eight or nine men from this sabotage unit are still free.
>
> It is discouraging that this event could take place, even though units had been warned after the arrest of the first two saboteurs. This proves that there exists a certain carelessness in certain areas and that troops have not been instructed properly with regard

to the danger of such enemy actions. Therefore the following has been ordered:

1. Each act of sabotage is to be communicated to all personnel so that each soldier knows what cunning methods of combat the enemy is using.
2. Sentry and patrol duties must not only be carried out according to the traditional methods, but greater versatility should be practised when on patrol. Unexpected checks, and raids and searches should be carried out. Special caution is required on holidays.
3. Acts of sabotage, attacks and even only the suspicion of sabotage must be reported to the relevant district headquarters as quickly as possible.
4. Offering suitable rewards for the prevention of acts of sabotage will promote initiative and attention to duty. On the other hand negligence must be punished very severely.

Future enemy attacks of this type will be prevented if soldiers are vigilant and the relevant district headquarters attentive to their duties.

Meanwhile at Wilhelmshaven on 26 December Hauptmann Heinz Corssen received instructions to travel to Bordeaux to interrogate four more captured British Royal Marines, two of whom were in German custody and two in French, in the town of La Réole, but who would soon be brought to Bordeaux. He was to accompany his immediate superior, Fregattenkapitän Dr Krantz, and to travel via Paris, where they would receive further instructions.

It was at the HQ FOIC in Paris that they were told by Fregattenkapitän Lange the astonishing news that the prisoners were to be executed once the interrogations were complete. Both Corssen and Krantz were especially shocked when they were told that Wallace and Ewart had already been shot. Asking to see a copy of the *Kommandobefehl* to verify these instructions for themselves, the two men were told that one was not available, having been destroyed on receipt. Not satisfied, they then visited Admiral Meisel, where they received the same story. Corssen testified to the war crimes investigator to the unusually intensive efforts he and Krantz had made to understand the nature of the interrogation that they had been tasked to undertake, and its outcome so far as the prisoners were concerned:

> Dr Krantz and I then drove to [see] Oberstleutnant [Wilhelm] Meyer-Detring at the OBWest in order to look at the Führer order. Meyer-Detring explained that there, too, the order had been destroyed in accordance with instructions. Either here, or later at the Counter Intelligence office in Bordeaux, Dr Krantz was told in my presence that the shooting of the first two prisoners had expressly been ordered by the Führer's HQ. According to a message passed by telephone, the report that the shooting had been carried out, had to be made to the Führer's headquarters by a stated time. The message was signed by Warlimont, WFSt. The third HQ to which Dr Krantz and I drove was the SD in Paris. Dr Krantz spoke there with Sturmbannführer Dr Knochen in my presence. There too, the Führerbefehl had already been destroyed.

It seems clear that both men were alarmed by what the SKL had already described as an 'innovation in international law', although their determination to get behind the truth of the *Kommandobefehl* did not prevent them from carrying out their duty as they had been instructed. The following night Dr Krantz and Corssen travelled to Bordeaux by train. Laver and Mills were already in the custody of the SD, and accommodated in the municipal prison. On their arrival Krantz and Corssen first received a briefing from Oberstleutnant Lohrscheider and members of the Abteilung IIIM, together with Kapitänleutnant Franz Drey, second-in-command of the local SD, on the attacks made on the blockade-runners. They were also able to view *Catfish* and *Crayfish*, which had been recovered from the river off Blaye.

Meanwhile, on 29 December two German NCOs from the Abwehr in Bordeaux arrived unannounced at La Réole police station. Gendarme Marcel Drouillard was on duty at the time. He told war crimes investigators in 1945 that they asked to question the two British prisoners. Drouillard pretended not to understand what they were talking about, but the two German visitors insisted that they speak to his superior. Reluctantly Drouillard reported the situation to Adjutant-chef Espère, who refused the Germans access to the prisoners. They were, he argued, being held in custody on behalf of the local prosecutor because they were in France without the proper documentation, and this required that they go through the correct legal process.

The two Germans, not to be put off, insisted on talking to the prosecutor. But he too refused their request. Furious, they stormed off, asserting that they would be back that evening. True to their word, at 11 p.m. truckloads of heavily armed German troops, about fifty in all, arrived at La Réole and surrounded both the police station and the hospital. Drouillard observed that about fifteen minutes before the Germans' arrival a telephone call was received at the police station from the Ministry of the Interior at Vichy, ordering the police to hand the prisoners over to the Germans.

Mackinnon and Conway were duly taken into German custody, joining Laver and Mills in the civil jail in Bordeaux. However, it is clear from the interrogation reports that, at the outset at least, the four men were kept separate and unaware of the presence of the other crew. The following day the two Royal Marines were interrogated by Dr Krantz and Heinz Corssen.

By 3 January Corssen had prepared his report. Whereas Mackinnon refused to divulge anything more than his name, rank and number, Laver and Conway, believing perhaps that with the attack behind them there was little danger in explaining what the Germans probably already knew, spoke more freely. They attempted to sow confusion in the minds of their interrogators, but by piecing together the various stories Corssen was able to build up a comprehensive picture of Operation Frankton. He stated explicitly, for instance, that Mackinnon and Conway 'did not mention the involvement of the other four boats'. Indeed, the report states that Mackinnon refused to talk throughout. Likewise, Mackinnon and Conway refused to divulge any information about the French people who had assisted their escape.

The German interrogation report, now in the National Archives, provides a remarkably comprehensive survey of No. 1 Section's recruitment, training and deployment, together with the names of those still on the run: Corporal Sheard, Major Hasler and Marine Sparks. It also contains information about the new types of harbour attack being developed by the RMBPD, Corssen noting: 'In future the use of special torpedoes should be expected, which would be steered by two men riding on them. Only the upper bodies of the men would be seen above water.' Likewise, it was clear that No. 2 Section had not yet been deployed on operations, indicating that a second raid was more than likely. 'A further deployment of demolition commandos against ships must be expected,' Corssen warned, adding: 'The training in Portsmouth was the same as for "Section One" . . . When and where the next mission is to take place could not be established, but the mission should be expected in the near future.'

Krantz and Corssen's business in Bordeaux was over by Tuesday 5 January 1943, the two men returning to Paris the following day. There the Abwehr's Dr Pheiffer demanded further questioning of the captured men, forcing Corssen to return to Bordeaux briefly. 'I learned nothing new,' Corssen complained, 'and returned to Paris, and thence Wilhelmshaven, on 13 January.'

Exactly when the four prisoners were finally transported to Fresnes prison in Paris is not recorded. What is clear is that on Tuesday 23 March Jack Mackinnon, along with Jim Conway, Bert

Laver and Bill Mills, were taken from their cells and executed, in full conformity with Hitler's precise instructions for the fate of captured commandos. Their final resting place remains unknown, although the Germans claimed in a document dated 1945 that their bodies were interred in Bagneux Cemetery, Paris. As with other German records attempting to cover up the *Kommandobefehl*, this claim is known to be a lie. The Admiralty attempted twice to gain information via the Red Cross from the German authorities in Berlin – who were normally forthcoming on these matters – as to the fate of the missing men, but on each occasion received a negative reply. They clearly had something terrible to hide.

SEVENTEEN

Home Run

The restaurant Hasler and Sparks had slipped into in Ruffec at midday on Friday 18 December 1942 was a working men's establishment owned by Yvonne Mandinaud called La Toque Blanche ('The Chef's White Hat'). Alix Mandinaud, her sister, was waiting on the tables and her brother René was working in the kitchen. Alix glanced up as the men entered, immediately noting their dirty and dishevelled state. Barely glancing at her, they made their way to the far corner of the room. Alix left them for a few moments before walking over and offering the compliments of the day. One of the men, tall and with a prominent blond moustache, responded haltingly, asking to see the menu. His accent was unusual, she thought. Could it be German?

She went over to the bar to collect the handwritten sheet, and when she returned something about the men's appearance prompted her to observe: 'Most of the food on the menu requires a ration card. However, the soup does not.' The strangers were silent for a few moments, before the tall one responded slowly, asking her for two bowls of soup and some wine. In the kitchen she mentioned the two men to René, suggesting that they were probably beyond the law as they did not seem to have ration cards. Her brother shrugged, observing that they might be German deserters, a not uncommon phenomenon in France at the time. In any case it was none of their business, and survival under the occupation was dependent to a large degree on seeing and saying nothing.

Hasler and Sparks were, by this stage, desperate. Cold, hungry and quite literally on their last legs, aware of their shabby state (they were still carrying their hessian bags over their shoulders) and uncertain about how they might go about engaging with a *résistant*, Hasler decided to risk their safety with the strangely understanding waitress. Scribbling a note, he enclosed it in the folded 500-franc note he passed to her after they had devoured their soup. Carefully they watched her return to the bar, look at the money and the scrap of paper, and calmly carry on.

Hasler had written: 'We are two escaping English soldiers. Do you know anyone who can help us?' Serving the two men with more soup, she told them to wait until the other guests had gone and she could close the restaurant. She then went out into the back. Hasler and Sparks looked at each other nervously. What if she had gone to inform the Germans?

But by the greatest of good fortune the two escapers had struck gold: the Mandinauds, while not members of any resistance group, were nonetheless determined to help the two men. But how could they be sure that they were not German agents provocateurs? Quickly, René contacted the local tax inspector, Jean Mariaud, who in turn asked a friend, one M. Pailler, for advice. Pailler was a retired teacher who had spent many years in England. On meeting Hasler and Sparks later that night in the flat above La Toque Blanche he was able to assert unequivocally that Sparks was who he said he was: 'He is a Cockney. No German could copy that accent.'

So the men were clearly British. But how could the small group gathered that night in the locked café make contact with the resistance *réseau* that Hasler was insistent they had been instructed to contact? What they did know was that M. François Rouillon, the manager of the Hôtel de France which the men had passed earlier in the day, was sympathetic to the Allies, and that Marthe Rullier, the local Red Cross representative, was friendly with the English Comtesse de Milleville. Perhaps they could help?

By luck they had stumbled on the key that would unlock the door into the otherwise secret world of the Marie-Claire *réseau*. Marthe Rullier could do more than contact Mary Lindell: she had been the Marie-Claire representative in Ruffec since 1940 and could arrange for the Mandinauds and Jean Mariaud to be taken to one of the safe-houses on a farm (known as 'Farm B') that lay on the demarcation line, run by Armand Dubreuille and his wife Amélie in the hamlet of Marvaud Saint Coutant. François Rouillon, likewise, was a member of Mary Lindell's *réseau*, and had looked after many escaping Allied servicemen in his hotel since 1940. So it was that the following afternoon, hidden in the back of a gas-powered baker's van driven by René Flaud (Mariaud's brother-in-law) and a young man called Fernand Dumas who knew the way to the safe-house, the men began the next stage of their journey. But now they were relying not on their own wits but on the courage, sacrifice and cunning of members of the French population whom they did not even know.

Hasler and Sparks, trusting entirely in their new friends, were driven by back roads some twenty miles to a wood deep in the countryside just south-east of the village of Benest, where they waited rather nervously until dusk. After making sure that there were no German or *gendarmerie* patrols about, the men were soon over the fields and standing, with their escort, in front of the farmhouse. The willingness of Dumas and Flaud to take risks that could have led to their execution, for men they did not know, spoke volumes for the latent patriotism in these men and women of Ruffec. The sudden arrival of the two Royal Marines had prompted immediate resistance to the occupying forces. Those associated with the Mandinauds were well aware, though, that Hasler and Sparks had been extremely lucky: there were many in Ruffec who would have betrayed them to the Germans. 'I knew I would be shot if caught,' recalled Mariaud. 'If I ever thought about the consequences of what I was doing I would have stopped. But I didn't. I know I was very lucky. People were afraid. You did not know who was your friend or your enemy. However, I got to know who the collaborators were.'

The appearance of the men on his doorstep at 8 p.m. that night came as a worrying surprise to Armand Dubreuille and his wife. He had agreed to provide refuge for escapers and evaders sent to him by Mary, but in this instance he had received no prior notification of their arrival. There in front of him were three men, at night, asking for sanctuary. His immediate concern was whether they were who they said they were. Why had not the Comtesse de Milleville told him of their imminent arrival? He knew Fernand Dumas, of course, although only vaguely: he had been to the farm once or twice before with the Comtesse. But what of the other two? Could it be that they were German agents, using the arrested Dumas to unravel the line?

The password 'Marie-Claire', however, settled him visibly, and he ushered them all inside. Dumas quickly explained in French the men's story and said that they had been vouched for by a range of people in Ruffec, and that for some reason knowledge of their arrival had been lost. In any case, could he get a message to the Comtesse while the men remained with them so that arrangements for their onward movement could be made?

Armand and Mme Dubreuille made Hasler and Sparks as comfortable as the requirements for security would allow. Armand told François Boisnier in 2002:

> It was the first time we had had any Englishmen. I told them not to leave their room during daylight hours and to keep the two doors locked. They could get fresh air in the courtyard at night. If they needed the toilet during the day, they were to use the small privy by the stable, but they had to check first that no stranger was around. My wife and I were obliged to carry on with our normal life, so they would not see us at all during the day. My wife brought them dinner in their room that evening and I said we would talk more the next day.

Neither Armand nor his wife could speak English, both parties having to rely on Blondie's somewhat rudimentary French to communicate. Mary Lindell had previously agreed with Armand Dubreuille that 'packages' moving along the *réseau* would stay for two or three days. On this occasion, however, Hasler and Sparks were to remain hidden on the farm, to the Dubreuilles' increasing alarm, for eighteen long days.

Being cooped up was difficult enough for the evaders, but even more worrying for the Dubreuilles. It was a dangerously long time to be harbouring such wanted 'terrorists'. The men were at least able to eat well and regularly: food was much more plentiful on farms than in the towns. It was the boredom that most irritated Sparks. Hasler was able to immerse himself in the few available books (in French and English) and the daily French-language newspaper, as well as the nightly BBC news bulletins, but this type of relaxation was largely alien to his companion. Hasler even used his penknife to sculpt from a piece of wood an elf blowing a trumpet.

The days dragged out, seeming to grow longer and longer. They had arrived on the evening of 13 December. Christmas had passed and then the New Year, all with no news from Mary Lindell. There seemed no end to their solitude, and to the complete lack of information. Then at last, at midday on 6 January, a courier arrived from the Marie-Claire *réseau*: it was Mary's son, Maurice. He was able to explain the reason for the delay. Mary and a colleague had been reconnoitring a crossing point over the demarcation line near the town of Loches, a hundred miles to the north of Ruffec, when she had been knocked down by a car driven, they thought, by local collaborators suspecting her of anti-German activities. Badly injured, she had barely survived, but had been fortunate to come under the care of sympathetic and patriotic French doctors and was even now recuperating in Lyon, which was where Maurice was about to take them.

Lyon, deep in eastern France only a few miles from the Swiss border and therefore far from being in a direct line to Spain, was nevertheless a relatively safe location, where Maurice and his mother could equip them with identity cards and prepare them for the journey to Perpignan and the final assault on the Pyrenees. It was also 110 miles from Geneva in neutral Switzerland, where Mary had arranged to deliver and collect messages from the British consul. Although the Germans had moved into the *Zone Libre* following the Allied invasion of French North Africa in November 1942, their presence was not yet as ubiquitous as it would later become. The greatest danger remained from overzealous Vichy officials on public transport and at checkpoints. But the nineteen-year-old Maurice seemed calm and unconcerned about the long journey, some 260 miles, to Lyon. They would cycle south through the countryside to the town of Roumazières-Loubert, where they would catch a night train to Lyon, travelling through Limoges and Clermont-Ferrand. Security checks were rare, and with luck they should get through without difficulty. They had little choice.

Saying a warm farewell to the courageous Dubreuilles, they promised to let them know, again via the BBC, when they were safely back in Britain. Following the theme of the message they planned to send the Pasquerauds, Hasler and Armand agreed that 'Les deux poulets sont bien arrivés' would be appropriate.* In a letter certifying Armand's help written on 3 August 1945 Hasler misremembered how long they had stayed, recording that it was 'about one month'. It had certainly felt a long time, for all of them.

They cycled that afternoon to Roumazières-Loubert, Maurice sitting on the cross-bar of Bill Sparks's bicycle (Maurice couldn't ride), arriving at the station as dusk was falling. Maurice went forward to purchase the three third-class tickets they required, instructing the two men to board the train from across the tracks rather than the platform, just as it was about to leave.

Maurice was right: no one paid them any attention, and they

* Both messages were eventually sent in late April 1943.

arrived safely and unmolested in Lyon the following morning. Sparks had a scare when they were exiting the station, however. He was carrying a packet of washed laundry with English labels that Hasler was keen they retain, in order, in the event of capture, to provide proof that they were not spies. Making his way through the ticket barrier, Sparks was accosted by a man in uniform whom he immediately thought to be a gendarme. Sparks panicked and, thrusting the packet at the man, hurried away through the crowd. 'The policeman's got my parcel,' he gabbled to Hasler breathlessly as they moved away, trying to put as much ground between them and the station as quickly and inconspicuously as possible.

But they weren't pursued. Maurice was keeping a discreet distance ahead, and they followed his every move, climbing on and off trams as they crossed the city, now bustling with early-morning activity. Eventually they reached a block of flats. Following the young Frenchman up the stairs, they entered one of the apartments. There, sitting on an easy chair, was Mary Lindell, her leg in plaster and heavy bandaging strapping her shoulder and collar bone. Her injuries, the men noticed immediately, in no way impeded the authority of this remarkable dynamo. Straight away she explained again the reasons for their enforced stay with the Dubreuilles and told them, almost incidentally, that they would need to stay in Lyon a bit longer. 'My route across the Pyrenees has been broken,' she added. 'You will need to stay here until I have made alternative arrangements.

Both men were immediately struck by the strength of Mary's personality. She was unequivocally in charge. Looking aghast at Blondie's now magnificent moustache she told him in no uncertain terms: 'That thing has got to go. It's too distinctive.' Handing Hasler a pair of nail scissors, she dispatched him to the bathroom to cut it off. Sparks was amused to see him meekly comply, although it took two attempts for Mary to be satisfied that the offending item had been entirely removed.

Hasler and Sparks were to remain in Lyon for a month, although they were forced to change apartments a number of times, the monotony of their imprisonment relieved only by the furtive business of moving somewhere new. Something of the nature of the Marie-Claire *réseau* is provided by Hasler's description of their accommodation, both men at times being separated, according to what lodgings were available:

> I was sent to live with Monsieur [Paul] and Mme Bonnamour. Mme Bonnamour is a daughter of Mr Barr, manager of Barclay's bank in Baker Street. I stayed with the Bonnamours for 6 days with the exception of one night, when I was sent to a flat belonging to Paul Reynauld. Carter* then obtained the use of a large villa on the northern outskirts of Lyons, belonging to Mr Barr. There Sparks rejoined me, and we were looked after by a young Frenchwoman who assists Carter [for a further six days].†

The business of securing identity cards was quickly organised. Mary then told Hasler that she needed to travel to Geneva to make contact with Victor Farrel about opening up another route across the Pyrenees, and that she would endeavour to take with her any message he wanted to have transmitted to London. Eagerly he agreed, but it was with a feeling of despondency when he sat down to write his missive that he realised that both he and Sparks had forgotten a part of the POW code that they had been taught in the weeks before their departure. So much had taken place since then that it had been entirely erased from their memories. Nevertheless, hoping that MI9 would be able to decipher what he was about to write, Hasler briefly summarised the operation.

It was the first formal confirmation to the watchers back home

* A French-speaking Englishman resident in Lyon, who worked for the Marie-Claire réseau.

† Paul Bonnamour had begun assisting evaders as early as 1941, and was closely associated with the PAO (the 'Pat Line') réseau. See Gilles Hennequin, *Résistance en Côte d'Or* (France: Société Darantière, 2010).

that at least some men had survived the operation, and were slowly returning. Combined Operations were otherwise completely ignorant of the fortunes of the ten members of the RMBPD who had been launched from HMS *Tuna* all those weeks before, in early December. It seemed a lifetime ago. It was clear from German decrypts and RAF reconnaissance reports that the attack had been at least partially successful, but there had been no news since then of the Royal Marines, with the exception of the German report that a 'small party had been finished off in combat'. Hasler gave Mary a note:

> COHQ. Tuna launched five cockles seven Dec. Cachalot torn in hatch. Pad hatches. In bad tide-race SW Pte de Grave Coalfish lost formation fate unknown. Conger capsized crew may have swum ashore. Cuttlefish lost formation nr Le Verdon fate unknown. Catfish Crayfish lay up in bushes Pte aux Oiseaux. Found by French but not betrayed. Ninth in hedges five miles north of Blaye. Tenth in field south end Cazeau. Eleventh in reeds thirty yds south on pontoons opp Bassens south. Attack eleventh. Catfish Bordeaux West three on cargo ship two on engines of *Sperrbrecher* two on stern of cargo ship one on stern of small tanker. Crayfish Bassens South five on large cargo ship three on small liner. Back together same night. Separate and scuttle cockles one mile north of Blaye. Sparks with me. Fate of Crayfish crew unknown. Hasler.

The message was sent, received and successfully decoded on 23 February 1943. 'Loud was the rejoicing in London and Portsmouth,' recalled Airey Neave, 'at the news of the two Commandos. [Brigadier] Crockatt [of MI9] at Beaconsfield was showered with congratulations, though it had only been by the merest chance that the two men had gone to the Hotel des Toques Blanches [sic] at Ruffec.'

Almost exactly a month before, all ten Royal Marines had been officially declared 'missing in action', and the men's families informed accordingly. At her home in Catherington, Hampshire, on 30 January Annie Hasler had received one of the impersonal telegrams from the Admiralty: 'Deeply regret to inform you that your son Captain (acting Major) HG Hasler OBE RM has been reported as missing on active service.' A few days later, on 2 February, arrived a formal letter enclosed in a brown envelope that postmen across the country came to recognise with dread, confirming the news in the telegram, but adding some hope. It explained that Hasler 'has been reported missing on active service while engaged in a raid against the enemy coast. My Lords [of the Admiralty] desire me to express to you their deepest sympathy in the great anxiety which this news must cause you, and to assure you that any further information which can be obtained will be immediately communicated.' There is no evidence in the Hasler papers that Annie Hasler was ever told of the decoded signal from Geneva on 23 February 1943, giving the first evidence that he had survived the attack.

Mary Lindell's return from Geneva (she had first gone to Berne) brought with it news that her charges were going to be handed over to another *réseau*, which the men were not to know was the Pat O'Leary Line, now being run out of Marseille by Albert-Marie Guérisse. Their contact was a small Frenchman called Fabien de Cortes, a tough young *résistant* in Lyon who since October 1942 had acted as a courier for Guérisse, who had agreed to escort the men to Marseille. It was now early February and they had been in Lyon for a month. They were to leave immediately.

Hasler and Sparks, now equipped with foolproof identity documents, boarded their third-class carriage for the Mediterranean port. The journey was uneventful, the two hundred miles being covered in five rattling hours. No one took any notice of the three men, not even the German soldiers with whom they shared their carriage. The travellers were too wrapped up in their own affairs to consider the possibility that two escaping Royal Marines might be right there in their midst. In the once bustling city of Marseille, on which the full weight of the occupation had begun to bear down since the arrival of the Germans three months earlier, the two men were escorted to a block of flats in the suburb of Endoume, a run-down quarter of the city overlooking the observatory gardens on the sea front. Their host was a housewife called Mme Martin. She and her husband, at huge risk to themselves, ran a hotel for escapers and evaders. They found themselves sharing the Martins' flat on the eighth floor of the apartment block with the first of the other escapers they had met: downed RAF aircrew and men who had managed to escape from POW camps in Germany.

The Martins were a remarkable couple. M. Martin worked in the docks and provided the income through which the guests in the 'hotel' could be fed. It was increasingly difficult in Marseille to secure food outside of the ration provided by the authorities, especially because, only the month before, the Germans, together with the Vichy authorities, had mounted a massive operation to clear the old port of 'undesirable' elements.

Marseille was now a very dangerous place. On 22, 23 and 24 January 1943 German troops and French police cleared some thirty thousand people from the 1st Arrondissement, claimed to be a haven for 'terrorists', sending two thousand to death camps in Germany and demolishing the ancient town. Fear now stalked the streets: the new Nazi jackboot, compared to the Vichy regime that it supplanted, was vicious and uncompromising. Prices on the black market increased inexorably as supplies dwindled, so that it became very difficult to find anything at all to supplement the increasingly meagre official ration. The Pat O'Leary Line provided what money it could, and forged ration cards were used extensively; but sacrifice by individual *passeurs* was also essential to enable the line to continue to function effectively. In particular, Mme Martin had to be very careful as to where she garnered her considerable daily requirement of provisions; she was forced to leave the flat at 5 a.m. each morning in order to acquire goods and foodstuffs from a variety of vendors across the city without raising suspicion.

For Hasler and Sparks, unaware of the efforts being made on their behalf, the Martin flat was a remarkable haven. It was in fact rented from a sympathiser, Mme Mongelard; it could accommodate twelve men, and was managed for Albert Guérisse by the selfless Martins and their two daughters, aged about seven and eleven. Sparks wrote:

> Monsieur and Madame Martin were lovely people, doing all they could to make us comfortable . . . Their younger girl took a shine to me and decided to try and teach me French, mainly because she thought my pathetic attempts were hilarious. She would carefully shape her mouth to show me how to pronounce a word, getting me to copy her. But each time she'd roll up with laughter as I came out with the wrong sounds, and that set the others off laughing too. I knew she was sending me up but she was adorable. The girls must have been experienced in the task of assisting escapees for they never spoke a word at school about it: to do so would have been our undoing, as well as their parents' . . .
>
> It became quite crowded in the flat, but there were plenty of beds or mattresses for us all to sleep on, and no-one went hungry. Sometimes friends arrived with a whole sheep, which they dumped in the bath and cut up.

The men's sojourn in Marseille lasted until 1 March. All the while they were hidden and sustained through the selfless efforts of the men and women of the Pat Line, many of whom were, and remain, anonymous. After several weeks with the Martins they were moved four miles across town, on 28 February, to the home at 12 Boulevard Cassini of another *passeur*, Maud Olga Andrée Baudot de Rouville – who, confusingly (given that the men had just left the home of M. and Mme Martin), used the non-de-plume of 'Thérèse Martin'. The resistance agent Louis Nouveau described her as 'very dedicated but [she] had an extraordinarily difficult character: for example, she forbade the pilots to smoke in case the smell gave them away during her absence'. More than a few escapers and evaders, though, had cause to be grateful for her remarkable diligence.*

The two Royal Marines joined the group that Albert Guérisse was bringing together to send over the Pyrenees, comprising, as well as the two Operation Frankton survivors, evaders Flight Sergeant Jack Dawson and a young Belgian aristocrat, Flying Officer Prince Paul Marie Ghislain Werner de Mérode of the RAF's No. 350 Fighter Squadron, whose Spitfire had crashed near Boulogne on 12 December 1942.† Guérisse's diary (in the United States National Archives in Washington) notes that on 1 March 1943 he helped 'with a last convoy to Perpignan in which there were: a Belgian (the Prince of Merode), an aviator in the RAF, a British Lieutenant belonging to a commando [Hasler], a British aviator [no – Marine Bill Sparks] and an American aviator'.‡ He was not to know that as he drafted these lines the Gestapo were closing in, and that he was nearly in their grasp. Indeed, by the time Hasler and Sparks's train chugged slowly out of Marseille en route for Perpignan – the two fugitives in the care of a courier by the name of Martineau – on 1 March, Albert Guérisse had himself only one day of liberty before he too was to become a guest of the Germans. Nor had Hasler or Sparks any idea that they were leaving in the nick of time: if they had remained even a day or two longer they would almost certainly have been captured in the great betrayal of the Pat O'Leary Line.

But their extraordinary luck still held. Within days of their

* She survived the war.

† De Mérode had previously escaped through Spain, in September 1941, after fleeing from Belgium in June, before making his way through Lisbon to Britain and joining the RAF. He later joined SOE and was dropped into Belgium in 1944. After the war he joined Belgium's diplomatic service and died in 1995.

‡ By the time the group reached the village of Céret, this man was no longer with the party.

departure from Marseille the *réseau* was rolled up by the Gestapo through the treachery of one man, Roger le Neveu. Mass arrests followed, including those of the courageous Fabien de Cortes and the Martin family, who had provided such invaluable succour to both men, and many others before them. On 2 March, the day after he had bade farewell to the group that included Hasler and Sparks on their journey to Perpignan, Albert Guérisse went to a restaurant in Toulouse to meet with Roger le Neveu, unaware that the man had betrayed his line, and himself, to the Gestapo.

Once an escaper or evader had managed to reach the south of France, the final challenge was to make it across the eastern Pyrenees. Many journeys, such as Airey Neave's, were made through the mountains that skirted the Mediterranean, using smugglers' and shepherds' tracks that avoided the road from Banyuls-sur-Mer that crosses the border at Cerbère, before climbing the mountains to cross the peak at the tiny village of Valletta, and then dropping down into the plain.

Even though the eastern Pyrenees represent the mountains at their mildest, this was a significant physical challenge even for the fittest of people, appropriately equipped. In wartime, when evaders were malnourished, exhausted physically by weeks and even months of deprivation, and without proper clothing or shoes – to say nothing of having to endure the constant fear of being caught – the crossing was a major hurdle. And for Hasler and Sparks it was even more demanding. The route took the party from Céret in Languedoc (where they had been taken by truck) over the Pyrenees some twenty miles – as the crow flies – from the coast, via the mountain villages of Las Illas and Maçanet de Cabrenys (where the border from France crosses into Spain), high above the valley that now carries the Autopista del Mediterráneo between Perpignan in Languedoc and Figueres in Catalonia.

The party now comprised five escapees: Hasler, Sparks, Dawson, Mérode and an unnamed Frenchman who had joined the group at Céret. Somewhere along the line the others who had started in Marseille had left them. Arriving at their point of disembarkation in the foothills beyond Céret late that afternoon to meet their two Catalan guides, Sparks was astonished at the beauty of the scene: 'Above us rose the towering mountains, snow-covered, awesome and magnificent; the only barrier between us and freedom.'

But it was over these mountains that they had to climb, and after two months of inactivity Sparks and his comrade were in a very poor condition to attempt something so arduous.

Each were handed a pair of espadrilles to wear, and a small parcel of food to last the duration of the journey. Once dusk had begun to fall they started to climb. Hasler and Sparks were soon struggling with the effort. Fortunately their first stop, after an hour of steep climbing, was at an old shepherd's hut where they spent their first, cold night on the mountain. It was an ominous start. They began to walk early the next morning, still relentlessly upward. Before long the two men were feeling the effects of the climb badly. 'I began to suffer the drain on strength that comes with high altitudes,' recalled Sparks. A combination of intense exertion and altitude acted to starve the men of both oxygen and energy, such that within hours they were holding the group up. It was only when they were able to drink freely in a mountain stream and to remain hydrated thereafter, sometimes by allowing snow slowly to dissolve in their mouths, that their agonies dissipated to an extent, and they were able to keep up with their guides.

Having walked through the first day, climbing ever higher and avoiding the German patrols known to be in the area, they spent their second night sheltering in a cave, huddled around a fire for warmth in the bitter cold, roasting garlic-infused sausages and bread that the guides carried with them. They were far too cold to sleep. And how the cockney Bill Sparks hated French cooking and its ubiquitous garlic! He grumbled good-naturedly but relentlessly to the long-suffering Blondie, who had eaten everything he had been given throughout their escape with relish. De Mérode recorded in his MI9 account of the escape that the dreadful journey took them four days of the most tiring walking. It was at the end of the third day that their guides showed them, in the clear night sky, the lights blinking in a distant Spanish village. They were standing at about eight thousand feet, the cold working its way to their bones.

The following morning, the exhausted men began to descend towards Spain, finding refuge at the end of their fourth day on the earthen floor of a peasant's dwelling. The next and final day entailed them walking to a point described by de Mérode in his MI9 debrief as 'about nine kilometres north of Banolas, where we spent 3 or four days in a hotel, seeing people who were in touch with the consulate in Barcelona. Through them arrangements were made for our journey to Barcelona by lorry.'

The greatest danger now that they were in Spain was their possible arrest by the police or the secret services of the openly Axis-leaning fascist state, which at best would lead to a long and uncomfortable sojourn in a transit camp and at worst to a handing-over, as had happened to the unfortunate Graham Hayes, to the Germans. Fortunately for the escapers, the Catalans had little love for the fascist government in Madrid, and most turned a blind eye to the weary men routinely seen trekking down from the mountains.

The first task of the couriers was to alert Henry Farquhar, the British consul in Barcelona, who would endeavour to bring the escapers secretly into the city and hide them out of sight of the authorities, before smuggling them onwards to Gibraltar where all evaders were debriefed by Donald Darling of MI6.

Farquhar did his utmost to rescue escapers and evaders. He had been doing so since 1940, despite the lack of funds for such enterprises and the opposition of the ambassador, Sir Samuel Hoare, an ex-career SIS agent, who resented the undiplomatic behaviour that the smuggling enterprise – for that was in truth what it was – entailed. When the SOE radio operator Denis Rake managed to escape to Spain in early 1943 he met Hoare after his release from the Miranda internment camp. The ambassador looked at him as though he had crawled out from under a rock, Rake recalled. 'Really,' he observed, 'I sometimes think you people are more trouble than you're worth.' Fortunately, Farquhar was supported by MI9's man in Madrid, Michael Creswell, who spent most of his time ferrying new arrivals from over the mountains, equipping them with clothes and lodgings in Spain, and arranging for their delivery across the border into Gibraltar.

With Hasler's party Farquhar did not disappoint. After three days of complete relaxation in a hotel in which they were the only guests, looked after by a man Sparks described as a 'very jovial Spaniard' who cooked the men large portions of food that even Sparks could stomach, the party were told by the *patrón* that a truck had arrived to transport them the eighty miles to Barcelona. Its cargo was porcelain sanitary ware, but enough room had been made at the front for the five men to sit, safely hidden from all but a detailed search of the vehicle. Safely navigating through the single checkpoint in the dark, the truck deposited the men at a boarding house in the anonymous back streets of the city in the early hours. The following morning they were driven to meet Farquhar, and although required to undergo an interrogation of sorts to validate their identities, they were to all intents and purposes safe. They had successfully achieved the 'home run', and were rightly jubilant at their achievement. They did not know that they were one of the few parties to escape via that route in spring; the weather had turned several others back.

The first thing Hasler did was to write to his long-suffering mother. Ever since his boyhood days when he had roamed the Solent in his little home-made boats, she had been sure that he would arrive home sometime, if not in time for tea. Now, following the sobering Admiralty telegrams of 30 January and 2 February, she was suddenly not so sure. Billeted at the Victoria Hotel in the Plaça de Catalunya under the pretence of being a commercial traveller, and aware of the awful pressure his absence would be causing his mother, Blondie sat down and wrote a somewhat laconic letter to Mrs Hasler, revealing nothing of his recent adventures:

Dear Mother,

I am taking this first opportunity of writing to let you know that I am still flourishing and happy. I am sorry not to have been able to let you know before, but you know how things are these days! I hope you haven't been too worried about me – I'm afraid it's not by any means the first time that you have spent waiting for news from me! I am very fit and happy as usual, and enjoying it all very much.

I am supposed to be on my way home, but anything may happen, and I expect this letter will get home before I do. Don't worry about me in any case.

I have had a most interesting time since I last saw you. I have only just arrived here, so the novelty has not yet worn off. I was here for a day in 1936, during the Civil War, but things are naturally much better nowadays.

There is quite a lot of food and drink to be had, but most of the things one can buy are rather expensive and appallingly bad quality. However, there are compensations not to be found in England – no black out, lots of bananas and oranges, and even quite a few eggs.

I hope you are keeping fit and happy. I am looking forward very much to seeing you again . . .

There is so little I can write about that I have now exhausted it. Hoping to be with you again soon.

Love,

George.

The first official indication in London that the two men had successfully negotiated their way over the Pyrenees and into Spain was a signal dated 25 March 1943 from the Naval Attaché at the British Embassy in Madrid: 'Major Hasler RM and Private [sic] WE Sparks arrived from France and will leave for Gibraltar as soon as possible.' No one knew, of course, except for the perpetrators, that two days earlier Mackinnon, Conway, Laver and Mills had been led from their cells in Fresnes. Cold-bloodedly, and in compliance with Hitler's instructions, the men had been executed, their remains hidden or destroyed to hide all trace of the crime.

The delay between the arrival of Hasler and Sparks in Barcelona and of the telegram in London on 25 March is instructive. The consulate in Barcelona was inundated with young men of military age fleeing from France, some genuine escapers and evaders, some Frenchmen fleeing military service or labour conscription back home and claiming French-Canadian citizenship, but unwilling to join the Allies as fighting men. There was also the possibility of deliberately planted Gestapo agents seeking to identify and then destroy the cross-Pyrenees *réseau*, so the consul staff needed all their wits about them to ensure that only legitimate escapers and evaders were passed back through the chain that led to Madrid and Lisbon or Gibraltar. Farquhar needed to be completely convinced that Hasler and Sparks were the genuine articles, and had not been turned by the Nazis – a difficult thing for him to do when both men resolutely refused to reveal why they had been in France in the first place. Hasler was shocked to hear from Farquhar some days after their arrival in the city that the tall, nameless Frenchman who had accompanied them over the mountains had disappeared. He was suspected of being a German agent because the *réseau* had subsequently been betrayed and the guides on the French side of the mountains arrested.

Because Farquhar had to work hard to keep his illegal activities under wraps and out of sight of the Spanish authorities (not to mention that of Sir Samuel Hoare), it took two further weeks for a car to be made available to drive Hasler to Madrid. As a 'priority' returnee he was forced to leave before Sparks, who was taken down to Gibraltar in slightly slower time. On 5 April 1943 confirmation of Sparks's arrival in Gibraltar arrived in a signal sent to Plymouth: 'Marine WE Sparks now reported to CORMORANT 031156Z.' Hasler had arrived a few days before. A car had driven him to Gibraltar from Madrid on 1 April, and the following day he had caught a long-range bomber flight destined for Britain.

Sparks's journey was far less easy. His identity still uncorroborated, he was observed closely by the authorities at every stage, a rightly paranoid security service watchful for swapped identities and agents provocateurs. He remained in Madrid until 1 April, when he left for Gibraltar by train with Pilot Officer Spittal RAF, his friend from the Pyrenees Sergeant Jack Dawson RAF, Sergeant Hodgson RAF and, as his MI9 report put it, 'several Frenchmen'. He arrived in Gibraltar on 2 April but it was a further month before Sparks, now somewhat lost without the guiding hand of Blondie Hasler, left Gibraltar, a virtual prisoner on a troopship returning to Britain.

Escorted by Military Police on the train from Liverpool to London, by this time Sparks had had enough of this draconian behaviour and gave his guards the slip at Euston Station. He was determined to get back to the East End to see his father, who he knew would be grieving the loss of now *two* sons. This done, the unrepentant Sparks reported back for duty two days later. At 1a Richmond Terrace, he received the rapturous reception he deserved. He was home.

Epilogue

Hasler and Sparks met a few days later in Southsea. It was a muted reunion, given the loss of so many of their comrades, but their feeling of satisfaction at completing such a difficult task was tangible. Their success, both in carrying out the attack and in achieving a home run, demonstrated most effectively that the sacrifices of the men who had been lost – Lieutenant Jack Mackinnon, Sergeant Sammy Wallace, Corporal Bert Laver, Lance Corporal Jan Sheard together with Marines Jim Conway, Bob Ewart, Bill Mills and David Moffatt – had not been in vain. British Royal Marines had boldly entered enemy territory and carried out an attack that cocked a snook at an enemy exulting in its apparent omnipotence. It was what they had been trained to do, and they had achieved their mission in spectacular fashion.

Unfortunately, Hasler's initial briefing to his men not to expect a long life, as Norman Colley recalled when they first mustered on the beach at Southsea, came all too true for many of them. Hasler felt their loss dreadfully. He cared passionately about his men and all who had helped him. The human cost had been appallingly high. Writing in 1982 Blondie remarked:

> Uppermost in my mind is the fact that eight out of ten men did not come back. It is easy to celebrate the glamorous side of the operation, but less easy to remember that, like most warfare, it took a tragic toll of young lives and left behind it a group of

heartbroken families. I can understand a little of their grief and pride because my own father was killed in World War 1 when I was three years old.

In Bordeaux the Royal Marines did enough damage to disrupt the harbour for months. It is claimed Winston Churchill later said that the raid helped to shorten the war by six months. This was hyperbole. But what is certain is that the raid made the Germans feel vulnerable in France, and it encouraged the French Resistance. Moreover, the tale of plucky British Marines fighting behind enemy lines was of immense morale value for a war-weary public at home – or at least, it would have been if it had been publicised.

So what was the purpose of Operation Frankton, and what did it achieve?

It took the war to the Germans at a time when opportunities to take offensive action in Europe were limited. In a letter to the French journalist Robert Chaussois on 3 January 1968 Blondie succinctly summarised the rationale for the raid, with an assessment of its impact on friends and foe alike:

> The psychological importance of small-scale raiding in 1942 was twofold: for the British, it was one of the few forms of offensive operations which we could carry out while our strength remained inferior to that of the enemy; it served to keep the offensive spirit alive, and to exercise not only the raiding forces but also the headquarters and planning organisations. For the Germans, it forced them to tie up a great number of fighting troops in patrols and sentries along a great length of coastline and these troops suffered from low morale because they had no operational initiative, and only a remote chance of seeing action.

In some respects Operation Frankton can be described as a classic 'Boy's Own' adventure, planned and executed by a classic adventurer, Blondie Hasler. In the sense that the events of December 1942 contained dash, high drama, personal courage, the outwitting of a Goliath by a puny David and the tragedy of judicial murder by an out-of-control and murderous police state, this is true. There was, of course, a deliberately adventurous culture within Combined Operations, led by the chief 'Boy Scout' himself, Lord Louis Mountbatten, who had been charged by the Prime Minister with mounting at least weekly raids against the enemy coast. But to see it merely as an adventure is to trivialise the Royal Marine Boom Patrol Detachment's achievement: the Cockleshell Heroes (again to borrow the title of the 1955 Paramount film and of C.E. Lucas Phillips's subsequent book) were most certainly not the equivalent of the Small-Scale Raiding Force, nor of the disorganised Commando raids of earlier in the war, nor even of the plethora of private armies that sprang up across North Africa in 1941 and 1942. These organisations could not have been more different from the Boom Patrol Detachment: the fact is that Blondie established, trained and led a tightly knit, well trained, purposeful and disciplined military team.

It is true, though, that the raid could not have taken place without the personal advocacy of Blondie himself. Likewise, his determination to build an effective harbour-busting weapon, as well as to take the war to the enemy, was always clear. He did not do this for his own ego, or for any warped sense of self-glory. Nothing could have been further from the true quality of Blondie's character. He had always been an independent-minded person: practical, energetic, single-minded, and undeterred by puny obstacles to his plans or dependent on other people's views for his sense of self-worth. He revelled in overcoming difficulties. Physically strong, he was also both physically and morally courageous, acting as his own guinea-pig in experiments with water and sail, and refusing to allow his men to take risks that he had not already taken himself.

But he was not reckless. Far from it, and in this respect he was infinitely more careful than the otherwise brave souls in the SSRF. He was also extraordinarily meticulous. As we have seen, everything he did was planned and measured, designed, drawn, and tested. Nothing – if it conceivably could be – was ever left to chance. He was an obsessive, immersing himself completely in the project at hand – and often several projects at a time – whether designing a new canoe, measuring the calorific content of new rations he had come up with, or trialling new underwater diving apparatus. Likewise, the planning and preparation for Operation Frankton was carried out in phenomenal detail – except for the escape arrangements, the responsibility of MI9, in which the raiders were let down badly.

If any blame can be attached to Hasler it lay in not testing robustly enough the arrangements for the return of the evaders through Spain. The plan for the Royal Marines' passage through enemy territory was perfunctory and ill thought through. Clearly, responsibility for this failure did not stop at Hasler's door, but at MI9's, as Airey Neave conceded. That the plan worked for Hasler and Sparks was as much down to luck as it was to Hasler's exemplary leadership. That, and his ability to find a way through problems that defeated men less well equipped than himself, as well as the remarkable courage of volunteers across France willing to sacrifice their lives and liberty to help the men escape.

The story of Operation Frankton remained forever a mystery to (now) Colonel Maurice Buckmaster of SOE. This is demonstrated by an extraordinary tale of bureaucratic incompetence at the heart of the organisation, revealed when a copy of a captured German document dated 18 December 1942 was received by SOE on 14 April 1944, fifteen months after the raid. The document, signed by Field Marshal Keitel, described how four valuable merchant ships had been slightly damaged in Bordeaux. The Germans clearly attributed this to a British sabotage party, and in the document railed against the Bordeaux authorities for allowing it to happen, demanding the 'sternest measures against saboteurs'.

The only comment that SOE could make was this: 'The operation can be identified with the often reported attack on the blockade runners, which was instigated originally by SCIENTIST [the SOE network] but never claimed by him officially as it could not be proved that it was his group that carried it out.' The organisation's response concludes with the astonishing comment that 'The two men arrested must have been local adherents, *because we do not know anything of their activities* [my italics].' The paper reveals that SOE had no knowledge whatsoever of who was behind the raid, not even that it was carried out by their colleagues in Combined Operations. These comments point to the confusion that reigned in SOE at the time, as elements of the organisation self-evidently did know of Operation Frankton, in particular those who had debriefed Claude de Baissac in March 1943. However, such knowledge never penetrated to Buckmaster's level.

One of the reasons for this, as the Foreign Office's former SOE adviser Duncan Stuart explains, is that in its infancy the organisation had no central filing system. It never recovered from this administrative calamity. 'Sections worked independently,' Stuart asserts, 'and were led by action-orientated individualists with a keen appreciation of the operational needs for close control and restrictive security but little concern for the filing systems.' Likewise, it seems clear that COHQ, and therefore Hasler, were entirely ignorant of SOE's activities in Bordeaux. It was instances like this that led to the establishment of a single clearance house for all raids, based in the Admiralty, early in 1943.

There was a further embarrassment for SOE. In his quarterly report to the Prime Minister in January 1943, written only weeks after the attack on Bassens and Bordeaux, the Executive Head of SOE Sir Charles Hambro claimed that the sinking by Hasler's Royal Marines of 'five merchant ships at Bacalan and Bassens' was carried out by SOE agents. Such a message would not have done much for the credibility of SOE, given that Churchill knew full well that Operation Frankton had been a Combined Operations raid, not one undertaken by SOE. What was SOE doing attempting to claim credit for an operation in which it had no involvement – and indeed the planning of which it had not the first idea?

Where Combined Operations and SOE failed at the operational level was fully to share their decisions about how the intelligence gained from third parties was going to be utilised in terms of military action. From the point at which Combined Operations decided that there was something in the idea of a canoe raid up the Gironde (21 September) to the point at which HMS *Tuna* left Holy Loch (30 November), there was more than enough time for SOE to be briefed on the plan, but it appears that it was not. This may have been because the usual SOE representative at the Examination Committee table (Major David Wyatt) had not returned from the Dieppe raid on 19 August, but the lack of dialogue between the two organisations was unforgivable.

On shore there was no inkling among the men of the Confrérie Notre Dame, F2, Phalanx-Phidias or Jade-Amicol networks (these groups, of course, knowing nothing of each other) in and amongst the docks and military-industrial complex of Bordeaux of the impending raid. Hidden in his secret bungalow in the eastern suburb of Cenon, on the hill overlooking the city and the docks lining the western bank of the river beneath, de Baissac's radio operator Roger Landes (codenamed 'Aristide') recalled: 'We did not know it was taking place – but then we were SOE and were not informed.' Aristide's complaint about being kept out of the loop, though, is not entirely fair. Even had Buckmaster known of the raid it is unlikely that he would have told any of his agents in the field, for fear of risking operational security.

The secret of security was silence. The fewer people who knew of an operation, the safer it was. Agents in the field with secret information about forthcoming operations might be tempted under torture to reveal what they knew, and it was for this reason that no one from the organising staff in Combined Operations or MI9 was allowed into enemy-occupied territory. The raiders, likewise, could be told of the generality of a resistance or escape group, but no names, precise locations or incriminating detail that might be squeezed out of them, however unwillingly, during a Gestapo interrogation. M.R.D. Foot and James Langley describe the occasion when an RAF escaper in 1940 received help in evading his pursuers from a French farmer and his wife near Amiens. Foolishly, he kept a record of their name and address on a scrap of paper in his wallet. When, a year later, he was shot down over the Western Desert his German captors took his wallet and, finding the scrap of paper, found and executed the French couple.* Combined Operations at least had assimilated this lesson, and the 'need to know' principle was vigorously enforced.

Nor is it true that members of 'Scientist' were on the docks on the night of the attack, preparing their own operation. Professor Foot described Frankton as a 'notorious occasion' when 'an SOE-controlled group [Scientist, under the control of Claude de Baissac] reconnoitring the dockside at Bordeaux for an attack that night saw its targets sink under the impact of limpet mines – provided, ironically enough, by SOE'. Elsewhere he asserts: 'The SOE were actually on the quay making their final recce before they attacked the following night, when they heard some quiet pops below the water and their targets started to settle into the water under their noses. They were furious.'

This claim has gone down in the mythology of Scientist, but it is simply not true. What *is* true is that Claude de Baissac had yet to formulate concrete or executable plans for launching his own attack on the blockade-runners, at that stage offering nothing close to practical proposals for action.

In his report when he returned to London in March 1943 he commented: 'In spite of the comparative lack of material SCIENTIST was well on the way to organising an attack on [its] shipping targets by the introduction of a reasonably large quantity of explosives through the dockers and the paint sealers working on the

* Langley first tells this story in *Fight Another Day* (1974), but developed the details with M.R.D. Foot in *MI9 Escape and Evasion*, published in 1979.

vessels.' There is no doubt that given time, perhaps another three or four months, de Baissac and his SOE network in Bordeaux could have launched their own operation to strike at the blockade-runners, but in the context of the need for immediate action Scientist was not in a position to attack in December 1942 (it did not have enough explosive, for instance). It is hard not to conclude that, had he been given the choice between an RMBPD raid in December 1942 and an SOE sabotage mission in March 1943, Lord Selborne would have not hesitated in supporting Mountbatten's decision to launch Operation Frankton when he did.

In Bordeaux, the Scientist network went on in 1943 to provide copious high-quality intelligence about the blockade-runners that, in the view of the Admiralty, forced the entire *Yanagi* trade to a standstill. But this, of course, was well after Operation Frankton. The volume and accuracy of the intelligence material provided by Scientist prompted the Admiralty to write in September that year:

1. The information . . . brought by Scientist on his last visit, was the most important he has had and enabled successful measures to be taken by the Admiralty.
2. Although air photography has contributed a little to the results, it is the ground intelligence from Bordeaux which has virtually put an end to blockade-running between Europe and the Far East this year. The stoppage of this traffic is of the highest importance as the supplies are vital to the Japanese.
3. Source has given better intelligence service than has been available from any other enemy port.

In the citation for the award of a Distinguished Service Order, which was authorised on 19 October 1943, SOE paid tribute to the success de Baissac achieved in tracking the blockade-runners, and planning their demise: 'Intelligence received from his organisation regarding blockade-runners operating from Bordeaux has been graded very high by the Ministry of Economic Warfare. The Admiralty have also expressed their appreciation of this information which they, too, rate very highly.' Claude de Baissac got over his disappointment at not being the first to attack the blockade-runners, and went on to play an important role in the establishment of resistance groups in the run-up to D-Day in June 1944. He died in 1974.

After his return Hasler was able to make his restaurant appointment with Dick Raikes, a few days later than anticipated, on Monday 12 April 1943 at Kettner's in Romilly Street, Soho. 'We thought the food was better,' remarked Raikes. Of Hasler he said: 'I didn't recognise him at first. He had aged ten years in those four months.' Later in the year both Hasler and Sparks were decorated by King George VI for their part in the raid. In one of those bland letters beloved of officialdom, Mountbatten wrote to the Admiralty on 15 June recommending Hasler for the DSO and Sparks for the Distinguished Conduct Medal:

> Captain Hasler and Marine Sparks undertook and carried through a dangerous and highly secret operation far within enemy occupied territory. They afterwards made their escape to this country.

The recommendation was approved by the King two days later, and the announcement appeared in the small print of issue no. 36072 of the *London Gazette* on 29 June 1943. The citations for the awards were slightly more detailed, Mountbatten stating:

> Major Hasler's cool, determined and fearless leadership was in accordance with the highest traditions of the Royal Marine Corps – and he is strongly recommended for the highest recommendation [sic] permissible for a feat of this nature.

And of Sparks:

> Major Hasler reports that Marine Sparks carried out his work in a cool and efficient manner and showed considerable eagerness to engage the enemy.

Other commentators have bemoaned the fact that Hasler was not awarded the Victoria Cross, but the thought never crossed Blondie's mind. Corporal Laver and Marine Mills were both awarded a Mention in Dispatches. There was no public recognition at the time for any of the other men who died at sea, or who were secretly executed by the Germans, as indeed there wasn't for many other brave, fearless warriors who died anonymous deaths fighting courageously for their country across many other fronts in this war. It was not until 1983 that a monument was finally erected, in Poole, to commemorate the lives, deeds and sacrifices of these gallant men. They have never been forgotten, however, by their families and those who understand the true value of their sacrifice. In March 2011 a magnificent new memorial to the men of Operation Frankton, and their French helpers, was unveiled at Le Verdon.

For the remainder of the war Blondie Hasler fought with great courage and distinction, continuing to design and operate canoes, some fitted with sails, against the Japanese in the Far East. In 1955 the RMBPD came to fame by virtue of the film *Cockleshell Heroes*, a tawdry piece of fiction that Blondie abhorred. He did not consider himself a hero, and wrote out a list of thirty-two alternatives titles, which he presented to Paramount Films. They rejected all of them, their eyes fixed firmly on the publicity and likely earnings, especially in the United States, that such a tale would generate, rather than the story's historical accuracy. In a letter to Professor James Kirschke of Villanova University in February 1987, Blondie wrote:

> In 1955 or thereabouts I co-operated with Brigadier C.E. Lucas Phillips in writing his book 'Cockleshell Heroes' – a dreadful title, linked to the premier [sic] of a film of the same name which was planned as a feature film, i.e., largely fiction and not a documentary.

> The book, but most emphatically not the film, is authentic and included virtually all I could remember about Frankton, plus a good deal of original research by Lucas Phillips.

Blondie regarded Lucas Phillips's book very highly and had contributed substantially to its preparation, considering it to be, in effect, his memoirs. After the war he was involved in the establishment of the Special Boat Service. Following retirement from the Royal Marines he occupied himself, amongst other things, with developing the art of single-handed ocean going yacht-racing, and is justifiably regarded as the father of the sport. He died in 1987. Bill Sparks later served in Burma, Africa and Italy and in Malaya as a police officer for a short while after the war. After a succession of jobs he settled down as a bus driver for London Transport. The prospect of poverty in his old age prompted by a reduction in his war pension forced him in 1986 to sell his DSM (it was bought by Lord Ashcroft). He passed away in 2002.

In Marseille, 1943 saw the bloody collapse of the Pat O'Leary *réseau*, with most of its members arrested or forced into hiding. By 22 April virtually all who had been intimately involved with it, including those who had helped Hasler and Sparks to escape, were either in prisons or concentration camps, or dead. The four stalwart members of the Martin family of Endoume were sent to the camps, and were never seen again. Only a handful lived to see the end of the war, one of whom was Albert Guérisse, who survived Dachau. He died in Belgium in 1989. The fearless Fabien de Cortes managed to escape from the train taking him and Albert, under Gestapo guard, to Paris. He reached Geneva, where he relayed to Victor Farrel what O'Leary had told him about the traitor Roger le Neveu. This information reached Langley and Neave in MI9 on 20 March 1943. De Cortes returned to France but was soon arrested and deported to a concentration camp in Germany. He nevertheless survived the war. Le Neveu reaped his reward with a Maquis bullet in the back of his head in 1944, but only after he had been tortured with a red-hot poker thrust up his backside.

Mary Lindell, the Comtesse de Milleville, survived the war by a whisker. On 25 November 1943 she was arrested at Pau by the Gestapo and taken by rail to Paris. During the trip she feigned sickness, made her way to a toilet, saw an opportunity and threw herself off the train. But her guards, alert to the possibility of an escape attempt by this most wily of enemies, were ready for her and shot first, hitting her in the head and neck as she fell. She was returned to the train and taken to a German military hospital where a German surgeon saved her life. Despite being extremely ill she was deported to Ravensbrück. Against the odds, she survived.

During 1943 Mary's son Maurice had been arrested and severely beaten by Klaus Barbie, the notorious 'butcher of Lyon', but was eventually released. Her other son Octave had been arrested in 1942 and deported to Germany, where he was murdered at Mauthausen concentration camp in Austria on 15 April 1945. The Comte de Milleville spent two years in prison, for his wife's activities. Their daughter Mary Ghita (Barbé) had also been deported to Germany in 1942, but had returned safely a year later. She survived the war. To carry on his mother's work while she had disappeared into the Nazi industrial killing machine, Maurice continued to work the Marie-Claire Line, escorting prisoners from Switzerland to Spain. He too survived the war, and died in Saarbrücken in 2007. Mary Lindell, after a postwar life dedicated to supporting the men and women of the Resistance, many of them the poorest of the poor but to whom no sacrifice was too great, died in Paris at the age of ninety-one in 1986.

The two eldest sons (Yves and Marc) of Clodomir and Irène Pasqueraud, who had escorted Hasler and Sparks to the bridge at Vinade, were deported to Germany in 1944. They did not return. Only their youngest son Robert survived. Nevertheless, most of those who helped Hasler and Sparks to escape lived on after the war, and some still survive in their old age, proud of their contribution to the safe return of the Royal Marines, and thus to the overall and eventual success of the Allied cause.

Back in Southsea Heather Powell, Bob Ewart's fiancée, had fallen ill with tuberculosis during the time the men were away, and died just before her seventeenth birthday. She never did read the letter Norman Colley was holding for her. Mrs Mackinnon received the letter sent by Marcel Galibert, the lawyer at La Réole, only a few days before her son was shot dead in Paris, his body dumped in an unmarked grave together with his three friends and colleagues, their lives extinguished by a brutal, blood-devouring regime for whom life existed only to be destroyed. It was for the destruction of this regime that the lost heroes of the RMBPD themselves died.

And what of their nemesis? Admiral Julius Bachmann retired from the Kriegsmarine in 1943. In 1945, serving with the *Volkssturm*,* the car in which he was travelling was attacked by an Allied fighter. He was killed instantly.

In another place – the 2nd Division memorial at Kohima, Nagaland, in India – far from the Atlantic coast, a memorial stands to the fallen. In words that echo the achievements and sacrifices of the Royal Marines of Operation Frankton, it offers a timeless, salutary challenge to those who pass by:

When you go home,
Tell them of us, and say,
For your tomorrow,
We gave our today.†

* A national militia established on Hitler's orders in October 1944, sweeping into its ranks all males between the ages of 16 and 60 not otherwise engaged in war work.

† The mountain village of Kohima in north-eastern India was the location, between April and June 1944, of the bloody repulsion of the Japanese invasion of India, the swansong of Japan's hegemonic delusions in Asia.

Glossary

Abwehr	German intelligence-gathering organization, focusing on human sources of intelligence, reporting to the OKW
BCRA	Bureau Central de Renseignements et d'Action (Free French Central Bureau of Intelligence and Operations)
C-in-C	Commander-in-Chief
Cdo	Commando
CO	Commanding Officer
CODC	Combined Operations Development Centre
COHQ	Combined Operations Headquarters
DCM	Distinguished Conduct Medal
DSEA	Davis Submarine Escape Apparatus
DSM	Distinguished Service Medal
DSO	Distinguished Service Order
FOIC	Flag Officer in Command (Kriegsmarine)
GIS	Geheime Staatspolizei (Gestapo)
GOC	General Officer Commanding (i.e., a divisional commander)
ISTD	Inter-Service Topographical Department

ISTDC	Inter-Service Training and Development Centre
KRRC	King's Royal Rifle Corps
MTB	motor torpedo boat
NCO	non-commissioned officer
NOIC	Naval Officer in Command (Kriegsmarine)
OBE	Order of the British Empire
OC	Officer Commanding
OBWest	German Army Command, West (*Oberbefehlshaber West*)
OKW	Supreme Command of the Armed Forces (Hitler's supreme military HQ)
passeur	a French helper in an escape network
RA	Royal Artillery
RE	Royal Engineers
réseau	Resistance or Escape and Evader network
RM	Royal Marine
RMBPD	Royal Marines Boom Patrol Detachment
RN	Royal Navy
RNVR	Royal Naval Volunteer Reserve
SD	Sicherheitsdienst (Security Service of Himmler's *Schutzstaffel* (SS))
SIS	Secret Intelligence Service (MI6)
SKL	German Naval Warfare Command, Berlin (*Seekriegsleitung*)
SNOIC	Senior Naval Officer in Command (Kriegsmarine)
SSRF	Small-Scale Raiding Force (No. 62 Commando)

WFSt	The operations department of the OKW (*Wehrmachtführungsstab*)
Zone Libre	free zone

APPENDIX 1

Hitler's *Kommandobefehl*, 18 October 1942

1. For a long time now our opponents have been employing in their conduct of the war, methods which contravene the International Convention of Geneva. The members of the so-called Commandos behave in a particularly brutal and underhand manner; and it has been established that those units recruit criminals not only from their own country but even former convicts set free in enemy territories. From captured orders it emerges that they are instructed not only to tie up prisoners, but also to kill out-of-hand unarmed captives who they think might prove an encumbrance to them, or hinder them in successfully carrying out their aims. Orders have indeed been found in which the killing of prisoners has positively been demanded of them.
2. In this connection it has already been notified in an Appendix to Army Orders of 7.10.1942 that in future, Germany will adopt the same methods against these Sabotage units of the British and their Allies; i.e. that, whenever they appear, they shall be ruthlessly destroyed by the German troops.
3. I order, therefore: – From now on all men operating against German troops in so-called Commando raids in Europe or in Africa, are to be annihilated to the last man. This is to be carried out whether they be soldiers in uniform, or saboteurs, with or without arms; and whether fighting or seeking to escape; and it is equally immaterial whether they come into action from

Ships and Aircraft, or whether they land by parachute. Even if these individuals on discovery make obvious their intention of giving themselves up as prisoners, no pardon is on any account to be given. On this matter a report is to be made on each case to Headquarters for the information of Higher Command.

4. Should individual members of these Commandos, such as agents, saboteurs etc., fall into the hands of the Armed Forces through any means – as, for example, through the Police in one of the Occupied Territories – they are to be instantly handed over to the SD. To hold them in military custody – for example in P.O.W. Camps, etc. – even if only as a temporary measure, is strictly forbidden.
5. This order does not apply to the treatment of those enemy soldiers who are taken prisoner or give themselves up in open battle, in the course of normal operations, large scale attacks, or in major assault landings or airborne operations. Neither does it apply to those who fall into our hands after a sea fight, nor to those enemy soldiers who, after air battle, seek to save their lives by parachute.
6. I will hold all Commanders and Officers responsible under Military Law for any omission to carry out this order, whether by failure in their duty to instruct their units accordingly, or if they themselves act contrary to it.

APPENDIX 2

The *Yanagi* Trade: blockade-runners between Japan and occupied France, 1942–5*

Operation Frankton was the first successful attack on the *Yanagi* trade. During 1943 the SOE 'Scientist' mission under Claude de Baissac contributed significantly to the gathering of precise intelligence about vessels in both the Gironde and the Garonne, but it was signals intelligence that revealed that the freighters were using 'safe lanes' some two hundred miles wide through what was otherwise a U-Boat 'free fire zone' in the middle of the Atlantic. This enabled Royal Naval and US Naval warships to begin to target the freighters more accurately on the high seas. The end of the seeming immunity of these fast freighters was nigh. Of the fifteen ships which sailed for Bordeaux from the Far East between August 1942 and May 1943 seven were sunk and four were forced to turn back, a failure rate of 73 per cent and a loss rate of 46 per cent. Of the seventeen which left Bordeaux during this period only ten got through (four being sunk and three turning back), a failure rate of 41 per cent and a loss rate of 23 per cent. These losses could not go on indefinitely.

* A comprehensive account of the blockade-runners can be found in Records of the National Security Agency, US Navy, COMINCH F-21, 'Memoranda, Reports and Messages on German Blockade Runners' SRH-260, National Archives, Washington DC, Record Group 457.

Then, a stunning cryptographical success by Bletchley Park in August 1943 gave the Allies direct access to the blockade-runners' own transmissions. As a result, in the five months between September 1943 and January 1944 six blockade-runners were sunk en route between the Far East and Bordeaux, only 20 per cent of the 33,000 tons of cargo that had set out on the journey being unloaded in France. With a loss of 80 per cent of the cargo, nearly double that of the previous period, the rewards of the *Yanagi* trade for Germany were no longer worth the effort, and on Hitler's instructions the trade then ceased, all remaining freighters being scuttled.

ships involved	24
attempted runs between France and the Far East	34
successful runs to the Far East	6
successful runs to Europe	4
sunk en route to the Far East	4
sunk en route to Europe	10
damaged in port in France; or made port, damaged	5*
sunk in port	1
departure cancelled before scuttling (1944)	8

What happened to the ships attacked by Operation Frankton?

1 SS *Alabama*. Bassens. Described by the Germans as a 'French ship being converted to cargo duties'. Five limpet mines exploded between 0700 and 1305 on 12 December 1942. Water penetrated through two hatches. Believed scuttled in 1944.

2 MS *Tannenfels*. Bordeaux. Two limpet mines exploded at 0830 on 12 December. The ship developed a list to 24 degrees but was prevented from capsizing. It was scuttled in the Gironde in 1944.

3 MS *Portland*. Bassens. Commanded by Captain Tünnemann, it

* Four of which were the result of Operation Frankton.

had just arrived from Yokohama before Frankton struck. One limpet exploded at 0955. Little water penetrated the ship and emergency repairs prevented any damage. Following repairs it left Bordeaux in March 1943, only to be sunk on 13 April off Dakar by the Free French cruiser *Georges Leygues*.

4 MS *Dresden*. Two limpet mines exploded, one at 0845 and one at 0855. Two small holes were made, leading to holds 4, 5, 6 and 7 filling with water, and the stern of the ship sinking to the bottom. The leaks were sealed by 9.30 p.m. on 12 December, and by 14 December the holds were pumped free of water and the ship refloated. She struck a mine on 6 November 1944 while on her way down the Gironde, and was wrecked.

5 *Speerbrecher* No. 5 (formerly the *Schwanheim*). A vessel of 5,000 tons, it was sunk by aerial attack off Royan on 13 August 1944.

6 Fuel tanker. The German accounts strangely ignore the tanker, which was sunk at the stern by one limpet and suffered fire damage.

APPENDIX 3

Combined Operations Raids, 1940–2

		Start date	
1940			
Collar	Boulogne	24.6.40	11 Independent Company, 374 Cdo
Ambassador	Guernsey	14.7.40	3 Cdo, 11 Independent Company
1941			
Claymore	Lofoten Islands	04.03.41	314 Cdo
Chess	Ambleteuse	27.07.41	12 Cdo
Acid Drop	Hardelot/Merlimont	30.08.41	5 Cdo
Chopper	St Vaast/St Aubin	27.09.41	5 Tp, 1 Cdo
Astrakhan	nr Calais	12.11.41	101 Troop, Special Service Bde
Sunstar	Ouistreham	23.11.41	9 Cdo
Anklet	Lofoten Islands	26.12.41	12 Cdo
Archery	Vaagso	26.12.41	2 and 3 Cdo

1942

Huckaback	Isle of Herm	27.02.42	SSRF
Chariot	St Nazaire	27.03.42	SS Bde, 2 Cdo
J.V.	Boulogne	11.04.42	101 Troop
Abercrombie	Hardelot	21.04.42	4 Cdo
Bristle	Boulogne	03.06.42	6 Cdo
Barricade	Pointe de Saire	14.08.42	SSRF
Jubilee	Dieppe	19.08.42	Canadians, 3, 4 & 40 Cdos
Gauntlet	Spitzbergen	25.08.42	
Dryad	Ile Casquets	02.09.42	SSRF
Brandford	Ile Burliou	07.09.42	SSRF
Aquatint	Port en Bessin	12.09.42	SSRF
Musketoon	Glor, Norway	20.09.42	12 Cdo
Basalt	Isle of Sark	03.10.42	SSRF
Fahrenheit	Pointe de Plouézec	11.11.42	SSRF
Frankton	Bordeaux	07.12.42	RMBPD

APPENDIX 4

Maps and Illustrations

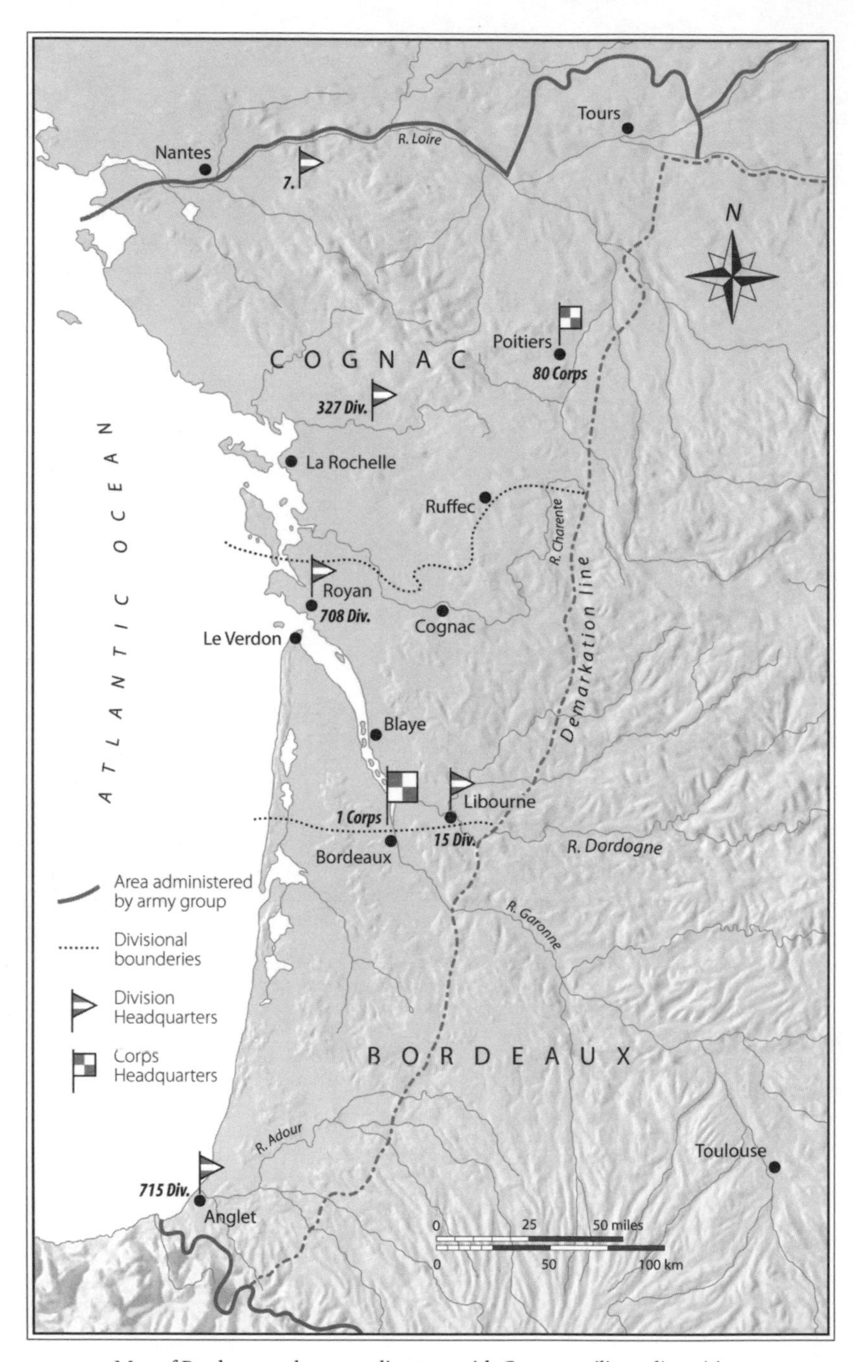

Map of Bordeaux and surrounding area with German military dispositions

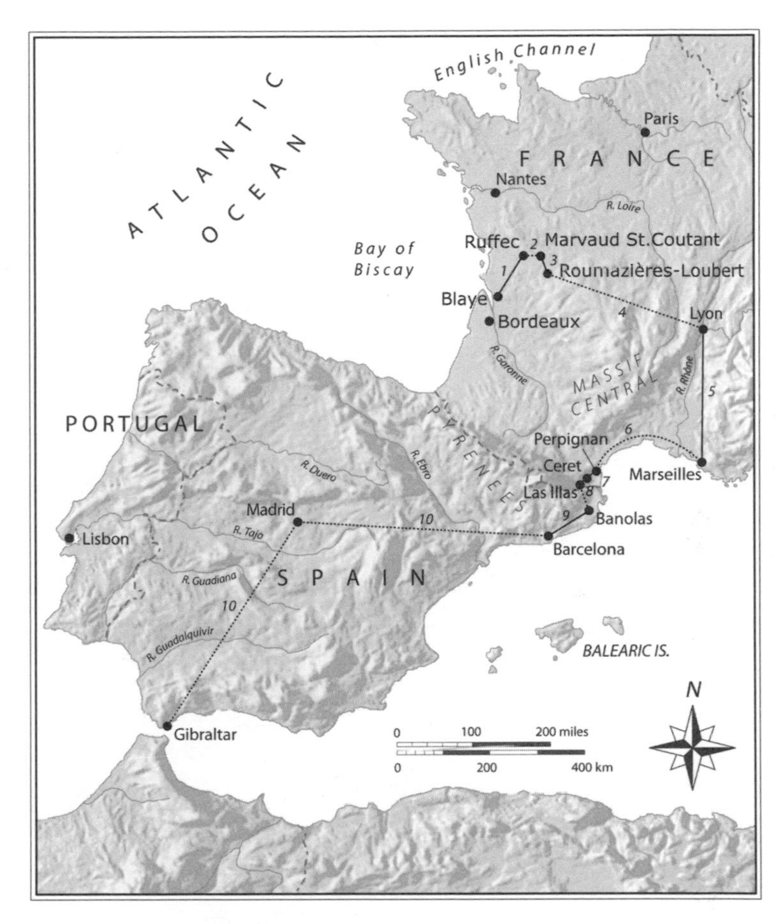

1. Blaye (Bordeaux) to Ruffec (foot)
2. Ruffec to the village of Marvaud Saint Coutant (in the back of a baker's van)
3. Marvaud Saint Coutant to the village of Roumazières-Loubert (by bicycle)
4. Roumazières-Loubert to Lyon (by train)
5. Lyon to Marseilles (by train)
6. Marseilles to Perpignan (by train)
7. Perpignan to the village of Ceret (in the back of a truck)
8. Ceret to Las Illas and then across the Franco-Spanish border in the Pyrenees to the area 9 miles north of Banolas (by foot)
9. Banolas to Barcelona (in the back of a truck)
10. Barcelona-Madrid-Gibraltar (by car)

Hasler's and Spark's escape route

The next three sketches were drawn by Hasler as part of his post-operational report. The first shows the route taken by the commandos up the Gironde estuary, the second and third show the disposition of the shipping in the harbour as well as indicating the positioning of the limpet mines.

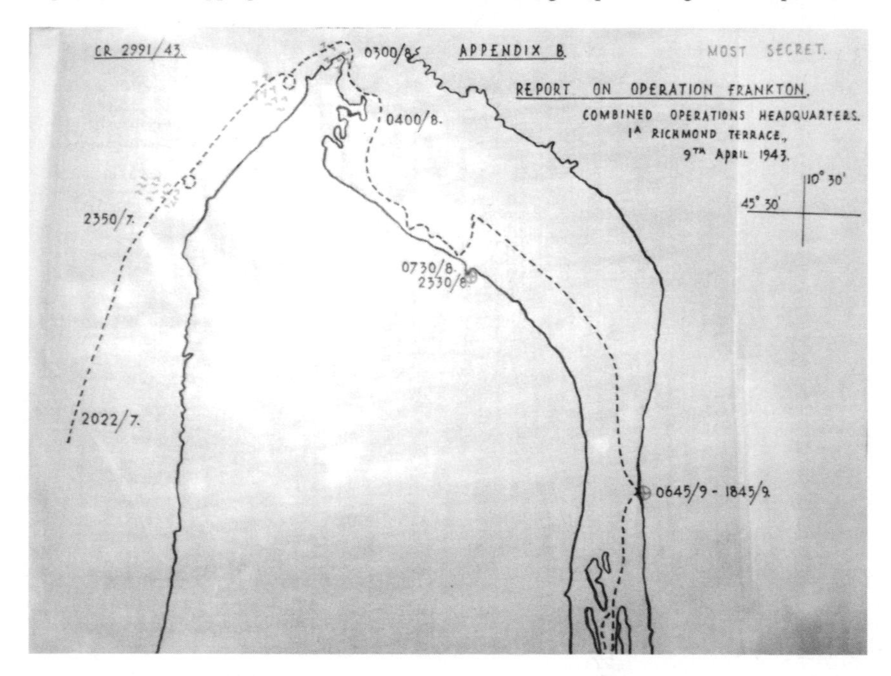

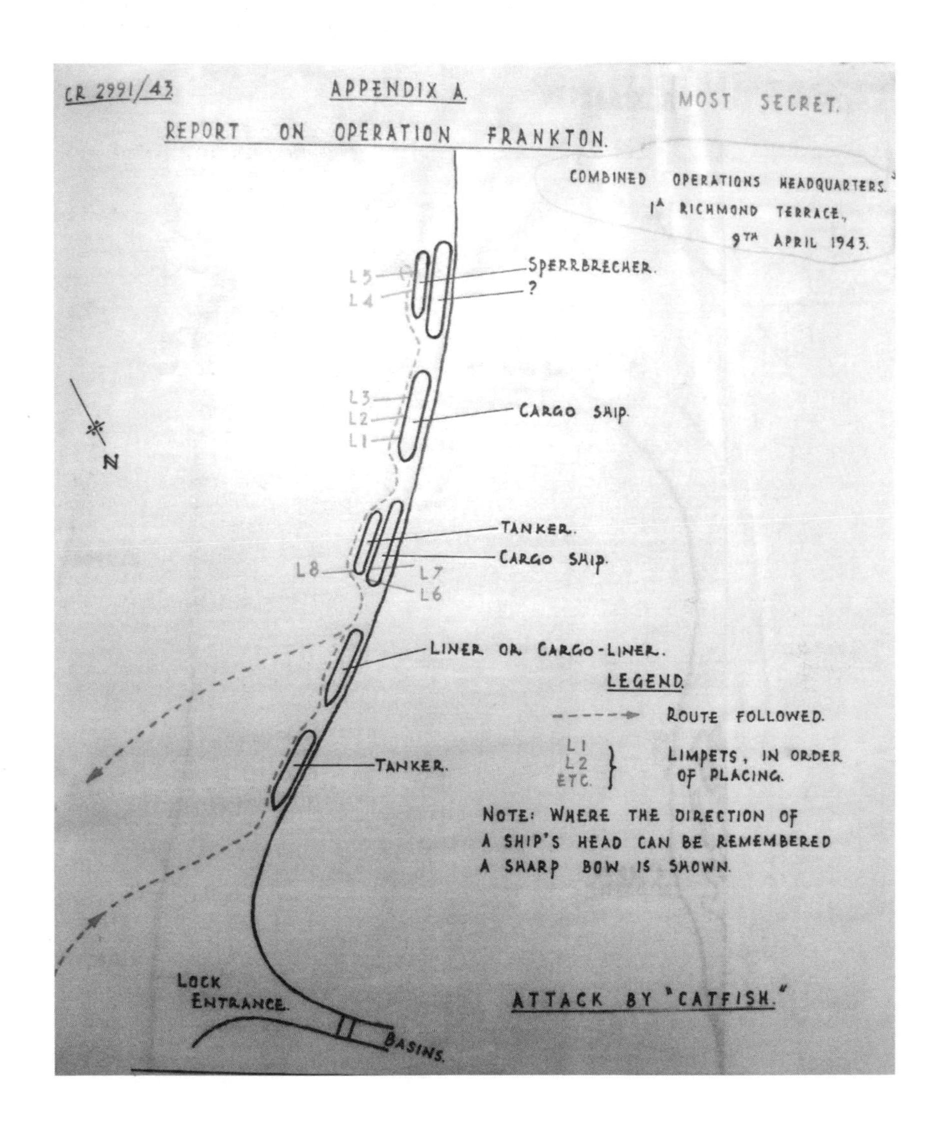
CR 2991/43.
APPENDIX A.
MOST SECRET.
REPORT ON OPERATION FRANKTON.
COMBINED OPERATIONS HEADQUARTERS.
1A RICHMOND TERRACE,
9TH APRIL 1943.
L5
L4
SPERRBRECHER.
?
L3
L2
L1
CARGO SHIP.
N
TANKER.
CARGO SHIP.
L8
L7
L6
LINER OR CARGO-LINER.
LEGEND.
ROUTE FOLLOWED.
L1
L2
ETC.
LIMPETS, IN ORDER OF PLACING.
TANKER.
NOTE: WHERE THE DIRECTION OF A SHIP'S HEAD CAN BE REMEMBERED A SHARP BOW IS SHOWN.
LOCK ENTRANCE.
BASINS.
ATTACK BY "CATFISH."

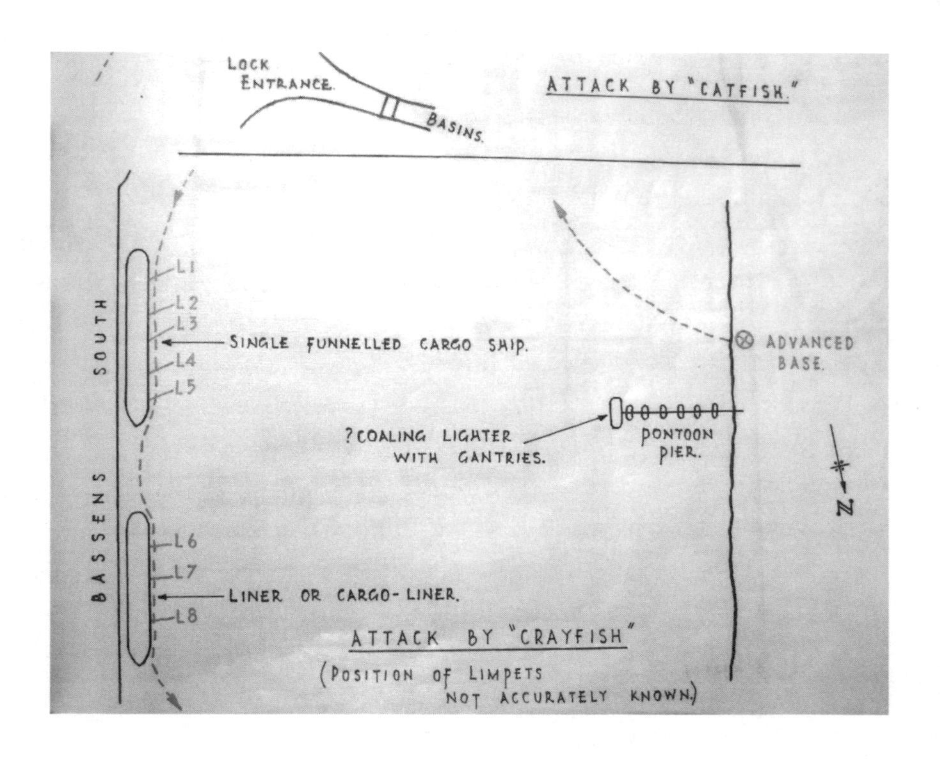
LOCK ENTRANCE.
BASINS.
ATTACK BY "CATFISH."
L1
L2
L3
L4
L5
SINGLE FUNNELLED CARGO SHIP.
ADVANCED BASE.
SOUTH
BASSENS
?COALING LIGHTER WITH GANTRIES.
PONTOON PIER.
N
L6
L7
L8
LINER OR CARGO-LINER.
ATTACK BY "CRAYFISH"
(POSITION OF LIMPETS NOT ACCURATELY KNOWN.)

Hasler's sketch of a Cockleshell MkII

Hasler's sketch of a tunny fishing boat

Sources

Broadlands Archives, University of Southampton (Mountbatten's Papers (MS62))

MB1/1202	Herbert Hasler
MB1/B53C	Operation Frankton
MB1/B55-9	Combined Operations

Bundesarchiv, Militärarchiv Freiburg im Breisgau

RH 24-80 Wehrmacht File 46a (Capture of Wallace and Ewart)
Subfile 390a, b, c
Subfile 392a, b, c
Subfile 401
Subfile 413
Subfile 415

RM 45 IV Kriegsmarine File 1148 (capture of Mackinnon and Conway)

RW 49 II Abwehr File 72 (Abwehr report of sabotage attack in Bordeaux)

Kriegstagebuch der Marinebefehlshaber West Frankreich – Admiral Julius Bachmann

Prozess gegen die hauptkriegsverbrecher von dem Internationale

Gerichtshof (IMT) Bd XXVI Nürnberg, 1949 S pp. 100–2
Hitlers Befehl vom 18 October 1942 über Vernichtung von Kommandotrupps Fallschirmspringern (Beweisstuck US501)

Mrs Bridget Hasler

Hasler's Diary
Various letters, photographs, sketches and papers, including two papers presumed to have been written by Blondie: the first entitled 'Blondie Hasler and the Cockleshell Raid on Bordeaux'; the second entitled 'A Look Back'.

Imperial War Museum, London

Sound Archives No. 8397, interview and transcript of William Sparks 14.11.1984
File 6349 96/56/1, the private papers of Lieutenant Commander RP Raikes DSO RN

Liddell Hart Archives

GB 0099 KCLMA	Papers of Brigadier Gerald Montanaro, late RE

National Archives, Kew, London

CAB/66/32/46	weekly résumé No.70
CAB/66/15/9	weekly résumé No. 77
CAB/66/16/10	weekly résumé No. 85
CAB/66/16/32	weekly résumé No. 90
CAB/66/18/30	weekly résumé No. 104
CAB/66/19/15	weekly résumé No. 111

CAB/66/14/24	weekly résumé No. 140
CAB/66/32/46	weekly résumé No. 174
CAB/66/17/15	War Cabinet meeting minutes 10 February 1941
CAB/66/16/23	Naval Military and Air Situation 8 May 1941
CAB/66/16/8	Lord Hankey's Committee on Preventing Oil from Reaching Enemy Powers
CAB 79/24/6	minutes of War Cabinet/Chiefs of Staff Committee Nos 301–61 MF
CAB 79/24/27	minutes of War Cabinet/Chiefs of Staff Committee Nos 301–61 MF
CAB 79/58/48	minutes of War Cabinet/Chiefs of Staff Committee Nos 151–212 MF
CAB 79/25/50	minutes of War Cabinet/Chiefs of Staff Committee Nos 1–50 MF
ADM 1/12	Loss of HM Ships
ADM 1/11710	Identification of Suspicious Merchant Ships
ADM 1/14353	Post-operational awards
ADM 1/18344	Shooting of captured marines and war crimes investigations
ADM 2	RM HQ
ADM 173/17676-8	Log of HMS *Tuna*
ADM 199/549	Letter from Lord Selborne to A.V. Alexander (Admiralty)
ADM 199/1844	HMS *Tuna* war diary
ADM 202/310	War diary of RMBPD Jan.–Dec. 1942
ADM 202/399	Frankton

ADM 223/3	Admiralty intelligence including information about Spanish iron ore from Bilbao travelling to Bordeaux/Bayonne
DEFE 2/1	Combined Ops HQ. June 1940–September 1941
DEFE 2/216	Operation Frankton. Photos, plans of area
DEFE 2/217	Operation Frankton. Hasler pre-attack appreciation (22 September 1942) together with minutes of COHQ Search Committee, 27 July 1942
DEFE 2/218	Operation Frankton kit list; aerials; hides and sketches
DEFE 2/842	Folbot/Goatley/Cockles
DEFE 2/952	RMBPD Reports of Operations
DEFE 2/953	Formation of RMBPD
DEFE 2/988	RMBPD 1942–8
HS 6	SOE Operations Western Europe
HS 6/ 416	Use of Limpets
HS 6/418	Barter mission MF
HS 6/589	Sabotage in France MF
HS 6/592	Liaison with FO: 'Action against Vichy shipping'
HS 7/244	France F Section Diary July–Sept. 1942 (pp. 1–144)
HS 7/245	France F Section Diary July–Sept. 1942 (pp. 145–315)
HS 8	SOE HQ Files
HS 8/203	SOE Council minutes

HS 8/244	Reports to the Chiefs of Staff Committee March–December 1942
HS 8/818/9	CCO/SOE Liaison Reports (Major David Wyatt RE)
HS 8/831	HMS *Fidelity*
HS 8/889/12	Quarterly SOE report to the Prime Minister (March–June 1942)
HS 8/889/13	Quarterly SOE report to the Prime Minister (July–September 1942)
HS 8/897	Letters from Lord Selborne to ministers
HS 8/1002	British circuits in France (Major R.A. Bourne-Paterson) (also HS 6/469 and 7/122)
HS 9/75	Debrief of Robert Leroy, 6 September 1943
HS 9/76	Claude de Baissac
HS 9/916/2	Robert Leroy
HS 9/1023/5	De Mérode
WO 165/39	Main HQ diary of MI9
WO 208/3242	Crockatt's Historical Record of MI9
WO 208/3268	MI9 Bulletin
WO 208/3312/1131	MI9 Evasion Report for de Mérode
WO 208/3312/1140	MI9 Evasion Report for Hasler
WO 208/3312/1160	MI9 Evasion Report for Flight Sergeant Jack Dawson RAF
WO 208/3312/1162	MI9 Evasion Report for Sparks
WO 208/324	Pre-capture training
WO 208/3494	Escapers and evaders
WO 252/118	Topographical report on the Gironde

WO 309/551	Killing of members of British raiding party from HM Submarine *Tuna*
WO 309/1604	Shooting of naval personnel in Bordeaux and elsewhere
WO 311/617	Killing of members of British raiding party from HM Submarine *Tuna*
WO 373/93	Award of DSO to Claude de Baissac
HW 1/1220	Signals Intelligence passed to Winston Churchill
HW1/1234	German Naval transcripts reporting heavy damage to steamships in Bordeaux
HW 14/61	Bletchley Park intercept of German report on Frankton
AIR 14/354	Escape Aids
Air 14/835	Operation Josephine 'B'
FO 837	Ministry of Economic Warfare
FO 954/8A	Eden's response
FO 954/31B/266-267	Selborne's letter to Eden

National Archives and Records Administration, Washington DC

SRH-260, Record Group 457 – Records of the National Security Agency, US Navy, COMINCH F-21, 'Memoranda, Reports and Messages on German Blockade Runners'

Kriegstagebuch des Oberbefehlshaber des Marinegruppenkommandos West: Admiral Marschall (1–15 December 1942). Pp. 4810–16; 4825–7; 4830–3; 4845–6. Führungsbefehl No. 14

Kriegstagebuch des Hafenkommandant Bordeaux 2–17 December 1942

Albert-Marie Guérisse (Pat Albert O'Leary) MIS-X file

Royal Marine Museum, Southsea, Portsmouth

2/15/4 RMBPD

7/19/13(1) Operation Frankton

Hasler Papers, 88/05

Select Bibliography

Marcus Binney *Secret War Heroes: Men of the Special Operations Executive* (London: Hodder & Stoughton, 2005)

Marcus Binney *The Women Who Lived For Danger: The Woman Agents of SOE in the Second World War* (London: Hodder & Stoughton, 2002)

Hugo Bleicher *Colonel Henri's Story* (London: William Kimber, 1954)

François Boisnier and Raymond Muelle *Le Commando de L'Impossible, Bordeaux 1942* (Paris: Trésor du Patrimoine, 2003)

Frederic Boyce and Douglas Everett *SOE, the Scientific Secrets* (Stroud: Sutton Publishing, 2003)

Martin Brice *Axis Blockade Runners of World War Two* (London: Batsford, 1981)

Donald Caskie *The Tartan Pimpernel* (London: Fontana and Oldbourne Press, 1960)

Matthew Cobb *The Resistance* (London: Simon & Schuster, 2009)

Richard Cobb *French and Germans. Germans and French* (New England: Brandeis, 1983)

François Cordet *Carnets de guerre en Charente* (Romagnat: Editions Gérard Tisserand, 2004)

G.B. Courtney *SBS in World War Two* (London: Robert Hale, 1983)

Cyril Cunningham *Beaulieu: The Finishing School for Secret Agents* (Barnsley: Leo Cooper, 1956)

Donald Darling *Secret Sunday* (London: William Kimber, 1975)
— *Sunday at Large* (London: William Kimber, 1977)
John Durnford-Slater *Commando* (London: William Kimber, 1953)
Bernard Fergusson *The Watery Maze* (London: Collins, 1961)
M.R.D. Foot *Resistance* (London: Eyre Methuen, 1976)
— *An Outline History of the Special Operations Executive 1940–1946* (London: BBC, 1984)
— *SOE in France: An Account of theWork of the British Operations Executive* (London: Routledge, Revised Edition, 2004)
M.R.D. Foot and J.M. Langley *MI9 Escape and Evasion 1939–1945* (London: Bodley Head, 1979)
Ken Ford *The Cockleshell Raid* (Botley, Oxford: Osprey: 2010)
Gérard Fournier and André Heintz *If I Must Die* (France, Editions Orep, 2006)
Betram M. Gordon *Collaboration in France During World War Two* (Ithaca, NY: Cornell University Press, 1980)
S. Hawes and R. White *Resistance in Europe, 1939–1945* (Harmondsworth: Penguin, 1976)
F.H. Hinsey *British Intelligence in the Second World War* vol 1. (London: HMSO, 1979)
C. Clayton Hutton *Official Secret* (Max Parrish, 1960)
Julian Jackson *France, The Dark Years* (Oxford: Oxford University Press, 2001)
Peter Janes *Conscript Heroes* (Paul Mould Publishing, 2004)
Keith Jeffery MI6 *The History of the Secret Intelligence Service 1909–1949* (London: Bloomsbury, 2010)
H.R. Kedward *Resistance in Vichy France* (Oxford: Oxford University Press, 1978)
— *Occupied France* (Oxford: Blackwell, 1985)
John Kennedy *The Business of War* (London: Hutchinson, 1957)
J.M. Langley *Fight Another Day* (London: Collins, 1974)
James Leasor *War at the Top* (London: Michael Joseph, 1959)
Admiral Lepotier *Commando dans la Gironde* (Paris: France Empire, 1957)

Helen Long *Safe Houses Are Dangerous* (London: William Kimber, 1985)
William Mackenzie *The Secret History of SOE – Special Operations Executive 1940–1945* (London: BPR Publications, 2000)
Airey Neave *They Have Their Exits* (London: Hodder & Stoughton, 1953)
— *Little Cyclone* (London: Hodder & Stoughton, 1954)
— *Saturday at MI9* (London: Hodder & Stoughton, 1969)
John Nichol and Tony Rennell *Home Run: Escape from Nazi Europe* (London: Penguin, 2007)
David Niven *The Moon's a Balloon* (London: Hamish Hamilton, 1971)
Henri Noguères *Histoire de la Résistance en France* (Paris: R. Laffont, 1969–81) 5 vols
Sherri Ottis *Silent Heroes* (University of Kentucky, 2001)
Robert O. Paxton *Vichy France: Old Guard and New Order* (Columbia University Press, 1972)
Guy Penaud *Histoire secrète de la Résistance dans le Sud-Ouest* (Editions Sud-Ouest, 1993)
Joseph Persico *Piercing the Reich* (New York: Viking Press, 1979)
Eric Petetin *Le père Antoine Dieuzaide* (Imprimerie Centrale de Bordeaux, 1984)
Janusz Piekałkiewicz 'Operation Frankton' in *Secret Agents, Spies and Saboteurs* (Newton Abbot: David & Charles, 1974)
C.E. Lucas Phillips *Cockleshell Heroes* (London: Heinemann, 1956)
Patrick Pringle *Fighting Marines* (London: Evans Brothers, 1966)
Anthony Read and David Fisher *Colonel Z. The Secret Life of a Master of Spies* (London: Hodder & Stoughton, 1984)
Robert Rhodes James (ed.) *Chips: The Diaries of Sir Henry Channon* (London: Weidenfeld & Nicolson, 1967)
Brooks Richards *Secret Flotillas: Clandestine Sea Operations to Brittany, 1940–1944* vol. 1 (London: HMSO, 1996)
Hilary St George Saunders *Combined Operations: The Official Story of the Commandos* (New York: Macmillan, 1943)

Hélie de Saint-Marc et Laurent Beccaria *Hélie de Saint-Marc* (Paris: Editions Perrin, 1988)
Francis Salaberry *Aquitaine Allemande* (J et D Publications, 1995)
Michel Slitinsky *Trois filles et vingt garçons* (Bordeaux: Editions des Cahiers de la Résistance, 1969)
— *La Résistance en Gironde* (Bordeaux: Editions des Cahiers de la Résistance, 1972)
Ewen Southby-Tailyour *Blondie* (Barnsley: Leo Cooper, 1998)
William Sparks *Cockleshell Commando* (Barnsley: Pen and Sword, 2002)
— with Michael Munn *The Last of the Cockleshell Heroes* (Barnsley: Leo Cooper, 1992)
Tess Stirling (ed.) *Intelligence Co-operation between Poland and Great Britain during World War Two* (London: Vallentine Mitchell, 2005)
John F. Sweets *Choices in Vichy France* (Oxford, 1986)
René Terrisse *Bordeaux 1940–1944* (Paris: Editions Perrin, 1993
Hugh Verity *We Landed by Moonlight* (Surrey: Ian Allen, 1978)
Richard Vinen *The Unfree French* (London: Allen Lane, 2006)
Barry Wynne *No Drums, No Trumpets, The Story of Mary Lindell* (London: Arthur Barker, 1961)
Philip Ziegler *Mountbatten* (London: Collins, 1985)

Articles

Tony Hunter-Choat and Mark Bentinck 'The Cockleshell Heroes Raid' *After the Battle* no. 118 (2002)
Tom Keene 'Plans, Targets and Secrets' *Royal Marines Historical Society Journal* (2005)
Duncan Stuart 'Of Historical Interest Only: The Origins and Vicissitudes of the SOE Archive' *Intelligence and National Security* vol. 20 no. 1 (March 2005)
Burke Wilkinson 'Cockles and Muscles: Operation Frankton'

Proceedings of the US Naval Institute vol. 80 no. 2 (February 1954)

Television/Film

Cockleshell Revisited Televideo Productions 1993
Frankton's Shadows BBC2 documentary Tom Keene 2004
It Happened To Me: The Story of Mary Lindell BBC 1959
The Last of the Cockleshell Heroes Jonathan Marland Meridian Television 2002
Mary Lindell Yorkshire Television 1980
Des Ombres dans la Nuit narrated by Ramon Maranon (in French) 2004
One Against the Wind 1991 (Drama)
Interview with Bill Sparks, Columbia-Gaumont (via Frankton Souvenir)

Document

Interview with Lt Cdr Dick Raikes DSO courtesy of Ewen Southby-Tailyour 2004

Acknowledgements

I could not have written this book without the active assistance of a wide range of people in Britain, France, the United States and Germany who generously gave me their time and access to material about the raid. I am particularly grateful to Mrs Bridget Hasler who opened up Blondie's extensive papers to me and allowed me their unrestricted use. These included interview transcripts, diaries, letters, articles, and in particular a long article possibly written by Blondie himself, but at the very least the product of a detailed interview with him, about the raid. Some of Chapters 10, 11, 12 and 14 have been taken verbatim from these detailed notes. I benefited especially from Bridget's insights into her remarkable husband.

I am especially obliged to a range of experts in their respective fields who helped me understand the broader context of military operations in Europe in 1942 and 1943. Professor M.R.D. (Michael) Foot, the SOE historian, explained the role and impact of special operations in France during those years as well as enabling me to understand something of the complicated relationships between MI6, the BCRA, MI9 and SOE. I am indebted to him for his time and observations. Dr Matthew Cobb of the University of Manchester and author of *The Resistance* has been of immense help in the detail of the Resistance in the Landes region, Aquitaine and the Charente, especially for bringing the diversity of the BCRA and SIS operations in and around Bordeaux to my attention, and for saving me from many errors. His provision of sources in French was of incalculable benefit to my knowledge of the various aspects of the resistance movement in the region. I was also helped in many ways also by Ewen Southby-Tailyour, Blondie's biographer, not least in his allowing me to view the full range of correspondence built up during his research for the biography. Ewen and Patricia's help and friendship as I wrote the book were a tremendous encouragement.

Likewise I am grateful for the generous assistance of the filmmaker Tom Keene, who in an article on the raid in the *Globe and Laurel Journal* in 2005 and in a BBC documentary exposed the 'Scientist' dimension to the story; Tom also explained the role that Major David Wyatt RE played in the relationship between SOE and CODC. I thank, too, Matt Little, archivist at the Royal Marines Museum; Malcolm Cavan OBE; the Combined Services Museum, Maldon, Essex; Mark Bentinck (the Royal Marine historian); Christopher Long, Keith Jane and Roger Stanton who patiently described to me the working of the Pat O'Leary escape line and answered all my questions; Duncan Stuart, lately the SOE adviser to the Foreign and Commonwealth Office (and whose wife Leonore translated the German text of Vice-Admiral Julius Bachmann's war diary), and the historian Nigel Perrin. Once again I have been supported throughout by the encouragement and editorial efforts of Philip and Isla Brownless.

In France I could not have managed without the wholehearted support of François Boisnier who for many years was President of the organisation Frankton Souvenir, and who maintains an active interest in all things associated with the Cockleshell raid. He, more than anyone else, has opened up the story of the raid to a wide audience and I am grateful for his permission to use his material (published or otherwise) for this book. Sitting in his ample study in the beautiful medieval town of Barbezieux, devouring his huge collection of material over several days in the autumn of 2010, was one the highlights of my writing year. His excellent *Le Commando de L'Impossible* (2002), written with his friend Raymond Muelle, is unfortunately available only in French. Much of the original research in Freiburg and Washington was prompted in the first place by François. I have been able to develop this research in places, but I pay testimony to him for his first opening the door.

I am also grateful for the assistance provided in different ways in France by Dr Hugues Maquis of the University of Poitiers; M. Francis Salaberry, M. Eric Poineau; M. St Marc; M. Furet; Mme Landreau (owner of the 'Fiery Woodman's Cottage' at Nâpres Farm, St Preuil), M. Jacques Loiseau in Bordeaux for his excellent record-keeping of the French Resistance in the Gironde area and the Centre Jean Moulin, Bordeaux. I am grateful, too, for the lovely accommodation provided for me in Barbezieux by Christopher and Audrey Raggatt at La Petite Champagne. I was fascinated to discover that I had written of Chris's father in one of my previous books. Sapper Raggatt of the Royal Engineers had fought against the Japanese in the ill-fated Arakan campaign of 1942/43, and his diary was of much use to me when I was writing *The Generals* in 2007/8. I was fortunate on another occasion to find myself at the magnificent Villa D'O at Saint Loubès, which can be heartily recommended for any visit to Bordeaux.

Finally, I pay testament to the assistance provided to me by Norman Colley, and to the families of the men who went on the raid. All but two did not return. These include Bridget Hasler, Peter Siddall, Ken and Judy Sims, Isabella Mackinnon, Janet Lafferty (née Ewart), John Connally, Eddie Ward, Brigid Legge, Jimmy Sparks and Gilly Clark (née Sparks). I was told by one of them that despite the passing of the years not a day went by when they did not mourn the loss of their loved ones, some of whom had died in the most despicable of circumstances. Nevertheless, they walked tall in the knowledge of what these extraordinary men, in this most gallant of generations, had achieved. I am especially grateful to Peter Siddall, the nephew of George Sheard, for helping to edit the manuscript of this book, to its great benefit.

It goes without saying that, grateful as I am to the many people who helped me, I alone am responsible for the contents and conclusions of this book and for any errors that may inadvertently have been included.

Note

For reasons of consistency and clarity all instances of the twenty-four-hour clock have been converted to the twelve-hour clock, and metric units have been converted to imperial.

Index